The *Titanic*
in Print and on Screen

The *Titanic* in Print and on Screen

An Annotated Guide to Books, Films, Television Shows and Other Media

D. BRIAN ANDERSON

McFarland & Company, Inc., Publishers
Jefferson, North Carolina, and London

LIBRARY OF CONGRESS ONLINE CATALOG DATA

Anderson, D. Brian.
 The Titanic in print and on screen : an annotated guide to
books, films, television shows and other media / D. Brian Anderson.
   p.   cm.
 Includes index.

 ISBN-13: 978-0-7864-1786-5
 softcover : 50# alkaline paper ∞

 1. Titanic (Steamship)—Bibliography. 2. Titanic (Steamship)—
In mass media—Bibliography. 3. Shipwrecks—North Atlantic
Ocean—Bibliography. I. Title.
Z6016.S55A53   2005   [G530.T6]
016.910'9163'4—dc22   2004030534

British Library cataloguing data are available

©2005 D. Brian Anderson. All rights reserved

*No part of this book may be reproduced or transmitted in any form
or by any means, electronic or mechanical, including photocopying
or recording, or by any information storage and retrieval system,
without permission in writing from the publisher.*

Cover illustration from Photofest

Manufactured in the United States of America

McFarland & Company, Inc., Publishers
 Box 611, Jefferson, North Carolina 28640
   www.mcfarlandpub.com

Acknowledgments

The author would like to thank those who have assisted him along the way, including Justine S., Bill Furlow, Mike Peters, Jeffry Lyon, Eric Paddon, George and Pat Behe, and Wendy Freedman. The author would also like to thank his family and friends for their support.

Table of Contents

Acknowledgments v
Preface 1

1. Nonfiction Books, Pamphlets and Audio 5
2. Novels and Short Stories 57
3. Children's Books 73
4. Narrative Films 94
5. Television Episodes/Anthologies 113
6. Documentary Films and Videos 118
7. Plays 143
8. Selected Essays and Articles 150
9. Selected Poems, Songs and Poetry Collections 154
10. Comic Books and Parodies 159
11. Multimedia Software 162
12. Selected Web Sites 167

Appendix A: Actors Who Have Appeared in More Than One *Titanic* Film 171
Appendix B: Brief Film and Television Appearances of the *Titanic* 172
Appendix C: Titanic Films Unrealized or Unreleased 174

Appendix D: Books Carried Aboard the *Titanic*   175
Appendix E: Books Written by *Titanic* Passengers
   (Unrelated to the Ship)   176
Index   179

Preface

Not long ago, an anonymous malcontent expressed his frustration at *Titanic* mania in a posting to an Internet newsgroup: "So it was a big ship that had the desperate misfortune to sink on its first voyage. A tragedy without a doubt. But why is that still so fascinating to so many people? Hasn't everything been said, every book been written and read, every theory been tendered, every movie been made that could be?"

The simple answer is no. We are no more finished with the *Titanic* than we are with Homer, the Civil War, or the Kennedy assassination. It has become a part of our mythology, firmly entrenched in the collective consciousness, and the stories will continue to be retold not because they need to be retold, but because we need to tell them. For the *Titanic* disaster is more than a metaphor for the collapse of class-based society and the hubris of man in the industrial age; it speaks to us on a primal, visceral level that defies explanation. And yet we continue to try to explain why the tragedy means so much, in the same way that we continue to try to explain why it is important to read *Huckleberry Finn* or *Moby-Dick*. The stories that explain who we are as humans are few and far between, and the story of the *Titanic* is one of them. It is an event that in its tragic, clockwork-like certainty stopped time and became a haunting metaphor. The *Titanic* is forever sinking in our imaginations.

Through books, films, stories, and songs, the archetypal shipwreck persists as an enduring metaphor for the perils of mankind's hubris and the siren lure of modern technology. Indeed, a beautiful, finely engineered ship was not the only thing lost on that fateful day in April of 1912. Edwardian society's fixation on class culture and its naïve worship of technology also fell victim to the cold, icy grip of the Atlantic. Two nations changed forever, and the world took note.

Through the years, interest in the *Titanic* has ebbed and flowed but has always maintained a solid base of enthusiasts drawn to the dramatic facts and myths of the disaster. In 1985, the discovery of the long-missing wreck two miles below the surface of the Atlantic revitalized interest in the *Titanic* and spawned a new generation of books, films, and, for the first time, Web sites and computer games. Recent years have seen the release of, among other things, a *Titanic* cookbook, a Broadway musical, and a traveling museum exhibit. None of this activity compares to the feeding frenzy created by James Cameron's blockbuster *Titanic*, however, which became the biggest movie of all time and whetted the public's appetite for all things *Titanic*.

The popularity of the movie has prompted the release of dozens of new and reprinted books, CD-ROM games, and several new television documentaries. Americans of a new generation have embraced the *Titanic* myth as their own.

This book is a survey of the narrative retooling that has grown out of history's most compelling and dramatic shipwreck. Organized in accessible categories and short entries, this bibliography includes everything from *Titanic*-inspired documentaries and narrative films to children's books, histories, novelizations, websites, and survivors journals, through the end of 2003. In films and song, the *Titanic* is often referred to as the "ship of dreams." It is an apt description when thinking about the ways the ship has been brought to life in literary and dramatic form. Each film or book exists as a dream or "imagining," a flickering of the collective psyche. This book, then, exists as a catalog of dreams or imaginings.

In any bibliography, the decision of what not to include is just as crucial as the decision of what to include. The following types of media sources are not included:

- *Newspaper and magazine articles.* Although I have included a listing of important articles and essays, the sheer number of newspaper and magazine articles written over the years would make a complete listing impractical and not particularly useful, given the tools for periodical research available at libraries. Other books have attempted to chronicle the news coverage of the wreck, both through facsimiles of actual newspaper front pages of the day and through more scholarly analysis.
- *Foreign language books and periodicals.*
- *Short television news or tabloid stories.* Capitalizing on renewed interest in the shipwreck after the success of James Cameron's film, many tabloid and news-magazine TV shows ran short pieces on the *Titanic*. Many of these pieces were simply retellings of well-

worn trivia packaged as "breaking news" stories. The stories themselves testify to the ease by which *Titanic* lore could be sold to the public in 1998. A man who locates a print of an old *Titanic* newsreel became worthy of a feature story, even though copies of the newsreel were already circulating. Generally, only those news shows at least a half-hour long and dealing exclusively with the *Titanic* are included. Some lightweight "news" shows are not included, however, such as the *Oprah* episode that gathered cast members and others involved with the James Cameron film.

- *Short TV parody skits.* Parodies prompted by the Cameron film are not specifically documented here. One *MAD TV* skit that fused the *Titanic* legend with *The Love Boat* was particularly amusing, as was a short animated CBS promotion that featured stick figures reenacting the *Titanic* story in 30 seconds in a celebrated send-up of the cost overruns and excesses of James Cameron's film.
- *Advertisements and brochures.* Original *Titanic* and White Star line literature and advertisements, at least as "works" in and of themselves, have been excluded.
- *Radio programs and broadcasts.* Original radio broadcasts, dramatic and otherwise, have been excluded as a category.
- *Puzzles, games, and models.* Although occasionally marketed alongside books, *Titanic* puzzles and games have not been included in this accounting. I have included several non-books that were packaged and marketed as books, in order to illuminate for readers the nature of these "sources" they may have encountered.
- *Dead media.* For the most part, I do not attempt to document the 8-mm film releases of *Titanic* movies (home-movie reels of selected scenes from both films of the 1950s were released) as long as the documentary or film in question is available on another, more accessible format.

It is also not my intention in this book to point out every historical inaccuracy in every film and book related to the *Titanic*. The mistakes abound, and I do try to note those errors when they seem egregious, especially when they are central to the filmmaker's or author's vision (e.g., the Molly Brown character in S.O.S. *Titanic* who upbraids several fellow passengers for calling her Maggie instead of Molly). That said, however, I would also argue that the myths of the *Titanic* are nearly as important as the facts of the disaster. No matter how many times we tell ourselves and others the real facts, Margaret Brown will always be the Unsinkable Molly and the last song heard as the ship goes down will always be "Nearer My God to Thee." Self-crafted *Titanic* experts have busied themselves with taking notice of the mistakes made most consistently over time: the first-class passengers dancing in the nonexistent ballroom on Sunday, flares that are the wrong color, various parts of the ship positioned in the wrong places. To paraphrase the grammarian John Benbow, if you take these inconsistencies too seriously, you will surely go mad.

Entries are organized to make information accessible and entertaining. Each section includes anywhere from five to dozens of entries, with each entry containing a brief review, bibliographic information, and technical details of a specific *Titanic* book, film, or other source. The short reviews are listed in alphabetical order according to the author's name or, in the case of films and multimedia products, the title of the work. Many of the reviews include subjective analysis meant to give researchers and scholars an idea of the overall usefulness or interest of the work.

Prices of books and videos are not included, as this is not, strictly speaking, a buying guide for collectors. ISBN are also not included.

Film listings include the most important production information and credits, and this may vary depending on the film itself and its strong points. Film entries (for both documentary and narrative films) also include information on the availability of the film on video, when appropriate.

1 Nonfiction Books, Pamphlets and Audio

1 Adams, Moody. ***The Titanic's Last Hero: Story About John Harper.*** Midnight Call, 1997; Emerald House, 1998. Paperback, 158 pp.

Story of a Baptist preacher who perished during the sinking, pieced together from older manuscripts, letters, and tributes originally published in pamphlet form in Scotland in 1912. The religiously toned story — in which Harper leads souls to salvation as the ship founders — positions itself as an antidote to tales of passengers selfishly ignoring cries from the water.

2 Andersen, Richard. ***Arranging Deck Chairs on the Titanic: Crises in Education.*** Amana Books, 1988. Paperback, 250 pp.

Although *Arranging Deck Chairs* is an education memoir and not a *Titanic* book at all, it presents a good example of how the doomed liner has worked its way into the vernacular as a metaphor for man's hubris in the face of the overwhelming forces of nature. The phrase in question, "it's like rearranging the deck chairs on the *Titanic*," once likely served as a colorful example of wordplay in the midst of heated political discussions. Switching agents in Hollywood, it has been said, is like changing deck chairs on the *Titanic*. Today the phrase has become a cliché, although still one of the most prominent examples of the *Titanic*'s influence on everyday language and culture. This bibliographic guide, for instance, does not document the many casual references to the *Titanic* in film and television. In an episode of the 1990s teen drama "Dawson's Creek," for example, a character named Pacey asks for his friend Joey Potter's opinion of his newly purchased second-hand boat. "Isn't it beautiful?" he asks. "Beautiful like the *Titanic* after the iceberg, maybe," she replies after surveying the weathered and beaten hull. Similarly, a religious pamphlet about the Ark notes, "The *Titanic* was built by professionals; the Ark was built by amateurs." The *Titanic* continues to be a convenient and powerful metaphor, and this is likely to continue as long as her memory lingers in the collective imagination.

3 Anderson, Roy. ***White Star.*** London: T. Stephenson, 1964. 236 pp. + xii.

Anderson's now hard-to-find story of the White Star Line includes a full fleet list of the line's sailing ships, steam ships, and motorized ships.

4 Archbold, Rick. ***Ken Marschall's Art of Titanic.*** New York: Hyperion, 1998. Hardcover, 160 pp. Illustrated by Ken Marschall; foreword by James Cameron.

This oversized and pricey coffee-table collection presents Marschall's realistic *Titanic* paintings in the order of historical events and with commentary by Archbold. The first chapter consists of a biography of Marschall alongside personal photographs, while a final chapter showcases some of Marschall's paintings of the *Lusitania, Mauretania, Olympic,* and *Britannic.*

5 Archbold, Rick, and Dana McGauley. ***Last Dinner on the Titanic.*** New York: Hyperion/Madison, 1997. Hardcover, 144 pp. Foreword by Walter Lord.

While many seized on the appearance of this *Titanic* cookbook as yet another sign of *Titanic* mania gone too far, the book was a natural outgrowth of the 1990s trend of hosting *Titanic*-themed banquets. Archbold and McGauley present not so much a book of recipes as a sprawling description of dining facilities and practices aboard the ship, from the lavish first-class restaurants to the spartan but commodious third-class dining saloon. The authors also offer suggestions for serving and setting the proper mood and, in an introductory essay, recount the events of the final evening from the point of view of the most well-known first-class passengers.

The actual recipes include Waldorf Pudding, Baked Haddock with Sharp Sauce, Turnip Puree, Coconut Sandwich, Roasted Squab on Wilted Cress, and Lamb with Mint Sauce.

The book includes a foreword by Walter Lord, a handful of black-and-white photographs, and many color Edwardian-style illustrations.

6 Baarslag, Karl. ***SOS: To the Rescue.*** Riverside, CT: 7 C's Press, 1986. Softcover, 40 pp.

This digest-sized pamphlet recounts the story of the *Titanic* from the perspective of Wireless Operators Bride and Phillips. The narrative unravels like fiction, with quite a lot of attention given over to typical *Titanic* story elements for such a short account.

The book was published, like many similar 7 C's titles, inexpensively for sale through the *Titanic* Historical Society at conventions and through its mail-order catalog.

7 Ballard, Robert D., and Rick Archbold. ***The Discovery of the Titanic.*** New York: Warner/Madison Press, 1987. Hardcover, 230 pp. Illustrated by Ken Marshall; with an introduction by Walter Lord.

Best-selling story of Ballard's discovery of *Titanic*'s wreck, as told to Archbold. A full-color slick photograph section originally included fold-out photographs.

In an epilogue to the 1995 edition, Ballard criticizes later expeditions that sought to salvage artifacts from the wreck site.

Other editions: Paperback, 1989; Revised edition, Warner Books, 280 pp., 1995; Softcover, 1998.

8 Ballard, Robert D., with Rick Archbold. ***Lost Liners: From the Titanic to the Andrea Dorea the Ocean Floor Reveals Its Greatest Lost Ships.*** New York: Hyperion, 1998. Hardcover/softcover, 224 pp. Illustrated by Ken Marschall.

Yet another repackaging of material from the Archbold/Marschall/Ballard camp, this oversized coffee-table book presents a catalog of information and illustrations on ships visited by wreck explorer Ballard, with chapters devoted to the *Titanic, Lusitania, Olympic,* and *Mauretania.* In two later chapters, Ballard laments the demise of passenger liners and makes his case for protecting wrecks from salvage operations.

9 Ballard, Robert D., and Malcolm McConnell. ***Explorations: My Quest for Adventure and Discovery Under the Sea.*** New York: Hyperion, 1995. Hardcover, 408 pp.

Ballard's memoir of his explorations of storied wrecks around the globe is most engaging when it touches on the often far-reaching implications of back-room politics and split-second decision-making. The book includes abundant color photographs.

Other editions: Softcover (Hyperion, 1995); retitled for a 1998 edition as *Explorations: From the Man Who Discovered the Titanic: A Life of Underwater Adventure.*

10 Balls, John. ***Titanic: The Norfolk Survivors.*** Norwich, UK: Publisher unknown, 1999.

Limited-run genealogical/ethnic history from the point-of-view of passengers hailing from Norfolk county on the east coast of England.

11 Bancroft, Caroline. ***The Unsinkable Molly Brown.*** Denver: Golden Press, 1956. Softcover, 26 pp.

This popular souvenir pamphlet-style book is cited by others as helping to create the "Unsinkable Molly Brown" myth. Includes photographs.

Other editions: Trade paperback (Boulder: Johnson, 1971).

12 Bancroft, Caroline, and May Bennett Wills. ***The Unsinkable Molly Brown Cookbook.*** Denver: Sage Books, 1966. Spiral-bound, 118 pp.

Recipes include Molly's Swiss Fondue, shrimp pate, Cannibal Canapes, and Miner's Casserole. Bancroft also authored a woman's magazine article on Brown, which she later turned into a booklet titled *The Unsinkable Molly Brown.*

13 Bebensee, Lyle, with Bill Muller. ***Titanic: The Last Male Survivor.*** HMS Press, 1991. Running time: Approx. 90 minutes, 1 cassette.

Confusing interview with German survivor Bill Muller, who was interviewed by Lyle Bebensee when Muller was in his mid–90s. The interviewer often has to repeat himself, and the answers are sometimes humorous:

> Q: What do you think about them going down and filming the wreck for TV?
>
> A: Well, they didn't have TV back then.

Other highlights include Muller's comments that the *Titanic* was trying to set a speed record and that if the ship had been a German ship with a German crew, "everyone would still be alive." Muller should not be criticized for the fact that an author tried to commercialize on his story so late in life; rather, the project raises ethical questions about the wisdom of soliciting interviews from survivors so many years after the event.

Note: The recording was reproduced and distributed on consumer cassettes.

14 Beesley, Lawrence. ***The Loss of the SS Titanic: Its Story and Its Lessons.*** Boston and New York: Houghton Mifflin, 1912. Hardcover, 220 pp.

Survivor Beesley penned his first-hand account at the behest of an editor who wanted to see a correct history to counterbalance the many spurious and cheaply printed accounts published in 1912. As a retired science teacher, Beesley is formal and thorough in his description of the *Titanic*'s construction, voyage, collision, and lifeboat embarkation. Beesley refutes newspaper illustrations that depicted the *Titanic* as breaking violently in two above the surface, while his description of the chaotic lifeboat-loading scene contrasts with Gracie's account. His famous recollection of the dying cries of drowning passengers gradually fading has chilled the imagination of readers since. In a final chapter reflecting on the aftermath of the disaster, Beesley absolves Captain Smith and the White Star Line while calling for changes to maritime regulations.

Other editions: In addition to being included in the Winocour anthology, Beesley's book has been reprinted several times by Houghton Mifflin and is available online as a public-domain work. 7 C's Press reprinted the book in 1973.

15 Behe, George. ***Titanic: Psychic Forewarnings of a Tragedy.*** London: Patrick Stephens, 1988. Hardcover, 176 pp.

Examination of alleged premonitions and other supernatural warnings of the *Titanic* disaster by an author well known in *Titanic*-enthusiast circles.

Other editions: HarperCollins trade paperback, 1989.

16 Behe, George. ***Titanic: Safety, Speed and Sacrifice.*** Polo, IL: Transportation Trails, 1997. Softcover, 88 pp. Foreword by Don Lynch. Drawings by Bonnie Berg.

In this digest-sized specialized history, Behe makes the case that blame for the *Titanic* tragedy can be placed squarely on the shoulders of bridge officers who ignored ice warnings as part of a plan to reach New York a day early. The officers' actions, Behe suggests, amount to nothing less than criminal negligence. Behe also presents evidence that lookout Frederick Fleet was bribed by the White Star Line as part of an orchestrated campaign to deny corporate responsibility.

Illustrated with black-and-white photographs from the author's collection as well as several curious drawings by Bonnie Berg depicting scenes on the night of the sinking.

17 Biel, Steven. ***Down with the Old Canoe: A Cultural History of the Titanic Disaster.*** New York: W. W. Norton, 1996. Hardcover, 300 pp.

Biel's scholarly tome traces the *Titanic*'s many manifestations as a metaphor in sermons, songs, film, and popular thought while placing its cultural meanings within larger contexts of literary theory. The title refers to a folk song "Down with the Old Canoe," recorded by cotton mill workers by a folk song collector.

Other editions: Paperback, 1997.

18 Biel, Steven, ed. ***Titanica: The Disaster of the Century in Poetry, Song, and Prose.*** New York, London: Norton, 1998. Softcover, 204 pp.

In this follow-up companion to his well received cultural study *Down with the Old Canoe,* Biel presents a selection of reprinted *Titanic*-inspired poems, sermons, journalism, essays, and songs. Most of the poems and songs are from 1912–1915, and hence public domain, while some of the essays date from the 1970s and 1980s. The collection of sermons from 1912 represents perhaps the book's most challenging and original offering. Biel's short preface reviews the *Titanic*'s significance as a symbol of divine judgment, race relations, gender relations, and class relations.

19 Bisset, Sir James, with P. R. Stephensen. ***Tramps and Ladies: My Early Years in Steamers.*** New York: Criterion, 1959. Hardcover, 334 pp. + xvii.

Memoir of the former commodore of the Cunard Line, including his passage aboard the *Carpathia* in April 1912.

20 Bonsall, Thomas E. ***Titanic: The Story of the Great White Star Line Trio: The Olympic, the Titanic and the Britannic.*** New York: Gallery Books (H. M. Smith), 1987. Hardcover, 64 pp. Cover art: Reproduction of a postcard originally printed by the White Star line.

This slim and unpretentious coffee-table book presents a breezy narrative account of the conception, design, first voyage, and sinking of the *Titanic* alongside archival black-and-white photographs, sketches, reproductions of White Star literature, and a few artistic illustrations. The publishers tout this book as the first "well-illustrated" *Titanic* book, and they are right in pointing out that the visual appeal of the disaster had been underestimated by publishers in previous years. In retrospect, though, it is refreshing just to see a *Titanic* book that does not rely on the esteemed art of Ken Marschall. The book seems almost quaint compared to the lavishly illustrated volumes of the 1990s, with its most appealing illustration being a subdued tinted photograph of the *Olympic*. Out of the book's nine chapters, three deal with the stories of *Titanic*'s sister ships *Olympic* and *Britannic*.

21 Booth, John, and Sean Coughlan. ***Titanic: Signals of Disaster.*** White Star, 1993.

Assembles a transcript of events based on wireless messages, including many previously unpublished.

22 Bown, Mark, and Roger Simmons. ***R.M.S. Titanic: A Portrait in Old Picture Postcards.*** UK: Brampton, 1987. Softcover, 98 pp.

This pamphlet-sized collection of nearly 100 period postcards follows the

Titanic's lifespan from her building and launching to her sea trials, maiden voyage, and sinking. The cards range from realistic black-and-white photographic representations of her fitting in Belfast to horrific and sentimental artistic images created for memorial cards in the aftermath of the disaster. Standout cards from the collection include a card memorializing the *Titanic*'s musicians, a card depicting a heroic Captain Smith rescuing a child before drowning, and a half a dozen cards emblazoned with the lyrics to "Nearer My God to Thee."

Other editions: Reprint, S. B., 1995.

23 Boyd-Smith, Peter. ***Titanic: From Rare Historical Reports.*** Southampton: Steamship, 1994. Hardcover, 246 pp.

Collection and analysis of media reports from 1912, with black-and-white photographs.

24 Braynard, Frank O. ***Story of the "Titanic" Cards: 24 Cards.*** New York: Dover, 1988. Softcover, 16 pp.

The slim book-like souvenir is actually a collection of modern postcards featuring photographs of *Titanic* scenes, including Captain Smith on deck with Lord Pirrie and lifeboats brimming with survivors. Each postcard can be detached for mailing.

25 Brinnin, John Malcom. ***The Sway of the Grand Saloon: A Social History of the North Atlantic.*** London: Macmillan, 1972. Hardcover, 600 pp. + xxii.

General history of the golden age of trans–Atlantic passenger liner crossings.

Other editions: Reprint edition (Barnes and Noble Books, 2000)

26 Bristow, Diana E. ***Titanic, R.I.P.: Can Dead Men Tell Tales?*** Detroit: Harlo, 1989. Paperback, 214 pp.

In this historical detective work, Bristow argues that the *Titanic* traversed the Atlantic on the shorter, "northern route" usually reserved for eastbound ships and that the nearby ship assumed to be the *Californian* was actually a German ship.

27 Bristow, Diana E. ***Titanic: Sinking the Myths.*** Fresno, CA: Katco Literacy, 1995. 505 pp. + iv.

Bristow probes "unanswered questions" of *Titanic*'s fateful voyage, such as why Smith only handed one ice warning to Ismay and why the officers did not fire "distress" rockets. The author, a retired flight attendant and member of the British *Titanic* Society, also argues against the "brittle steel" theory and derides decades of "theorizing when the facts were known in 1912."

The first chapter introduces readers to 1912-era nautical terminology and history.

28 Brown, David G. ***The Last Log of the Titanic.*** New York: International Marine/McGraw-Hill, 2001. Hardcover, 234 pp.

In this account based mostly on U.S. Senate hearings, Master Captain Brown attempts to root out the true causes behind the *Titanic* disaster from the point of view of the bridge. Among Brown's "startling" new assertions are that the *Titanic* collided with a submerged ice shelf rather than a simple iceberg and that First Officer Murdoch ordered an "All Stop" rather than a "crash stop" (a reverse of the engines), in hopes of maneuvering around the berg while avoiding further damage.

The title of the book is ironic; the ship's last log was not recovered. Thus, Brown's book positions itself as a reconstruction of the log by an expert ship handler.

29 Brown, Richard G. B. ***Voyage of the Iceberg: The Story of the Iceberg That Sank the Titanic.*** Toronto: J. Lorimer, 1983. Hardcover, 152 pp.

The title of marine biologist Richard Brown's natural history may be misleading. It is not so much a speculative narrative of a specific iceberg as it is an ambitious survey of the natural processes, animals, and people who, in one way or another, help to shape the story of the iceberg and its infamous role. As Brown describes the journey of the iceberg from its initial calving in Baffin Bay to its collision with the *Titanic* 18 months later, he digresses into description, fiction-like passages about the native people and animals of the North Atlantic. Alternating, shorter chapters relate the story of the *Titanic*'s construction, voyage, and sinking.

Other editions: UK edition (Bodley Head, 1985)

30 Brown, Rustie. ***The Titanic, the Psychic and the Sea.*** Lomita, CA.: Blue Harbor Press, 1981. Hardcover, 163 pp. + xii. Foreword by Alan Vaughan.

Review of the alleged psychic premonitions and omens surrounding the disaster.

31 Bryceson, David. ***The Titanic Disaster, As Reported in the British National Press April–July 1912.*** New York and London: W. W. Norton, 1997. Hardcover, 312 pp.

Survey of early British news coverage of the disaster, including lengthy articles, news tidbits, photographs, memorial tributes, and editorial cartoons.
Other editions: Original UK edition (Patrick Stephens, 1997).

32 Bullock, Shan F. *A Titanic Hero: Thomas Andrews Shipbuilder.* London: Maunsel, 1912; Baltimore: Norman, Remington, 1913. 80 pp. + xvi. Introduction by Sir Horace Plunkett.

Consideration of and tribute to the shipbuilder from an early vantage point.

The book includes an introduction by Sir Horace Plunkett, an Irish politician and agriculture expert who commissioned the work, as well as an appendix of letters and cablegrams sent after the sinking.

Other editions: Reprint, 7 C's Press, 1973; Blackstaff Press with introduction by Michael McCaughan, 2000.

33 Butler, Daniel Allen. *Unsinkable.* Mechanicsburg, PA: Stackpole Books, 1998. Hardcover, 292 pp.

This footnoted and scholarly effort touches on aspects of the *Titanic* ranging from her building to her discovery at the bottom of the Atlantic some 70 years later. An epilogue reveals the fate of many of *Titanic*'s passengers and crew after the disaster, while three appendices condense information on matters of specific interest. The first appendix lists various facts and figures related to the *Titanic* in table form. Appendix II addresses the role of the *Californian*, with some damning conclusions, and a final short appendix explores the more obvious, but often ignored, question of the culpability of Captain Smith. A black-and-white photograph section includes a snapshot of the iceberg believed to be the one struck by *Titanic*.

34 Caesar, Pete. *Titanic!* Green Bay, Wis.: Ocean and Great Lakes Marine Press, 1988. 146 pp.

Basic history by author known for a series of self-published books on wrecks of the Great Lakes.

35 Cahill, Richard A. *Disasters at Sea: Titanic to Exxon Valdez.* London: Century, 1990; Kings Point, NY: American Merchant Marine Foundation, 1990. Hardcover, 274 pp.

The scope and technical aspects of Cahill's analysis provide interest, as he attempts to find common threads in history's most famous and costly shipwrecks, with the aim of providing insight to those involved in the shipping industry .

Other editions: San Antonio: Nautical Books, 1991.

36 Caplan, Bruce M. ed. ***The Sinking of the Titanic.*** Seattle, WA: Hara, 1997. Paperback, 222 pp.

This attractive paperback is an updated reprint of the 1912 book usually attributed to Logan Marshall. The editor omits all but one of the last 12 chapters dealing with the aftermath of the disaster, as well as the original's sentimental "memorial" illustrations. Additions include an index, bold subheadings, and a dedication to Captain Rostron of the *Carpathia* and the citizens of New York. Caplan also keeps the color and photograph of the original cover.

37 Caren, Eric, and Steve Goldman, eds. ***Extra Titanic: The Story of the Disaster in the Newspapers of the Day.*** Edison, NJ: Castle Books, 1998. Hardcover, 190 pp.

Oversized collection of facsimile newspaper pages from the days and weeks after the disaster, most notable for the gothic artistic renderings not often seen elsewhere.

38 Carter, Jennifer, and Joel Hirschhorn. ***Titanic Adventure: One Woman's True Life Voyage Down to the Legendary Ocean Liner.*** Far Hills, NJ: New Horizon Press, 1999. Hardcover, 1999. Foreword by William F. Buckley, Jr.

In this "true-life adventure story," Carter recounts escaping an abusive marriage to become the first woman to join a dive expedition (as a dive coordinator) to *Titanic*'s wreck site, with a 1987 French-American team aiming to recover artifacts. (The expedition provided the basis for the Telly Savalas television special *Return to the Titanic — Live!*) Much of Carter's story dwells on business politics and personal squabbles.

Hirschhorn, the book's ghost writer, is known for his work as a songwriter, including the score for the film *Seven Brides for Seven Brothers.*

Includes color photographs.

39 Chapin, Howard Millar. ***Bibliotheca Titanicana: A List of Books Relating to the Loss of S.S. Titanic.*** Metuchen, NJ: 1926. 20 pp. 50 copies "printed for the American collector." Illustrations: One reprint of photograph of the iceberg that sunk the *Titanic*, taken by Mrs. Chapin aboard the *Carpathia.*

This early annotated listing of *Titanic* books and pamphlets was culled from the personal card catalog of Howard Chapin, a passenger aboard the rescue ship *Carpathia* at the time of the disaster. In the preface, Chapin notes that he includes 39 of a possible 43 items (actually the book contains 40); he omits a few variant and foreign editions. Chapin's reference pamphlet provides an interesting window into the state of *Titanic* lore at this early stage, for most of the cataloged works are short nonfiction accounts, including two by Chapin, poetry chapbooks, and official reports. The bibliographic notes are concise and the subjective comments brief (he terms some of his contemporaries' accounts "sensational"). Chapin's book is held in the collections of the U.S. Library of Congress.

40 Chernow, Ron. ***The House of Morgan: An American Banking Dynasty and the Rise of Modern Finance.*** New York: Simon and Schuster, 1990. Hardcover, 832 pp.

This ambitious economic history of the Morgan dynasty traces its mysterious and sometimes dark rise from Victorian England (and its machinations of the White Star Line) to the stock market crash of 1987. An earlier family biography by the same name, Lewis Corey's *The House of Morgan: A Social Biography of the Masters of Money* (New York: G. Howard Watt), appeared in 1930.

41 Clary, James G. ***The Last True Story of Titanic.*** Enniskillen, N. Ireland: Domhan Books, 1998. Softcover, 152 pp.

The "last true story" of Clary's title surfaces in the final chapter of this otherwise standard collection of *Titanic* lore and history. In this chapter, Clary asserts that after the *Titanic* struck the iceberg, the captain ordered the ship to resume forward direction at half-speed. This assertion is based on brief testimony during the U.S. senate inquiry and on Laurence Beesley's statement that the ship "resumed her course" after striking the iceberg. According to Clary's calculations, the move caused the ship to sink more rapidly, thereby costing many more lives than was necessary. The theory has been dismissed by other *Titanic* experts.

The book's earlier chapters focus on *Titanic*'s building, fitting out, launching, and sea trials. Another lengthy chapter analyzes various *Titanic* questions and mysteries, such as whether the ship broke in two pieces before spiraling to the bottom of the ocean and why passengers did not attempt to construct rafts from deck chairs. Of more interest is the collection of "survivor's tales," which includes the author's interview with survivor Edwina McKenzie and the strange saga of *Titanic*'s two canine survivors.

The author, who also penned a well-known volume on sea superstitions, served as historian and artist for Jack Grimm's unsuccessful expedition to locate the *Titanic*'s wreck.

42 Cohen, Leo. ***The Titanic Revisited.*** La Jolla, CA: L. Cohen, 1981. 78 pp.

In this self-published account, engineer Cohen reconstructs the final hours of *Titanic*'s voyage, focusing on the technical aspects of the ship's faltering and breaking apart as well as the relative position of the *Californian*.

43 Coleman, Terry. ***The Liners: A History of the North Atlantic Crossing.*** London: Allen Lane, 1976. Hardcover, 232 pp.

General history of the north Atlantic passenger trade, with some emphasis on *Titanic*.

Other editions: Penguin paperback, 1977.

44 Cooper, Gary. ***The Man Who Sank the Titanic?: The Life and Times of Edward J. Smith.*** Witan Books, 1992. Hardcover/softcover: 180 pp.

Other editions: Reprint, 1998.

45 Cox, Stephen. ***The Titanic Story: Hard Choices, Dangerous Decisions.*** Peru, Illinois: Open Court, 1999. Softcover, 152 pp.

Literature professor Cox aims to refute many cherished beliefs about the *Titanic* disaster — namely that it was the result of arrogance and greed and that many more lives could have been saved by the provision of more lifeboats. Such an argument naturally proceeds as a defense of White Star director J. Bruce Ismay, who in surviving the disaster became a kind of living symbol for the blind arrogance of the ship line. To do so, Cox examines the proceedings of both the American and British inquiries and revisits the evidence and testimony that essentially exonerated Ismay in both hearings. In a more general sense, Cox argues that the *Titanic* doomed by man's technological hubris and corporate greed is a ship of myth, created by the forces of hindsight and cultural mythology. The facts of the disaster, he contends, suggest a confluence of other causes, including the unpredictable nature of the events, the conservative training of the officers, and the "incalculability of certain risks."

Supplemental material includes the verbatim testimony of Daniel Buckley, Emily Ryerson, and Frederick Barrett. Includes index and black-and-white photographs.

46 Davie, Michael. ***Titanic: The Death and Life of a Legend.*** New York: Alfred A. Knopf, 1987. Hardcover, 245 pp.

Comprehensive account focusing on the economics of the ship's construction, the official inquiries following the disaster, and Ballard's discovery of the wreck.

Other editions: British edition under title *Titanic: The Full Story of a Tragedy* (London: Bodley Head, 1986); Henry Holt paperback library edition, 1988.

47 Downs, David, and Ken Beck. ***Titanic Trivia.*** Nashville, TN: Premium Press America, 1998. Softcover, 128 pp.

Pocket-sized square book with 424 esoteric facts about the ship, her passengers, and her legacy. The most obscure (and unnecessary) fact mentioned may be that Robert Ballard was reading Chuck Yeager's autobiography when the sunken ship was discovered.

48 Dodge, Washington. ***The Loss of the Titanic.*** Springfield, MA: 7 C's Press, prob. 1974. Softcover, 36 pp.

Reprint of first-class passenger and *Time* magazine editor Dodge's address to the Commonwealth Club in 1912. In an otherwise formal and staid account, often written in passive voice, Dodge attempts to answer a few questions probably common to the ears of survivors, such as "Why didn't passengers lash together rafts from deck chairs?" (His answer: There was not enough time once passengers comprehended the true peril of the situation.)

The digest-sized booklet with card cover was printed, along with other 7 C's titles, as an item of interest to *Titanic* enthusiasts and convention-goers. Additional material includes a photograph of Dodge in later years, a photograph of passengers being taken aboard the *Carpathia*, and detailed deck plans.

49 Duff-Gordon, Lady Lucile. ***Discretions and Indiscretions.*** New York: Frederic A. Stokes, 1932.

Best-selling memoir of the twice-married dress designer and first-class survivor Duff-Gordon.

50 Duncan, Jody, ed. ***Cinefex, No. 72.*** Riverside, CA: No publisher, 1997. Softcover, 180 pp.

This special issue of the quarterly film special-effects journal is certainly substantial and informative enough to qualify as a book. The two main articles by Don Shay touch on a myriad of special-effects concerns, including the construction or large-scale and small-scale replicas, the employment of computer-generated effects, and the decision to use an older actress rather than an artificially aged Kate Winslet for the part of the modern-day Rose. A final chapter by editor Duncan relates how the business of Cameron's special effects came together (ultimately 17 companies and some 1,200 name credits were involved) and muses on the effects the monumental impact the film had on film budgets generally and the special-effects industry in particular.

51 Eaton, John P., and Charles A. Haas. ***Falling Star: Misadventures of White Star Line Ships.*** London: Patrick Stephens, 1989. Hardcover, 256 pp.

This history of the 62 years of White Star's existence, in addition to summarizing the story of the *Titanic*, also relates the fates of such liners as the *Olympic, Atlantic, Britannic,* and *Republic*.

Other editions: American edition (Norton, 1990).

52 Eaton, John P., and Charles A. Haas. **Titanic: Destination Disaster—The Legends and the Reality.** New York: W. W. Norton, 1987. Hardcover, 160 pp. Cover art: Painting by Chris Mayger, who the authors note has taken "artistic license" with the fact. Illustrations: 60+ black-and-white photographs and sketches, including many from the authors' personal collection and many culled from news archives.

Emerging from the wave of *Titanic* interest spurred by Bob Ballard's discovery of her wreck in 1985, J. P. Eaton and Charles Haas provide a concise summary of the events leading up to the wreck while analyzing and dispensing with some of the *Titanic*'s most enduring legends. In fact, with 160 pages and plenty of photographs, the book can be recommended as a brief and general overview of the *Titanic*'s most essential facts and myths. Among the myths the authors lay to rest are that the *Titanic* was cursed because it was not christened (in fact, no White Star ship was christened), that a worker was accidentally welded into the ship's hull during the frantic construction process (this apparently grew out of the inspector's hammering the hull each evening), and that Lucky Tower, the greaser who had supposedly survived the *Lusitania* and the *Empress of Ireland*, was aboard the *Titanic* (his name does not appear in the official crew list). The authors wisely demur when it comes to the popular legend of the orchestra's final encore performance, though. After considerable hand-wringing over the possibilities, the authors conclude that it really isn't possible to know which tune the heroic musicians chose as their last. "What difference?" they ask. To *Titanic* lore-seekers, of course, it is all the difference in the world.

Other editions: Revised and expanded edition (Norton, 1996; 184 pp.). An added chapter in this edition summarizes the salvage expeditions to the *Titanic* and the controversies they stirred. The cover illustration has been replaced with a painting by E. D. Walker.

53 Eaton, J. P., and Charles A. Haas. **Titanic: The Exhibition.** Memphis: Wonders, 1997. Softcover, 222 pp.

Souvenir book published in conjunction with the Memphis RMS *Titanic* exhibition. Includes color photographs of artifacts as well as a passengers list and cargo manifest.

54 Eaton, John P., and Charles A. Haas. ***Titanic: Journey Through Time.*** New York and London: W. W. Norton, 1999. Hardcover, 248 pp. Foreword by William MacQuitty.

In this fifth effort by collaborators Eaton and Haas, the authors reveal new angles and perspectives on the disaster through a chronological diary of events from the birth of shipbuilder William James Pirrie in 1847 to the release of James Cameron's film in 1997. Along the way, the authors touch on lesser personalities and some trivial matters not covered in their earlier works, such as the testimony of Antarctic explorer Sir Ernest Shackleton, the fate of an earlier ship named *Titanic* (a freight carrier), and the question of how many dogs sailed aboard the doomed liner. A middle section includes eight pages of color photographs and illustrations, including the evocative but often overlooked painting *RMS Titanic Life-Ring* by E. D. Walker.

55 Eaton, John P., and Charles A. Haas. ***Titanic, Triumph and Tragedy: A Chronicle in Words and Pictures.*** Wellingborough, Northhamptonshire: Patrick Stephens, 1986. Hardcover, 320 pp.

This encyclopedic, comprehensive work has, with its subsequent editions, emerged as the consummate *Titanic* reference guide. Presented in chronological order with many accompanying black-and-white photographs, the book presents events from the fitting out and sea trials of *Titanic* to the wreck's discovery and exploration. Chapters in between cover the *Californian* controversy, the American and British inquiries, and the disposition of lawsuits and insurance claims. The disaster itself is summarized in one concise chapter with dozens of helpful mugshots to identify the cast of characters as the action proceeds. The book's appendices round out the reference value of the work in their summary of such information as the cargo manifest, passenger data, and collectibles.

Other editions: Second edition (London: Patrick Stephens, 1994; Hardcover, 352 pp.); American editions (W. W. Norton, 1986, 1995).

56 Everett, Marshall, ed. ***Story of the Wreck of the Titanic, the Ocean's Greatest Disaster: 1912 Memorial Edition.*** L. H. Walter, 1912. 320 pp.

This so-called "instant book" or "dollar book" was rushed to press, along with at least four other books, in the months following the disaster to capitalize on early public interest; publishers assumed this interest would be short-lived. The books often included the subtitle "memorial edition" and were sold for around a dollar in the streets and by door-to-door salesman. (The Galveston Storm of 1900 and the San Francisco Earthquake were other popular subjects for these quick-and-dirty books.) Most of these early accounts were printed on pulp paper and in great numbers; even though volumes in excellent condition are difficult to find, the books are not considered rare or unusual within the book trade. A complete description and analysis of the "dollar book" trade related to the *Titanic* can be found in an article by Jay White in the Spring 1999 issue of *Acadiensis*.

Like the other volumes, Everett's book makes liberal use of short chapters, telegraphic subheadings, and sentimental, breezy prose. The narrative essentially recaps journalistic accounts of the event, with abundant quotations from survivors and assorted eulogistic passages on the well-known first-class passengers. As in other early journalism related to the disaster, the numbers in Everett's book are slippery, yet it remains a noteworthy relic of its time.

Interesting stand-out chapters center on the hazard of icebergs in the Atlantic and the grim voyage of *Titanic*'s dead. A chapter by the Rev. Andrew Johnson titled "The Tragedy at Sea" typifies early attempts to explain the event by mythicizing it, a practice that has scarcely abated.

The book's epigraph is "Nearer My God to Thee," and Everett quotes survivor Mrs. W. J. Douton as recalling the hymn being played as the ship sank. The book also plays up the self-sacrifice of those who awaited death on board and "exemplified" the tenet of *John 15:13*, a biblical passage more often used in connection with fallen soldiers (this theme was later picked up by *Titanic* novelists such as Danielle Steel).

Everett (a pseudonym of Henry Neil) also edited quick volumes on William McKinley's assassination, the San Francisco Earthquake, and the Chicago Iroquois Theater fire. As Neil, the author wrote on the Japanese-Russian war and Theodore Roosevelt's hunting adventures.

Other editions: Hardcover reprint, Castle Books, 1998.

57 Foster, John Wilson. ***The Titanic Complex.*** Vancouver: Belcouver Press, 1997. Softcover, 92 pp.

Scholarly and footnoted survey of *Titanic*-inspired poetry, art, and drama. In this thesis-like effort, Wilson traces the slipping meaning of the *Titanic* as a modern and postmodern symbol, arguing that the meaning of the disaster and the way artists respond to it has shifted with each generation's changing ethos. His comment that the *Titanic*'s sinking was in some way a "dynamite career move" calls to mind the familiar saying about Paris: "If it didn't exist, we'd have to invent it."

58 Foster, John Wilson, ed. ***The Titanic Reader.*** New York: Penguin, 1999. Softcover, 364 pp.

Foster's anthology of *Titanic* journalism, fiction, poems, letters, and transcripts includes roughly 100 individual pieces and excerpts. Some of the more unusual and rewarding items in the eclectic mix include several excerpts from

Filson Young's lyrical *Titanic*, Arthur Conan Doyle's reaction to George Bernard Shaw's essay, Herman Melville's 1888 poem "The Berg," and a scholarly essay on the gender myths of the *Titanic* disaster.

59 Fredricks, Henry, ed. ***The Tragic Story of the Titanic.*** Philadelphia, PA: International Bible Press, 1912. Hardcover, 352 pp.

Early bibliographer Chapin notes that this book is largely the same as that published under the name Logan Marshall (q.v.). This version has become harder to find for modern collectors.

60 Gardiner, Robin, and Dan van der Vat. ***The Titanic Conspiracy: Cover-ups and Mysteries of the World's Most Famous Sea Disaster.*** New York, NY: Carol, 1996.

In this loose threading of conspiracy theory, Gardiner and maritime historian van der Vat argue that the *Titanic*'s fate was tied not to fate or accident but to the malicious wills of a few power-mad capitalists. The authors build this house of cards primarily on the theory that the *Titanic* was replaced by the *Olympic* in a last-minute scheme to recover through insurance fraud money lost on the problem-plagued *Olympic*. As evidence to bolster this claim, the authors point to incomplete and inaccurate passenger survivor lists, the loss of the *Titanic*'s log, and a hole near the bow of the ship that resembles damage from an explosion. The authors also suggest that the *Californian* was presented as a suitable scapegoat and distraction and that the White Star Line bribed key witnesses in the U.S. and British inquiries.

Other editions: First published in the UK as *The Riddle of the Titanic* (London: Weidenfeld and Nicholson, 1995).

61 Gardner, Martin, ed. ***The Wreck of the Titanic Foretold?*** Buffalo: NY: Prometheus, 1986. Hardcover, 158 pp.

Collection of evidence surrounding the possibility that the *Titanic* disaster was foretold through numerous supernatural channels. Gardner, known for his work in skepticism, presents the case of Morgan Robertson's novel *Futility*, reproduced as a major portion of this book. Another chapter deals with the numerous premonitions and after-death "appearances" by journalist and spiritualist W. T. Stead, whose novel *From the Old World to the New* describes the sinking of a ship in the North Atlantic; a reproduction of the final portion of Stead's novel is included. Gardner's third offering is the reproduction of a short story, "The White Ghost of Disaster," concerning the sinking of a liner named *Admiral* and published just before the *Titanic* disaster. An appendix includes reproductions of poems dealing with iceberg collisions, including Celia Thaxter's "A Tryst."

Other editions: Paperback (with new preface), 1998.

62 Garrett, Richard. ***Atlantic Disasters: The Titanic and Other Victims of the North Atlantic.*** London: Buchan and Enright, 1986. Hardcover, 286 pp.

Overview of maritime disasters on the North Atlantic shipping lanes; includes 16 pages of black-and-white photographs as well as maps and line illustrations.

Other editions: Seven Hills Book Distributors, 1987.

63 Garrison, Webb. ***A Treasury of Titanic Tales.*** Nashville, TN: Rutledge Hill Press, 1998. Softcover, 240 pp.

The author of this standard collection of profiles and point-of-view narratives professes to favor focusing on the lesser-known personas over the well-documented lives of the "rich and famous" involved in the disaster. To that end, there are profiles of Lord Mersey, Frank Millet, Harry Widener, W. T. Stead, and Guglielmo Marconi. Other chapters on Maggie Brown, John Jacob Astor, and Bruce Ismay seem to indicate that is nearly impossible for authors to steer clear of the larger-than-life figures of *Titanic*'s story.

64 Geller, Judith B. ***Titanic: Women and Children First.*** New York/London: W. W. Norton, 1998. Hardcover, 224 pp.

Geller profiles more than 50 women and children passengers, grouped by class and ranging from first-class celebrities as Lady Duff Gordon and Molly Brown to such unknown steerage passengers as Amy Stanley, Rosa Abbott, and Celiney Yasbeck. Illustrations include family photographs and heirloom photographs from private collections and a handful of original drawings.

65 Gibbs, Philip. ***The Deathless Story of the "Titanic."*** London: Lloyd's Weekly News, 1912. Softcover/Newsprint, 40 pp.

Essentially a "special edition" of Lloyd's Weekly News published soon after the sinking, Gibbs' journalistic account resembles others at the time with its reliance on sentimental tone ("greater than the tragedy is the glory") and emphasis on the chivalry and heroics of first-class millionaires ("there were many noble actors upon that dark stage of the death-ship"). The 20-page narrative is rounded out in book form through the inclusion of survivor and victim photographs, a two-page cross-sectional ship illustration, a facsimile reprint of the sheet music for "Nearer My God to Thee" and 10 pages of survivor and crew lists. The book does not provide a list of victims, although a curious sidebar lists the first-class passengers who were forever separated from their wives.

Other editions: Facsimile reprint sold through the *Titanic* Historical Society (Riverside: 7 C's Press).

66 Gillespie, John, and Vera Gillespie. *The "Titanic Man"—Carlos F. Hurd: How the World First Received the Complete Stories of the Titanic Disaster.* Amereon, 1989. Softcover, 98 pp.

Story of *St. Louis Post-Dispatch* journalist Hurd, a passenger aboard the *Carpathia* at the time of the *Titanic*'s sinking. Sidestepping orders from Captain Arthur H. Rostron to not interview the 705 *Titanic* survivors picked up by the *Carpathia*, Hurd secretly gathered notes with the help of his wife Katherine, who hid his notes in her undergarments. Hurd's resulting effort was perhaps the most famous journalistic account of the disaster, a 5,000-word story adopted by the Associated Press and telegraphed around the globe. The article is reprinted in facsimile form herein and accounts for a goodly portion of the book.

Other editions: As *A Newsman's Dream Come True: Carlos F. Hurd Covering the Most Famous of All Shipwrecks, R.M.S. Titanic* (abridged, 65 pp.), 1993; softcover reprint (J. & V. Gillespie), 1996.

67 Giuliano, Geoffrey. *That Fateful Night: True Stories of Titanic Survivors—In Their Own Words!* Bantam Doubleday Dell Audio, 1998. Running Time: Approx. 144 minutes on 2 cassettes. Narration: Geoffrey Giuliano.

Slickly produced and packaged audio presentation delivers as promised, although its credibility is hampered by the overwrought narration style of the author (who calls Captain Smith, for instance, "more myth than man"). The slick production style also makes it frustrating for listeners to identify speakers, as each interviewee is not clearly identified. Nonetheless, rock-biographer Giuliano brings a good deal of new (or at least underreported) information to light, including interviews with historian John Boothe, who argues that the final ice warning was not carried to the bridge, and survivor Edith Russell, who recounts how she barely made it on the lifeboat because her dress was too tight. Other survivors interviewed include Millvina Dean and Eva Hart, who gives her standard recollections retrofitted with superstitious forebodings, recalling that both her parents had strange premonitions of doom. Overall, although interesting, the interviews leave one wondering whether survivors—very young at the time—make the best witnesses: One survivor gives the insightful comment that the ship was "too near the icebergs" while Eva Hart asserts that everyone would have been saved had there been enough lifeboats. One curious though extraneous interview focuses on the story of a woman who claims to have been conceived on the *Titanic* as a result of an extramarital dalliance during the ship's final hours.

Other interviewees include the great-nephew of Cosmo Duff-Gordon, who defends the actions of his uncle, and Tim Lightoller, the grandson of Officer Lightoller, who recalls the time his uncle cruised his yacht into a World

War II battle to rescue survivors. Perhaps the most compelling material, however, is the narrative of Captain Rostron of the *Carpathia* and the various obstacles he overcame in rescuing the *Titanic* survivors.

Other editions: CD and abridged versions.

68 Goldsmith, Frank. ***Echoes in the Night: Memories of a Titanic Survivor.*** Indian Orchard, MA: *Titanic* Historical Society, 1991. Softcover, 130 pp.

Autobiography of *Titanic* survivor Goldsmith, aged 9 at the time of the disaster.

69 Goss, Michael, and George Behe. ***Lost at Sea: Ghost Ships and Other Mysteries.*** Amherst, NY: Prometheus, 1994. Hardcover, 359 pp.

This anthology includes a rather lackluster chapter titled "RMS *Titanic*: The Unsinkable," in which the authors examine the various reports of psychic premonitions and other paranormal activity surrounding the famous wreck. The chapter, a companion piece to Behe's other writings on the *Titanic*'s supernatural angles, draws on references from psychic journals of the time as well as manuscripts and reports from the *Titanic* Historical Society. The reports vary from the mundane to the truly hair-raising, including survivor Anna Ward's vague presentiments as told to her father, M. Abrahams' dream of his nephew's white face the night before the young man went down with the ship, and passenger Bert John's spooky dream on board the ship 24 hours before the wreck, in which he saw himself leap from a coffin into a lifeboat (as a steerage passenger, John apparently survived the wreck only by jumping over the side of the ship into a departing lifeboat). The authors attempt to present a balanced report — within the context of a supernaturally-tinged book. What the authors fail to note is the extent to which any ocean journey at the time would have conjured up ominous feelings of impending doom. More interesting for maritime readers are the book's account of the Goodwin Sands (the final resting place for scores of 19th-century English ships) and its cultural history of the legendary *Flying Dutchman*.

70 Gracie, Archibald. ***The Truth About the Titanic.*** New York: Mitchell Kennerly, 1913. Hardcover, 330 pp.

Lively and famous first-person narrative that has become a valuable source for, among other questions of debate, investigating the position of passengers in the various lifeboats. Gracie's style is a curious anachronistic mix of Edwardian politeness (he describes the lifeboat loading as "orderly") and politically incorrect insensitivity (he refers to the actions of a "crazed Italian").

Gracie died before its publication. The original edition remains a scarce collector's item.

Other editions: Reprint (7 C's Press, 1973), with foreword by Robert H. Gibbons; *Titanic, A Survivor's Story* (Alan Sutton, 1986), 324 pp.; Reprint, Academy Chicago, 1996; Sutton, 1998; Blackstone Audio; collected in Winocour (q.v.).

71 Groff, John M., and Jane E. Allen. ***Titanic and Her Era.*** Philadelphia: Philadelphia Seaport Museum, 1982. Card cover, 32 pp.

Pamphlet-type contextual history produced for sale in museums.

72 Haisman, David. ***I'll See You in New York: Titanic, the Courage of a Survivor.*** Brisbane: Boolarong Press, 1999.

Biography of Edith Haisman (Brown), 15 years old at the time of the disaster, by her son.

73 Harrison, Leslie. ***Defending Capt. Lord: A Titanic Myth, Part II.*** Malvern: Images, 1996. Hardcover, 191 pp.

A second part to Harrison's defense of Captain Lord, issued in limited press runs. Harrison's arguments have also been repackaged under the titles *The Case for Captain Lord: An Echo of the Titanic Disaster* (1997) and *Captain Lord's Plight to Remember* (1997).

74 Harrison, Leslie. ***A Titanic Myth: The Californian Incident.*** London: William Kimber, 1986. Hardcover, 282 pp.

Exhaustive defense of Captain Lord.

Other editions: paperback (HarperCollins, 1986); paperback (Sutton, 1991); second revised edition (self-published, 288 pp., 1992).

75 Hart, Eva M., as told to Ronald C. Denney. ***Shadow of the Titanic: A Survivor's Story.*** Dartford, UK: Greenwich University Press, 1994. Softcover, 192 pp.

This memoir of one of the most well known and often interviewed survivors begins with some brief, yet tauntingly harrowing family history (Eva's mother survived an abusive first marriage) and quickly moves through the disaster as seen through the eyes of 7-year-old Eva. Ms. Hart, while decrying the inaccuracies and injustices perpetrated in so many other *Titanic* accounts, gives heavy credence to her mother's ominous premonitions and severe misgivings about traveling on the liner. As Eva remembers it, her mother believed calling the ship unsinkable was "flying in the face of the Almighty." Denney, more known as a technical author, balances Ms. Hart's memories with facts and figures regarding the ship's accommodations, speed, and survivors. Roughly a third of the book concerns events leading up to and including the sinking; the remaining pages are devoted to Ms. Hart's later life in politics, volunteer work, and civil service. Of particular interest is her account of dealing with the *Titanic* victims' relief fund, a subject not often addressed elsewhere.

Other editions: New York University Press, 1997.

76 Herring, Susan Davis. ***From the Titanic to the Challenger: An Annotated Bibliography on Technological Failures of the Twentieth Century.*** New York: Garland Science, 1989. Hardcover, 460 pp.

Bibliography of technical articles, books, and technical reports related to maritime disasters, chemical plant explosions, aerospace accidents, and automotive manufacturing failures such as the Ford Pinto. The section on *Titanic* spans about five pages and covers mostly citations of early articles from *Scientific American, the New York Times,* and *Nature.*

The author also produced a volume called *Encyclopedia of Technological Failures* (Garland, 2004).

77 Heyer, Paul. ***Titanic Legacy: Disaster as Media Event and Myth.*** Westport, CT: Praeger, 1995. Hardcover, 200 pp.

Heyer, a professor of communication, explorers the media coverage of what he terms "our century's first collective nightmare" over 80 years. In tracing these murmurs and echoes, Heyer touches on the effects of the wireless telegraph, the first rushed newspaper reports, and the disaster's manifestation in song, literature, drama, and film.

78 Hilton, George Woodman. ***Eastland: Legacy of the Titanic.*** Stanford, CA: Stanford University Press, 1995. Hardcover, 366 pp.

Scholarly history of the 1915 sinking of the steamer *Eastland* in the Chicago River. More than 800 men, women, and children were killed as the ship capsized carrying employees and their families to a company picnic. The disaster ranks as the worst in Great Lakes history. The subtitle is cruelly ironic: To comply with new maritime safety regulations spurred by the *Titanic* disaster, nine lifeboats were added to the *Eastland* near the end of her completion; the author argues that this additional weight aggravated the ship's top-heavy design and accelerated the disaster. Interestingly, the *Eastland*'s crew launched none of the lifeboats, additional or otherwise, because of the proximity of other vessels and shore-based operations.

Other editions: Paperback, 1996.

79 Hoffman, William, and Jack Grimm. ***Beyond Reach: The Search for the Titanic.*** New York: Beaufort Books, 1982. Hardcover, 206 pp.

Official account of millionaire Grimm's attempt to locate the wreck of the *Titanic* aboard the Texas A&M University research vessel *Gyre* in 1981. As a document of the journey, the book remains without a climax, but it does provide a one-side portrait of a self-styled megalomaniac. When speaking of the *Titanic*, Hoffman reveals, Grimm's "eyes sparkle." When asked what he would do if the wreck were not found, Grimm says, "I'll probably kill myself." The narrative of the search, along with the technical descriptions of the equipment involved, takes just a few chapters. Spliced in with these are a brief retelling of the disaster, a description of life aboard the *Titanic*, a survey of news coverage and books following the disaster, a general encyclopedic survey of the business of shipwreck searches, and word-for-word brief interviews with Grimm and survivors Ruth Blanchard and Eva Hart.

Illustrations include historical black-and-white photographs and modern black-and-white photographs, mostly of some of the equipment used in Grimm's undertaking.

80 Howard, John. ***Foundering of the "Titanic."*** Melbourne, 1912. 8 pp.

Early pamphlet history.

81 Howells, Richard Parton. ***The Myth of the Titanic.*** New York: St. Martin's Press, 1999. Clothbound, 214 pp. + xii.

Cultural analysis of the *Titanic* as psychological metaphor and myth, including how the disaster parallels the myths of preliterate societies.

82 Hubbard, Elbert. ***The Titanic.*** East Aurora, NY: Roycroft, 1923. Softcover, 32 pp.

Limited-run of Hubbards's famous essay, originally published in his book *Hollyhocks and Goldenglow*.

83 Hustak, Alan. ***Titanic: The Canadian Story.*** Montreal, Quebec: Vehicule Press, 1998. Softcover, 172 pp. Foreword by John P. Eaton.

This attractive, high-quality book recounts the voyages and fates of 130 passengers bound for Canada on the *Titanic* (82 of these passengers perished). Hustak uses sources such as newspaper accounts, letters, and testimony to reconstruct the stories of such passengers as Alice Fortune of Winnipeg, who is said to have been warned of her fate by a clairvoyant in Cairo just two months before sailing on the *Titanic*. The account progresses through the timeline of the disaster, sometimes speculating on the activities of various Canadian passengers during time-marking events. Probably because of the availability of source material, Hustak tends to focus more on stories of the first-class passengers, many of whom made their fortunes in Canada and had vacationed in Europe before booking passage on the *Titanic*.

A center fold-out sketch shows the positions of various Canadian passengers at various times during the sinking. Appendices list basic biographical information and burial locations for all the Canadian passengers. Also includes various black-and-white photographs.

84 Hutchings, David F. ***RMS Titanic: A Modern Legend.*** Southampton: Kingfisher, 1987; Portsmouth, NH: Maiden Voyage Booksellers, 1987. Softcover, 48 pp.

Magazine-style history with black-and-white photographs covering the construction, sea trials, sinking, and aftermath.

85 Hutchinson, Gillian. ***The Wreck of the Titanic.*** Greenwich: National Maritime Museum, 1994. Softcover, 48 pp.

A museum guide to an artifact exhibit at the National Maritime Museum. With color illustrations.

86 Hyslop, Donald, Alastair Forsyth, and Sheila Jemima, eds. ***Titanic Voices: Memories from the Fateful Voyage.*** Southhampton: Southampton City Council, 1994.

This oversized and heavily illustrated volume attempts to recreate the atmosphere of shipboard life and the immediacy of the disaster through a reliance on oral histories, many previously unpublished photographs, and letters. It is a labor of love, the kind of research-intensive document that could only be put together by those dedicated to the importance of preserving local history in the voices of those involved. Photographs reveal the streets where passengers and crewmembers lived, the pubs where crewmembers might have drank, and the intimate comforts of the staterooms and common facilities aboard the ship. The second half of the book details, through photographs, art, and quotations, the reaction of Southampton to the disaster, the outpouring of charity and sentiment, the proceedings of U.S. and British investigations, and the disposition of certain passengers and memorials.

A color section includes early artistic renderings of the ship by George Washington Sandell and Walter Dane Bryer, as well as color photographs of a few pre–Ballard mementos and artifacts. Photographs by John Lawrence.

Other editions: New York: St. Martin's Press, 1997; UK: Sutton, 1997.

87 Iverson, Kristen. ***Molly Brown: Unraveling the Myth.*** Boulder, CO: Johnson Books, 1999. Hardcover, 294 pp. Foreword by Muffet Laurie Brown.

The first two chapters of Iverson's biography, with a foreword by Muffet Laurie Brown, use Brown's adventures aboard the *Titanic* as an introduction to her bold and indefatigable character. The first chapter unravels in narrative, somewhat speculative form, touching on encounters with Capt. Smith, Harold Bride, Lightoller, and Ismay. The second chapter details Brown's passage on the *Carpathia* and traces her growth to legendary status. Iverson notes that the "Unsinkable Molly Brown" moniker was put forth by the press as a satirical poke at Brown's increasingly outspoken views on issues such women's suffrage and workers' rights.

Iverson extensively references Marcus (q.v.) and Brown's own newspaper account.

88 J. B. K., ed. ***Morgan Robertson, the Man.*** New York: Metropolitan Magazine, 1915. Hardcover, 132 pp.

Early biography of the author of the novel *Futility*, who also worked as a sailor, clock repairer, and inventor, with significant contributions from the author himself. Chapters include "Morgan Robertson's Famous Recipes" and "My Skirmish with Madness."

Other editions: Reprints (7 C's Press, Buccaneer Books, 1991; Amereon, 1995) have typically offered the biography in a single volume with *Futility*. Blackstone Audio has produced an audio version (2002).

89 Jessop, Violet. ***Titanic Survivor: The Newly Discovered Memoirs of Violet Jessop Who Survived Both the Titanic and Brittanic Disasters.*** Dobbs Ferry, NY: Sheridan House, 1997. Hardcover, 238 pp. Introduced, edited and annotated by John Maxtone-Graham.

Memoir of an Irish stewardess who served on the fateful voyages of White Star's two most tragic liners (as well as the *Olympic*). The sometimes disjointed string of memories touches on the author's early childhood, her bouts with smallpox and tuberculosis, and her family's journey to Dublin. She relates her experiences with the White Star Line in honest fashion, recounting a life of hard labor, unrelenting management, and ill-mannered passengers, although she calls "Tommy" Andrews "one of the finest and kindliest of men."

The *Titanic* incident is related in three chapters. Real crew members and passengers who make appearances include the Strauses ("a delightful old couple"), John Jacob Astor and his young wife ("sad-faced" and "dull"), Thomas Andrews, and violinist Jock Hume ("eager and full of life"). (Although Jessop originally used pseudonyms, Maxtone-Graham is able to decipher most of the names.) As the ship goes down, Jessop recalls that most of the passengers seemed reassured by lights of another ship on the horizon and by the relative steadiness of the ship.

The memoir was never truly lost but only reached publishers through the efforts of Jessop's surviving nieces some 25 years after her death. The original working title of the memoir was *Neptune's Greenroom*. Jessop, who planned to use the pseudonym Constance Ransom, later changed the title to *While I Remember*.

The editor is the author of *The Only Way to Cross* (Macmillan, 1972), a general history of passenger life aboard luxury liners. Violet Jessop's story appears in shorter form in that book.

Other editions: Paperback, 1998; Audio, 2001 (Margaret Sircom, narrator).

90 Kaharl, Victoria. ***Water Baby: The Story of Alvin.*** New York: Oxford University Press, 1990. Hardcover, 256 pp.

Behind-the-scenes scientific account of the development and initial journeys—through scientific squabbles and political wranglings—of the Woods Hole manned submersible.

91 Keith, William H., Jr., and Nina Barton. ***Titanic: Adventure Out of Time: Hints and Solutions.*** Indianapolis: Brady, 1996. Softcover, 192 pp.

This strategy guide for the popular late–1990s interactive computer game (q.v.) includes a 30-page history of the ship as well as a three-page rumination on quantum mechanics and the mind-bending possibilities of time travel.

92 Kludas, Arnold. ***Passenger Liners of the World—Vol. 1: 1858–1912.*** Patrick Stephens, 1975.

First in a six-volume set by a German maritime historian.
Other editions: Reprint, 1986.

93 Kuntz, Tom, ed. ***The Titanic Disaster Hearings: The Official Transcripts of the 1912 Senate Investigation.*** New York: Simon and Schuster Pocket Books, 1998. Paperback, 572 pp.

This mass-market edition was released to capitalize on the consumer frenzy prompted by the success of James Cameron's film. The appendices to the Senate's original final report, including a digest that omitted the testimony of third-class passengers that they were briefly prevented from accessing the upper decks during lifeboat loading, are here printed with a few changes to reflect the abridged form of the book. Additional material includes an introductory essay by Kuntz, which emphasizes the dramatic nature of the proceedings, and a center section of black-and-white photographs and sketches.

94 Lacey, Pat. ***Master of the Titanic.*** Sussex: Book Guild, 1996. Hardcover, 360 pp.

This biography written-as-novel has met with criticism for its poetic licenses. Lacey is a great-niece of Smith.

95 Lightoller, Charles Herbert. ***Titanic and Other Ships.*** London: Ivor Nicholson and Watson, 1935. Hardcover.

Lightoller's lively, informal storytelling style belies his position as a keeper of order and routine. His memoir relates the life of a seaman with color and detail, taking Lightoller from his first voyage as a fourteen-year-old ship's apprentice rebelling against his father's life as a cotton grower to his service in the Great War aboard the *Oceanic.* Of the forty-five chapters, six concern Lightoller's brief time in service on the *Titanic.* In these chapters, Lightoller gives an uncanny character sketch of Captain Smith (known to Lightoller as "E. J."), describes famous encounters with the Strauses and Major Peuchen (who offered to attend a departing lifeboat as an experienced yachtsman), and details the harrowing hours spent balancing with other survivors atop an overturned collapsible lifeboat. Of the *Titanic* myth, Lightoller muses, "Certainly there was no sailor who ever sailed salt water but who smiled—and still smiles—at the idea of the 'unsinkable ship.'"

Other editions: Softcover, 1939. Also reprinted in pamphlet form as *Titanic* (Ludlow, MA: 7 C's Press, 1975; 40 pp.) and available as a free online text.

96 Littlejohn, Philip. ***Titanic: Waiting for Orders.*** Crescent, 1999. Hardcover, 64 pp.

The author relates the story of his grandfather, First Class Steward Alexander James Littlejohn, who survived the sinking after being ordered to man a lifeboat.

97 Lord, Walter. ***The Night Lives On: New Thoughts, Theories and Revelations About the Titanic.*** New York: William Morrow, 1986. 272 pp. Includes black-and-white photographs, deck plans.

In his second, more literary take on the *Titanic* disaster, Walter Lord attempts to explain the hold the shipwreck continues to have on the public imagination. His arguments now seem secondhand, because they have been so oft-repeated since: the *Titanic* was the biggest news story of the time; it held an embarrassment of riches for lovers of trivia and supernatural; it was connected to many celebrity-status first-class passengers such as John Jacob Astor and Molly Brown; and it could be viewed as a microcosm of Edwardian society (and the fall of that society). The book includes detailed accounts (not often seen elsewhere) of Captains Rostron and Lord and the roles of the *Carpathia* and *Californian*. Lord also addresses some of the neglected points of his earlier book, including the issue of whether the ship went down intact (he rightly points out that the issue itself shows the unreliable nature of eyewitness accounts). Among the many *Titanic* "myths" tackled in this book, Lord most convincingly presents his case that an officer did in fact kill himself on deck that night; he further argues that that officer would have most logically been Murdoch. Overall, the book is more eloquent in tone and more expansive in its content than the first book, although it has not achieved the first book's classic status.

Other editions: Paperback, Avon Books, 1998; Audio Edition (abridged): *The Night Lives On: The Untold Stories and Secrets Behind the Sinking of the "Unsinkable" Ship — Titanic!* HarperCollins, 1998.

98 Lord, Walter. *A Night to Remember.* New York: Holt, Rinehart & Winston, 1955. Hardcover, 209 pp.

Walter Lord's journalistic, chronological treatment of the *Titanic* disaster has become the classic *Titanic* narrative, revered among enthusiasts and lay persons alike. Indeed, Lord, whose has also written books about the Alamo and Pearl Harbor, was probably the first author to approach the *Titanic* disaster as a serious historian, attempting to carefully document the events of the night and to separate fact from myth. Many of the previous histories had either been haphazardly researched collections of myths and survivor accounts, or had emphasized the "moral import" of the sinking as a lesson for all mankind. This is not to say that Lord succeeds on all counts. His dry style serves as a remedy to the glut of sentimental *Titanic* histories, but it may also fail to spark interest in modern readers already familiar with the most basic facts of the disaster. Whatever factual lapses exist in this account cannot be attributed to poor research (e.g., Lord describes the ship as sinking intact, but there was only marginal evidence to believe otherwise until the wreck was discovered in 1985). In such a complicated narrative as the *Titanic*, a narrative that must be reconstructed from widely varying survivor accounts and official documents, it is scarcely possible to address all the myths and facts seamlessly. Lord attempted to fill in the gaps with a follow-up book, *The Night Lives On* (q.v.).

The first six chapters present a straightforward chronological account of the events leading up to the *Titanic*'s sinking. Later chapters blend survivor perspectives and the continuing narrative with news analysis (Lord was one of the first to point out how biased the early coverage was). A final chapter, "Facts About the *Titanic*," gathers the hard numbers of the ship's construction and the events of April 1912. Lord also addresses the validity of a number of the *Titanic* myths in this chapter. A passenger list is included as an appendix. The endpapers are illustrated with boat deck diagrams. Other illustrations include black-and-white photographs of the passengers and facsimiles of documents and letters.

Other editions: Holt edition, 9 printings through May 1961. Condensed in Reader's Digest, 1956. Book-of-the-Month Club, 1956. Bantam, 164 pp., 1956 (45 printings through 1983). Bantam reissue paperback, 209 pp., 1997. Abridged audio book, read by Martin Jarvis (Auburn, CA: Audio Partners, 1997).

99 Louden-Brown, Paul. ***The White Star Line: An Illustrated History 1870–1934.*** Norfolk: Ship Pictorial, 1991. Softcover, 138 pp.

Handbook-like guide to the White Star Line's most celebrated period, with black-and-white photographs or color pamphlet reproductions on nearly every page. Seven plates are dedicated to *Titanic*, including reproductions of her information card, photographs of the ship in port, and a photograph of the Southampton Engineers Memorial. The book's introduction, a brief text history of the line, runs six pages.

100 Lynch, Don (text), and Ken Marschall (illustrations). ***Titanic: An Illustrated History.*** Madison Books/Hyperion, 1992. Hardcover/softcover, 228 pp. Cover art: Ken Marschall. Illustrations: Include original paintings by Ken Marschall, color photographs by Peter Christopher, and numerous archival photographs and illustrations. Special illustrations include a three-page foldout cutaway of the *Titanic*'s layout.

The *Titanic* myth packaged as an attractive, richly illustrated coffee-table tome seems so obvious an idea as to be disingenuous. What better format to tell the classic Edwardian disaster tale of class culture and tragedy, of a majestic ship that drowned John Astor along with third-class waifs and immigrant peasants?

But the *Illustrated History* is a different kind of coffee-table book. To borrow the lingo of anthropologists, *Titanic: An Illustrated History* reworks an oft-told story by focusing on the material culture of the ship. Chapter 3, for instance, devotes entire pages, filled with oversized illustrations and photographs, to the sumptuous first-class lounge, staircase, dining saloon, and swimming pool. Through stunning visuals, we are reminded again that the *Titanic* was no ordinary ship, and that even the steerage accommodations were well above average. The first part of the book leans toward the sentimental, with facsimile reproductions of scrapbook items such as tickets, invitations to the official launching, telegraph messages, and family photographs. But Marschall's mournful watercolors add an appropriate air of solemnity, and by the end of the book, the reader is confronted with the grim, tragic irony of the underloaded lifeboats, the recovered bodies in pauper's caskets, and a finely preserved deck chair (which nicely restates the cliché about the futility of rearranging). Finally, in the book's closing pages, the *Titanic* is seen in full-blown reality, a rusty shell at the bottom of the Atlantic.

As Bob Ballard points out in his introduction, Marschall was the first artist to capture the eerie essence of the *Titanic* wreck (and did so after only a brief telephone conversation with Ballard). Don Lynch, who wrote the book's engaging and breezy text, has been associated with the *Titanic* History Society.

101 Lyons, Nathan. ***Riding 1st Class on the Titanic!*** Andover, MA: Addison Gallery of American Art/MIT Press, 1999. Softcover, 234 pp.

This collection presents photographer Lyons's work from 1974 to the time of publication. Much of his work consists of paired images and "found language." The title photograph, the only image having to do with the famous ship, captures the phrase spraypainted on a brick wall; as such, it restates the irony of the *Titanic*'s dual role as a symbol of modern elegance and inevitable destruction.

102 MacInnis, Joseph B. ***Titanic in a New Light.*** Charlottesville, VA: Thomasson-Grant, 1992. Hardcover/softcover, 96 pp.

Companion book to the first IMAX film, with color and black-and-white photographs.

103 MacQuitty, William. ***A Life to Remember.*** London: Quarter Books, 1991. Hardcover, 390 pp.

Autobiography of *A Night to Remember*'s film producer, titled after his most famous work. Among other things, MacQuitty reveals details of famous friendships with psychiatrist Wilhelm Stekel and entertainer Beatrice Lillie.

Other editions: Softcover, 1995.

104 Maddocks, Melvin. ***The Great Liners.*** The Seafarers series. Alexandria, VA: Time-Life Books, 1978. Hardcover, 176 pp.

Typical of the attractive, heavily illustrated volumes in Time-Life series,

The Great Liners condenses the *Titanic*'s building and demise into about 12 pages of narrative within a chapter called "A Litany of Disasters on the Devil Sea." Illustrations include a facsimile of a wireless transmission, 1912 newspaper drawings, and photographs of Captain Smith and Molly Brown. The brief story of the *Titanic* holds more interest here as it fits into the history of north–Atlantic maritime tragedies.

Other editions: Revised (1982, 1984).

105 Marcus, Geoffrey. ***Titanic! The Maiden Voyage.*** New York: Viking Press, 1969. Hardcover, 320 pp.

Although any nonfiction account of the *Titanic* predating Bob Ballard's expedition to the wrecksite would be by definition incomplete and possibly prone to error, Marcus's book was hailed at the time as an evocative story of the disaster that meshed reportorial facts with a strong human interest angle. In short, it was the most complete account of the disaster to date, surpassing Walter Lord's classic tome in the breadth of its scope and the force of its narrative (Walter Lord himself praised the book as "penetrating and all-inclusive.")

The account of the disaster begins with the departure of the boat train at Waterloo Station and progresses through the events with a particular focus on the maritime and technical points-of-view (Marcus was a British naval historian). Subsequent chapters deal with public reactions, the American and British inquiries, the *Californian* controversy, and the venerable myths and legends.

Abundant illustrations and photographs include historical editorial cartoons, shipboard photographs, and a few maps and charts.

In his preface, Marcus frames the story of the disaster with the scattering of the ashes of Fourth Officer Joseph Boxall near the site of the sinking. It is as if Marcus knew revisiting the site would someday yield the secrets and unravel the mysteries of the *Titanic*.

Other editions: Paperback, Manor Books, 1974; Easton Press, 1987.

106 Marriot, Leo. ***Titanic.*** New York: Smithmark, 1997. Hardcover, 160 pp.

Coffee-table recounting of the events of the *Titanic*, from conception and building to sinking and legacy. Printed in China and designed to be sold as an inexpensive catch-all book, Marriott's tome is most noteworthy for its collection of black-and-white shipboard photographs detailing the interior of the ship. However, many of the photographs, as Marriott acknowledges, are actually of the *Olympic*. Other illustrations include movie stills and facsimiles of death certificates and telegrams.

107 Marsh, Ed, and Douglas Kirkland. *James Cameron's Titanic.* HarperCollins, 1997. Hardcover, 178 pp. Foreword by James Cameron.

This oversized souvenir book showcases color stills from the movie, balanced with some behind-the-scenes shots and set and costume design sketches. The text (by Marsh) is an overview of the film's conception and production, while the captions provide gossipy tidbits from cast and crew.

Kirkland is credited with original photographs for the book.

Other editions: Softcover, 1997.

108 Marshall, Logan, ed. *Sinking of the Titanic and Great Sea Disasters.* L. T. Myers, 1912. 351 pp., with 32 pages of illustrations.

More straightforward account than Mowbray's book (q.v.), and more in keeping with what would be the traditional account of the disaster for many years to come, Marshall's early book was probably the most popular account of the year. This would account for the fact that the copies of the book are not hard to find, although *Titanic*-mania has elevated the going price for even the most ragged copies in recent years. Among the many myths that would persist for decades, Marshall describes the ship disappearing beneath the sea with a "quiet, slanting dive" and cites survivor accounts to support the theory that Murdoch shot himself amidst the confusion of the lifeboat loading. Although presented more objectively than some of the other earlier accounts, Marshall's account is not without its 1912 sensational biases: In one seamy tale, the author transforms the person who attempted to steal the wireless operator's lifejacket into a "negro stoker" (in fact, no blacks were aboard the *Titanic*).

The rest of this newspaper-like account (set with a large typeface and many subheadings) is fleshed out with a physical description of the ship, biographies of notable passengers, verbatim accounts of the sinking by Lawrence Beasley (*sic*), Jack Thayer, and Harold Bride (all of which have been collected elsewhere), and lesser-known brief accounts by passenger James McGough and a steward aboard the *Carpathia*. The final chapters include collections of telegrams of condolences from world leaders and noted personalities, a financial accounting of the mail and cargo lost aboard the ship, a detailed list of other maritime disasters, an analysis of the "dangerous trend" in shipbuilding toward sacrificing safety for luxury, and an account of the U.S. Senate inquiry.

A preface by Rev. Henry Van Dyke includes an interesting analysis of the "women and children first" rule, wherein the author notes that there is no real logic to this rule, since a man is intrinsically "worth more than a woman." The rule, he notes (regardless of whether it was actually followed), comes out of the Judeo-Christian tradition of self-sacrifice.

Chapin notes that Marshall's book is virtually the same as Fredricks (q.v.).

In addition, modern enthusiasts claimed to have seen six different editions of this book (including different colored covers). See Everett for more information on the dollar books issued in 1912.

Editions: Abridged and edited version (Bruce Caplan, ed.), Seattle, WA: Hara, 1997. The public-domain text has also been made available online.

109 Marshello, A. F. ***Titanic Trivia.*** R. P. Communications/Reese Press, 1987. Softcover, 100 pp.

This self-published, pamphlet-style book presents 10 questions on each recto page, with the 10 answers following directly on the reverse page. Questions range from the straightforward ("In what city was *Titanic* built?") to the mundane ("At whose table did Thomas Andrews have his last dinner?"). Ten questions alone deal with Morgan Robertson's novel *Futility*.

110 Martin, Simon. ***The Other Titanic.*** London: David and Charles, 1980. Hardcover, 207 pp.

Account of the early White Star Liner *Oceanic*.

111 Mauro, Philip. ***The Titanic Catastrophe and Its Lessons.*** London: Morgan and Scott, 1912. Clothbound, 28 pp.

In this thin tract, Philip Mauro, an attorney and passenger on the *Carpathia*, builds a religious metaphor using the dying passengers on the *Titanic* as a symbol for those humans who trust in the works of man, and those saved on the lifeboats as those who put their trust in Christ, or "God's Lifeboat." Mauro argues that there was no real need for the *Titanic* to cross the ocean at all and that the disaster did not receive so much attention because of the loss of life. Rather, it was the loss of a great symbol of man's technological achievement that was mourned in the aftermath of the tragedy.

112 Marx, R. F., and Jenifer Marx. ***The Search for Sunken Treasure: Exploring the World's Great Shipwrecks.*** Key Porter Books, 1996. Softcover, 192 pp.

School-library collection of descriptions of various famous wrecks, including the *Andrea Doria* and *Titanic*.

113 Maxtone-Graham, John. ***The Only Way to Cross.*** New York: Macmillan, 1972. Hardcover, 434 pp. + xiii.

Seminal history of the north Atlantic golden age of first-class travel, detailing the opulence and luxury aboard such liners as the *Titanic, Lusitania, Queen Mary, Mauretania, Amerika,* and *Normandie*. Includes foreword by Walter Lord.

Other editions: Special edition reprint (Macmillan, 1986); Barnes & Noble reprint (1999).

114 McCaughan, Michael. *The Birth of the Titanic.* Ireland: Blackstaff Press, 1998. Hardcover, 184 pp.

Heavily illustrated retelling of the disaster, drawn from Harland & Wolff archives, newspapers, and White Star publicity materials. The size of the *Titanic* is perhaps nowhere more apparent than in photographs from her construction, in which funnels, propellers, and crankshafts outsize workers by nightmarish proportions. Besides photographs, McCaughan includes facsimiles of White Star documents, Marconi telegrams, and letters. The endpages reveal color reproductions of *Titanic*'s design drawings and floor plans as approved by Bruce Ismay in 1908.

115 McCaughan, Michael. *Titanic.* Ulster Folk and Transport Museum, 1982. Paperback, 32 pp.

Pamphlet-sized earlier effort by McCaughan includes photographs, ship plans, and an event chronology.

116 McCluskie, Tom. *Anatomy of the Titanic.* San Diego, CA: Thunder Bay Press, 1998. Hardcover, 160 pp.

This coffee-table book, published in the midst of the publicity created by Cameron film's (on which McCluskie was a consultant), reconstructs the design, building, and fitting of the *Titanic* through plans and photographs mostly drawn from Harland & Wolff's archives. The text addresses such technical topics as boiler operation, refrigeration, navigation equipment, cargo handling, and the watertight compartments. A series of interior concept drawings, reproduced in color, is particularly evocative.

117 McCluskie, Tom. *The Wall Chart of the Titanic.* Barnes and Noble Books, 1998. Hardcover.

This oversized book-like item was produced by Barnes and Noble to sell in its retail outlets. The book folds out to reveal a 15-foot wall chart containing exterior cutaway rigging and deck plans, augmented with photographs to illustrate the location of various amenities and machinery. An introduction tells the basic story of *Titanic*'s planning and construction, while the flip side of the chart includes a timeline, a lifeboat informational table, a crew list, and a copy of the cargo manifest.

118 McMillan, Beverly, and Stanley Lehrer, with the staff of the Mariners' Museum. *Titanic: Fortune and Fate: Letters, Mementos,* *and Personal Effects from Those Who Sailed on the Lost Ship.* New York: Simon and Schuster, 1998. Hardcover, 192 pp.

This busy volume showcases items on display as part of a special exhibition at the Mariners' Museum in Newport News, Virginia, in 1998. These mostly consist of items carried from the sinking ship by passengers and mementos that have been long ensconced in private family collections. The scarcity of such items outside of salvagers' hands permits the occasional period steamer trunk, *Olympic* staircase, reproduction deck chair, or general purpose White Star dinner plate to serve as acceptable stand-ins. As seen in light of the salvage exhibitions, this collection of items differs in both tone and emotional effect, offering a sad scattering of pocket watches, silk scarves, a 2,700-year-old Egyptian talisman belonging to Molly Brown, Douglas Spedden's famous polar bear, postcards, and letters.

119 *Memorial to the "Titanic" Engineering Staff, the members of which were all lost with the Steamer on April 15th, 1912.* Bradford: Percy Lund, Humphries, The Country Press, 1913. Softcover, 54 pp.

This memorial pamphlet was published by the Institute of Marine Engineers Inc., in conjunction with its 1912-1913 session. Each of *Titanic*'s 35 marine engineers, plumbers, boilermakers, and electricians, along with designer Thomas Andrews, is remembered with a brief, half-page biography and official dress photographs. (All the engineers as well as Andrews perished.) Prefatory material includes updates on contributions for the engineers' memorial .

Other editions: Facsimile reprint, 7 C's Press, 1990.

120 Merideth, Lee W. ***1912 Facts About Titanic.*** Mason City, IA: Savas, 1999. Softcover, 224 pp.

Merideth's 1912 detailed "facts," each one running a paragraph or more, together constitute a rough chronology of events, beginning with the design and construction of the ship and leading to recovery operations and the aftermath of the disaster. A generous supply of black-and-white photographs includes portraits of Violet Jessop, Jacques Futrelle, and the Navratil children.

121 Mills, Simon. ***The Titanic in Pictures.*** Chesham, UK: Wordsmith, 1995. Softcover, 136 pp.

This well-illustrated and history reviews the complicated relationship between *Titanic* and the movie industry over the years. In each chapter devoted to a separate film, Mills reviews the motivations, back story, complications, successes, and legacy of each film. The films covered include *Saved from the*

Titanic, Atlantic, In Nacht und Eis, Hitchcock's unmade film, *Titanic* (1943), *Titanic* (1953), *A Night to Remember, S.O.S. Titanic,* and *Raise the Titanic.* Illustrations include black-and-white publicity stills, conceptual drawings, and behind-the-scenes photographs. A final chapter touches on the several contributions *Titanic* has made in the annals of anthology television.

Includes appendices and a full filmography with production credits.

122 Molony, Senan. ***The Irish Aboard Titanic.*** Merlin, 2000. Softcover, 256 pp.

Cultural analysis and history from unique ethnic perspective.

123 Molony, Senan. ***Titanic: A Ship Accused, Case of the S.S. Californian Re-Examined.*** Cedric Information Services, 2002. Clothcover, 238 pp.

Argues that the *Californian* could not have been the mystery ship in the vicinity that night.

124 Morris, Richard. ***The Unsinkable Molly Brown.*** New York: Putnam, 1961. Hardcover, 160 pp.

Souvenir book published in conjunction with the musical.

125 Mowbray, Jay Henry. ***Sinking of the Titanic: Thrilling Stories Told by Survivors.*** Harrisburg, PA: Minter, 1912. Hardcover, 288 pp.

One of the first accounts of the disaster, Mowbray's "memorial" book serves more as a tribute to those who perished than as an informational account. The book not unexpectedly brims with Edwardian sentimentality, with Mowbray describing the disaster as "a heart-rending story, redeemed and ennobled by the heroism of the victims." Stepping up to meet the expectations of those who idealized the shipwreck as the epitome of Anglo-Saxon chivalry, Mowbray glosses over the more unseemly aspects of the lifeboat loading, writing how "men stood aside ... and gave place not merely to the delicate and the refined, but to the scared woman from the steerage." For the facts of the disaster, Mowbray relies on the accounts of survivors such as Lady Duff-Gordon and Mrs. William R. Bucknell, and pads out his narrative with hymns, sentimental artwork that borders on being morbid, and such empty descriptive passages as "the star-sprinkled dome of heaven and the phosphorescent sea alike breathed forth peace."

Among the many myths that the book gives credence to is that the ship was trying to break a speed record and that Captain Smith may have committed suicide. To his credit, Mowbray does note that the "women first" rule was followed to such an extent that boats were lowered half-filled and that the ship might have survived had she plunged head-first into the iceberg.

The book also includes a brief account of the memorial service of Archibald Butt, a list of great marine disasters from 1866 to 1911, a summary of the U.S. Senate inquiry, a passenger list, and an account of the funeral ship *Mackay-Bennett*.

Despite the factual shortcomings, and the book's many typographical and spelling errors, *Sinking of the Titanic* stands with the other early *Titanic* accounts as a fascinating representation of how the disaster was quickly sanitized and appropriated by Edwardian myth-makers as an affirmation of the venerable class system — quite the opposite of what the *Titanic* disaster often represents today.

For more information on "memorial" books released in 1912, see Everett.

Reprint editions: Softcover reprint under the title *Sinking of the Titanic: Eyewitness Accounts* (Dover, 1998; 288 pp.). The text of the book, which has fallen into the public domain in the United States, has also been available online at times.

126 Murray, John Norman. ***The Titanic: A Sign Prophecy to England, the Unites States, and the New International Order.*** Wilkes-Barre, PA: J. Murray, 1993. Paperback, 42 pp.

Self-published religious tract connecting the disaster to conservation religious teachings.

127 Newell, Gordon. ***Ocean Liners of the Twentieth Century.*** New York: Bonanza, 1958. Hardcover, 192 pp.

Well-regarded general history of the modern ocean liner industry, with significant attention paid to forebear *Titanic*. A prolific maritime historian, Newell's has also written works on Pacific tugboats, the U.S.S. *Missouri*, crew racing, Puget Sound, and famous sea rogues.

Other editions: Reprint (Bonanza, 1963; Seattle: Superior, 1963).

128 Nummi, Gerald E., and Janet A. White. ***I'm Going to See What Has Happened.*** Nummi and White, 1996. Softcover, 44 pp.

Self-published, spiral-bound notebook history of the disaster from the point-of-view third-class Finnish survivor Elin Hakkarainen, mother of Gerald Nummi. The booklet is similar in tone and production to many privately produced genealogical histories and is illustrated with photocopy-quality family photographs, news clippings, and passage documents. Nummi died before the booklet's publication.

129 O'Connor, Richard. ***Down to Eternity: How the Proper Edwardian and His World Died with the Titanic.*** New York: Fawcett, 1956. Paperback, 192 pp.

Romantic account largely based on original newspaper accounts. The pulp paperback cover was taken from the Hollywood film *Titanic* (1953), although the book was not directly inspired by the film.

130 O'Donnell, Edward Eugene. ***The Last Days of the Titanic.*** Dublin: Wolfhound Press, 1997. Hardcover, 120 pp.

Remarkable collection of photographs taken by Francis Browne aboard the *Titanic* and *Olympic*. The photographs are presented first in a partial facsimile of Father Browne's *Titanic* album, assembled in 1920 and containing 63 pages and 159 photographs. The photographs are then presented in enlarged form with annotations and corrections to Browne's original captions. Many of the best photographs are of the *Olympic*, but this does not lessen the value of the collection. Also included are reproductions of an essay and poem by Browne as well as some of his press clippings and correspondence.

Other editions: American edition (Niwot, CO: Roberts Rinehart, 1997).

131 Oldham, Wilton J. ***The Ismay Line, The White Star Line, and the Ismay Family Story.*** Liverpool: Journal of Commerce, 1961. Hardcover, 284 pp. + xviii.

Well-remembered account of the rise of the line and the triumphs and tribulations of its founding family.

132 Ostrow, Lonnie, and Zina Saunders. ***Titanic: A Postal Collection.*** Inter-Governmental Philatelic Corporation, 1998. 28 pp.

Presented as a collector's album, this "book" includes six postal sheets of legal *Titanic* photographic stamps issued by various countries around the world. Also includes a brief history, blueprint, and trivia list.

133 Padfield, Peter. ***The Titanic and the Californian.*** London: Hodder and Stoughton, NY: John Day, 1965. Hardcover, 318 pp. Foreword by Captain Stanley Lord.

Noted maritime historian Padfield systematically challenges long-standing allegations that Captain Stanley Lord of the *Californian* ignored repeated distress calls from the *Titanic*.

134 Parisi, Paula. ***Titanic and the Making of James Cameron: The Inside Story of the Three-Year Adventure That Rewrote Motion***

Picture History. New York: Newmarket Press, 1998. Hardcover/softcover, 234 pp.

Entertainment reporter Parisi, who followed the making of the *Titanic* from its inception, paints James Cameron as a visionary who would stop at nothing to make certain that his artistic vision was not compromised. Those entranced by the movie and the trivia connected with it will find much to enjoy about the book (such as the fact that Linda Hamilton was originally asked to play Molly Brown, and Claire Danes was auditioned for the role of Rose). The early chapters on Cameron's voyages to the bottom of sea are particularly engaging, as cultural clashes between the Russian mariners and American filmmakers come to the fore. Illustrated with color photographs taken on the set.

135 Pellegrino, Charles. ***Ghosts of the Titanic.*** New York: Avon Books, 2000. Paperback, 340 pp.

In a follow-up to his best-selling *Her Name, Titanic,* Pellegrino pursues the answers to such mysteries as Captain Smith's missing hour and the silence of the nearby *Californian* from the perspective of a researcher on the team of Bob Ballard's expedition group. The ghosts of the title are those that have pursued Pellegrino since, like so many others, he became obsessed with the disaster in the midst of a life-threatening illness. With obvious admiration and fondness, Pellegrino blends into his scientific account the stories of such colorful passengers as high-diving champion Frank Prentice, "*Titanic* waif" Michel Navratil, chief baker Charles Jougin, and Howard Irwin (who Pellegrino compares to the fictional Jack Dawson). Pellegrino has held pieces of the *Titanic*'s hull and has seen the intact jars of olives resting at the bottom of the ocean; he has met with and spoken to aging survivors. Most entertaining, perhaps, are Pellgrino's highly parenthetical and tangential footnotes, including one in which he reveals the fate of the ship's only known cat (who survived by disembarking at Southampton) and notes that although thousands of rats most likely populated the ship, none is none to have survived. A center section includes diagrams of the ship's deckplan and the site of the wreck. As a scientist haunted by the remains and memories of the *Titanic,* he makes a strong case for the value of remembering and thinking about the disaster.

Other editions: Avon Books. Paperback, 2001.

136 Pellegrino, Charles. ***Her Name, Titanic: The Untold Story of the Sinking and Finding of the Unsinkable Ship.*** New York: McGraw Hill, 1988. Hardcover, 270 pp. + xvii. Cover art: courtesy of the Bettmann Archive.

Paleobiologist Charles Pellegrino casts himself in alternating roles as probing scientist-philosopher and stirring storyteller in this work, which has been criticized by some *Titanic* aficionados for its speculative bent. The book begins with an imaginative recounting of a shipyard conversation between Thomas Andrews and his young bride as Halley's Comet trails across the backdrop of the morning sky. The second chapter fast-forwards to December 1985, as Pellegrino recounts his experiences aboard the *Melville*, Bob Ballard's research vessel. This time out, Bob Ballard is using the robot submarine *Argo* and its baby-sub *Jason* to explore the bottom of the East Pacific Rise (where Ballard and his fellow scientists discover a dark yet teeming world of lava ruin fields and sea lilies). The book continues in this way, alternating between Pellegrino's workmanlike retelling of the events of 1912 and his romantic musings on the scientific possibilities of deep-sea exploration. Much of the book hinges on Pellegrino's fascination with the contradictory persona of Ballard (who discovered *Titanic*'s wreck in 1985); as Pellegrino recalls, it was the awe of seeing the televised, ghostly video images of the *Titanic*'s hull that sent the publicity-hungry Ballard into an emotional spiral of mournful grief, cutting off media contact and satellite links.

Most engaging are the verbatim transcripts of conversations between Ballard and Pellegrino, who spent some years working with NASA in developing rocket systems and dreaming of anti-matter rockets capable of attaining speeds of 92 percent the speed of light. Ballard and Pellegrino argue over the relative merits of visiting the equally alien worlds of deep ocean and deep space (Pellegrino's initial contact with Ballard arose as a result of his interest in the possibility of deep oceans on the icy satellites of Jupiter and Saturn). Pellegrino's far-flinging narrative encompasses many other worthwhile bits, including a chance encounter with Walter Lord on the island of St. Thomas and Bob Ballard's eerie prediction of a *Titanic*-like disaster in space just a month before the *Challenger* explosion.

Illustrations include sketch of mid–Atlantic Ridge and approximate sites of Bob Ballard's exploration dives, sketch of five-deck layout, progressive sketches showing the effects of the sinking on the ship itself, sketches and diagrams of Bob Ballard's various research vessels, and approximately 20 black-and-white photographs of Ballard's trips to the bottom of the Atlantic ocean and the rusting hull of the *Titanic*'s ghostly form.

In the book's preface, Pellegrino notes that *Her Name, Titanic* is meant to be a companion to Bob Ballard's *Discovery of the Titanic*.

Other editions: Avon Books paperback, 1990.

137 Pellow, James, with Dorothy Kendle. ***A Lifetime on the Titanic: The Biography of Edith Haisman.*** London: Island Books, 1995. Softcover, 128 pp.

Biography of survivor Edith Haisman (maiden name Brown), who was 15 at the time of the sinking and whose fame grew, along with other aging survivors, according to public interest in the disaster. Haisman died in 1997.

138 Quinn, Paul J. ***Dusk to Dawn: Survivor Accounts of the Last Night on the Titanic.*** Hollis, NH: Fantail, 1999. Hardcover, 290 pp. Foreword by Edward Kamuda.

Quinn's expanded timeline version of events begins at 8 P.M. the night of the disaster.

139 Quinn, Paul J. ***Titanic at Two A.M.: Final Events Surrounding the Doomed Liner.*** Saco, ME: Fantail, 1997. Hardcover, 128 pp.

Drawing on survivor testimony, Quinn attempts to reconstruct the final desperate minutes aboard *Titanic*, from the hour when nearly all of the lifeboats had left the ship. Illustrations include black-and-white photographs and paintings by the author.

140 Reade, Leslie. ***The Ship That Stood Still: The Californian and Her Mysterious Role in the Titanic Disaster.*** New York: Norton, 1993; Somerset: Patrick Stephens, 1993. Hardcover, 384 pp. Edited and Updated by Edward P. De Groot. Foreword by Eva Hart.

This indictment of Captain Lord takes the form of a narrative aboard the ship, reconstructing the actions of the crew of the *Californian*. Reade began the work in the 1960s; when he died in 1989, De Groot prepared the manuscript for publication. The book has since become scarce and much sought by those interested in *Californian* lore. Includes appendices and a bibliography.

141 Rivett, Norman C. ***Some Aspects of R.M.S. Titanic (1912) and Her Sister Ships.*** Sydney: The Naval Historical Society of Australia, 1993. Softcover, 26 pp.

Technical pamphlet by Australian naval historian.

142 ***Report on the Loss of the S.S. Titanic.*** Belfast: Blackstaff Press, 1990; New York: St. Martin's Press, 1990. Hardcover, 74 pp.

Reprint of the official British government report on the disaster, with an introduction consisting mostly of snippets of survivor testimony and a section of large black-and-white photographs.

143 Rostron, Arthur. ***Loss of the Titanic.*** 7 C's Press. Date unknown. Softcover, 36 pp.

Account of the disaster from the unique perspective of *Carpathia* captain Rostron, taken from his 1931 autobiography *Home from the Sea* (Macmillan). This pamphlet-style reprint was produced in conjunction with the *Titanic* Historical Society.

Other editions: Audio edition (*Titanic* Historical Society, two cassettes), with an introduction by Rostron's daughter. Audio CD edition: *RMS Titanic: The Captain's Log* (Brentwood, TN: KRB Music, 1998).

144 Ruffman, Alan. ***Titanic Remembered: The Unsinkable Ship and Halifax.*** Formac, 1999. Softcover, 72 pp.

Story of the aftermath, with special attention to the recovery and burial of *Titanic*'s victims. Visuals, including photographs of the grim recovery efforts, are drawn from the permanent *Titanic* exhibit at the Maritime Museum of the Atlantic in Halifax.

145 Russell, Thomas H., ed. ***Sinking of the Titanic.*** L. H. Walter, 1912; Chicago: Laird & Lee, 1912. Hardcover, 312 pp.

Variant reprint of Everett (q.v.) printed with a red cover.

146 Sabella, Casey. ***Titanic Warning: Hearing the Voice of God in This Modern Age.*** Green Forest, Arkansas: New Leaf Press, 1994. Softcover, 174 pp.

Breaking from the traditional mode of using the *Titanic* as a metaphor for man's hubris in the face of the Almighty, Sabella compares the ship, a manifestation of invincibility and pridefulness, to the state of the modern church as a whole. While retelling the story of the disaster in breezy fashion, Sabella uses aspects of the event as metaphors for issues of discipleship and church leadership in the modern age. The underutilized lifeboats, for instance, represent the ways in which churches fail to reach out to those in the community who do not come to church asking for salvation. Churches, he argues, must strive to model themselves after the dutiful and charitable *Carpathia*, which launched into a mission of rescue without hesitation and without the expectation of reward.

Each chapter concludes with study and discussion questions.

147 Sandler, Kevin S., and Gaylyn Studlar, eds. ***Titanic: Anatomy of a Blockbuster.*** Piscataway, NJ: Rutgers University Press, 1999. Clothbound/Softcover, 288 pp.

Although the title implies this might be a "making of" account, it is instead a collection of scholarly essays on the film and its place in cinema from a wide range of sociocultural perspectives.

148 Santini, Steve. ***Titanic: Touchstones of a Tragedy.*** Lincoln, NE: Writers Club Press, 2000. Softcover, 102 pp.

More than 60 photographs of various artifacts related to and recovered from the *Titanic* serve as windows into life aboard the ship and the human drama behind the disaster. The artifacts are not those collected by RMS *Titanic*, but rather comprise an odd collection of mementos and other small items rescued by passengers, including menus, ticket stubs, dinnerware, a pocket watch, postmortem photographs, and a cigarette case. The unusual perspective of the book provides a valuable material-culture study in accessible prose and format. Includes index.

The author serves as curator of the private *Titanic* Concepts Inc. collection, from which the artifacts were drawn.

149 Sauder, Eric, and Hugh Brewster. ***The Titanic Collection: Mementos of the Maiden Voyage from the Archives of the Titanic Historical Society.*** Chronicle Books, 1998. Paperback, 32 pp.

This novelty product sold in bookstores was not so much a book but rather a boxed collection of *Titanic*-related memorabilia reproductions, including a first-class ticket, menus, postcards, a telegram, and luggage stickers.

150 Schults, Raymond L. ***Crusader in Babylon: W. T. Stead and the Pall Mall Gazette.*** Lincoln: University of Nebraska Press, 1972. Cloth, 278 pp.

Scholarly biography of passenger and famed editor Stead.

151 Sebak, Per Kristian. ***Titanic: 31 Norwegian Destinies.*** Oslo, Norway: Genesis, 1998. Hardcover, 190 pp.

This genealogical history traces the cultural roots and influences of Norwegian immigration through the fates of 31 Norwegian passengers. Sebak presents detailed background information for all the passengers, including photographs and family history. The disaster unfolds from the perspectives of the Norwegian passengers, and a parallel narrative traces the voyage of a Norwegian sealer that was in the vicinity. The book's final chapters deal with the fate of the seven Norwegian survivors, the disposition of bodies, the effect of the disaster on Norwegian families, and impending lawsuits. Appendices document passenger fares and the lifeboat-launching chronology. Abundant illustrations include black-and-white photographs and maps.

Sebak writes that he was inspired to write the book after seeing the television movie *S.O.S. Titanic* when he was 10.

152 Shapiro, Marc. ***Total Titanic.*** New York: Pocket Books, 1998. Paperback, 190 pp.

Accessible, mass-market paperback book was one of many "quick and dirty" books released in 1998 to capitalize on the success of James Cameron's movie. Although this book contains little new information (and a few factual oversights), its low cost and easy-to-read text make it hard to fault. One can glean all the basic facts of the disaster, as well as trivia about the most well-known *Titanic* movies, in just a couple of hours by scanning the heavily bulleted chapters of this book. Includes 16 pages of photographs, comprehensive passenger and crew lists, and a bibliography. A companion CD-ROM (q.v.) was packaged similiarly, but has more to do with the film *A Night to Remember* than Marc Shapiro's book.

153 Shilts, Randy. ***And the Band Played On.*** St. Martin's Press, 1987. 630 pp.

This book on the rise of the AIDS epidemic uses the *Titanic*-inspired metaphor of the band playing during the great sinking to draw a damning comparison — that medical and government authorities remained oblivious to the potential impact of the disease and allowed the spread to continue unabated. See also *Andersen, Richard.*

154 Shubow, Leo. ***Iceberg Dead Ahead! The Heroic Work of the Ice Patrol.*** Boston, MA: Bruce Humphries, 1959. Hardcover, 204 pp.

This history of the U.S. Coast Guard's Ice Patrol, which was established after the *Titanic*'s demise, includes a chapter titled "What Happened to the *Titanic*?"

155 Smith, Ken. ***Tyne to Titanic: The Story of Rescue Ship Carpathia.*** Newcastle Upon Tyne: Newcastle Libraries and Information Service, 1998. Softcover, 28 pp.

This attractive, official-type account of the *Carpathia*'s role in the disaster focuses on describing the rescue ship and how she came to *Titanic*'s aid, with not much new revealed concerning the voyage to New York. Illustrations include photographs of *Carpathia* and survivors aboard the rescue ship, as well as a reproduction of a soap advertisement that invokes *Titanic*'s good name.

156 Spignesi, Stephen J. ***The Complete Titanic: From the Ship's Earliest Blueprints to the Epic Film.*** Secaucus, NJ: Carol, 1998. Hardcover, 436 pp.

This broad, accessible reference compiled by a general nonfiction author, *The Complete Titanic,* like many of the books released in 1998–1999, aims to be a utilitarian book for non-specialized readers. Much of the book's content reproduces official documents or earlier efforts, including the ship's official certificates and registers, menus, telegraph transcripts, and the U.S. Senate hearing transcripts. A section of 1912 writings offers the accounts of Harold Bride and Washington Dodge, newspaper articles, and Joseph Conrad's famous essay. Another section of the book addresses the myths and legends of the disaster, from the unknown last words of Captain Smith to the true causes of the sinking. Other sections describe the work of Robert Ballard and the myth-making efforts of James Cameron and *Titanic: A New Musical.* Appendices include a bibliography and the *Titanic*'s cargo manifest.

157 Stacey, Thomas. ***The Titanic.*** See 318.

158 Stead, Estelle. ***My Father: Personal and Spiritual Reminiscences.*** New York: George H. Doran, 1913. Hardcover, 352 pp. + xii.

Early biography of Stead by his daughter.

159 Stenson, Patrick. ***Lights: The Odyssey of C. H. Lightoller.*** New York: Norton, 1984. Hardcover, 326 pp.

Biography of second officer Lightoller, detailing among other things his early service on clipper ships and windjammers and the loss of his two sons in World War II.

160 Stevenson, Jay, and Sharon Rutman. ***The Complete Idiot's Guide to the Titanic.*** New York: Alpha Books, 1998. Softcover, 332 pp.

The familiar, orange-covered Idiot series became a staple in bookstores during the 1990s and, along with the similar "for Dummies" books, provided easy-to-follow information on an increasingly bizarre range of topics, including roses, prayer, philosophy, sex, motorcycles, fly fishing, handwriting analysis, Yiddish, gene decoding, the Mafia, and NASA. As embarrassing as these books may have been to own, with their cartoon graphics and multitudinous sidebars, most were written by acknowledged experts; the title of the series simply played on the notion that Americans often *felt* ignorant in the face of increasing amounts of information. *The Idiot's Guide to the Titanic,* coauthored by a nonfiction tradesman and Rutman, a cofounder of *Titanic* International, covers the predictable touchstones with an abundance of gray boxes and bulleted lists. Each chapter, whether describing the lives of first-class passengers, the building of the ship, or the so-called *Titanic* prophecies, ends with a "Least You Need to Know" box to provide easily accessible cocktail-party facts. Like the rest of the books in the series, the book suffers from a flippant tone and comical style, all the more obvious when dealing with a somber subject. Chapter and section titles brim with alliteration and puns; the result is neither clear nor very amusing: "Deep Sea TV," "Spin Cycles," "A Bad Scrape," "Salt-Water Staffers." Besides the cartoons, illustrations include black-and-white photographs, sketches, and a fold-out back cover showing the layout of the ship.

161 Stone, Peter. ***Titanic: The Complete Book of the Musical.*** New York: Applause Books, 1999. Hardcover, softcover, 176 pp.

Souvenir book for the 1990s Broadway musical. The original text tells the story of the musical's conception, writing, and production, while the second half of the book contains a reproduction of the script alongside color performance photographs. The book's final pages include a list of those lost in the sinking. In answer to the famous question of why anyone would want to make a musical about 1,500 people dying, Stone writes, "In the show Maury Yeston and I wrote, those deaths are not the end of the story; the lost are followed by survivors with their dreams and hopes and their memories of courage, sacrifice and yes, survival, inspiring them, and, we hopes, us as well." Yeston is credited on the book's cover for his work on *Titanic*'s music and lyrics.

162 Stormer, Susanne. ***Good-bye, Good Luck: The Biography of William McMaster Murdoch.*** Germany: Stormer, 1995.

This comprehensive biography of controversial officer Murdoch was well received by enthusiasts yet has only been printed in limited runs.

Other editions: American edition title *William McMaster Murdoch: A Career at Sea* (1998). Revised edition *William McMaster Murdoch: A Career at Sea — The Complete and Documented Version* (Germany: Stormbreakers, 2002; 428 pp.; with foreword by Scott Murdoch).

163 Thayer, John B. ***The Sinking of the S.S. Titanic.*** Ludlow, MA: 7 C's Press, 1974. Softcover, 32 pp.

Digest-sized reprint of Thayer's eyewitness account.
Other editions: Limited private run (500 copies), 1940.

164 Thompson, Frank. ***Lost Films: Important Movies That Disappeared.*** New York: Citadel Press, 1996. Softcover, 298 pp.

Film historian Thompson estimates that at least half of the films made before 1950 have been irrevocably lost, due to nitrate film decay and the lack of funding to preserve the films not casually misplaced. In this scholarly study, Thompson provides as much insight as possible into the making and reception of 27 of what he considers to be some of the most important of these lost works, relying mostly on reviews, publicity materials, and other studio documents. One of the films reviewed is Dorothy Gibson's *Saved from the Titanic*, perhaps, because of general interest in the *Titanic*, the most famous lost silent film of all. Much of his information is taken from articles originally printed in *Moving Picture World* just a month after the disaster.

165 Thresh, Peter. ***Titanic: The Truth Behind the Disaster.*** Greenwich, CT: Brompton Books, 1992. Hardcover, 80 pp.

This standard, thin coffee-table history touches on events from *Titanic*'s construction to the discovery of her wreck 70 years later. Illustrations include reproductions of postcards and advertisements, photographs, and drawings.
Other editions: Reprint (Book Sales, 1998).

166 Throckmorton, Peter, ed. ***The Sea Remembers: Shipwrecks and Archaeology from Homer's Greece to the Rediscovery of the Titanic.*** New York: Weidenfeld & Nicholson, 1987. Hardcover, 240 pp.

This collection of essays on underwater archeology is augmented with photographs, maps, notes, a bibliography, and glossary.

167 Tibballs, Geoff. ***The Titanic: The Extraordinary Story of the Unsinkable Ship.*** Pleasantville, NY: Readers Digest, 1997. Softcover, 128 pp.

Colorful rendering of the disaster, illustrated with an abundance of color photographs, watercolors, movie poster reproductions, cartoons, and information boxes. Unusual or noteworthy selections from the text include a section on passengers who "missed the boat," an inventory of foodstuffs, cutlery, and linen, and a sampling of insurance claims (ranging from a $100,000 oil painting to five chickens valued at $207).

168 ***Titanic.*** Ludlow: Mass.: 7 C's Press, 1974. Running time: Approx. 3½ hours on 3 cassettes.

This audio recording was packaged and distributed by the *Titanic* Historical Society in cooperation with 7 C's Press. The first cassette, labeled "*Titanic*, Vol. 1" consists of an award-winning Canadian Broadcasting Company radio program written and narrated by Neil Copeland. The monophonic program begins with the story of Morgan Robertson's novel *Futility*. Survivor interviews are interspersed with such eerie sound effects as the tapping of the wireless telegraph. Aging survivors interviewed or featured in the program include Eva Hart and 94-year-old steerage passenger Gus Cohen. A good portion of the program is given over to examination of the *Californian* controversy, with author Peter Padfield providing a persuasive argument in Capt. Stanley Lord's defense. Lord himself is also featured in an older recording.

The second cassette, labeled "*Titanic*: Vol. II," provides a sequel of sorts to the CBC program, with a collection of survivor interviews not included in the original broadcast. The program begins with a history of the formation the *Titanic* Historical Society, which was set up in the early 1963 as an antidote to the growing tendency to fictionalize and embrace myths and legends of the *Titanic*. The tape provides invaluable oral histories from survivors not often heard elsewhere. Edwina Celia Corrigan (maiden name Troutt) in a 1957 interview remembers agreeing to take charge of a 3-month infant and jumping to safety into a lifeboat, incidents transformed for James Cameron's *Titanic*. Also in 1957, Mrs. Frederick Kenyon recalls fond exchanges with Capt. Smith and curiously remembers observing nobody onboard being intoxicated. During a 1973 interview at the THS 10th anniversary convention, attended by seven survivors, Frank Goldsmith (age 9 in 1912) recalls his father not wanting to don a life preserver and poignantly compares the cries of drowning passengers to the cheers at a baseball game following a home run.

A third cassette, titled "Remember the *Titanic*," presents sound bites from the 1973 meeting, including recollections from survivors (with some repetition from the second cassette) on such topics as why passengers were leery of boarding the lifeboats and society members musing on the reasons for their interest in the disaster.

169 *Titanic, the Official Story: April 14–15, 1912.* Random House, 1997.

Although not technically a book, this boxed collection of documents was marketed and produced by Random House and sold in bookstores. A guide to the documents provides a short history of the disaster and follows the trail of official documents that sprang from the inquiries and other heated exchanges in the aftermath of the wreck. The assortment of documents, taken mostly from the British Public Record Office and the archives of Harland and Wolff, includes facsimile reproductions of the *Titanic*'s shipping certificates, the original construction drawings, distress telegrams sent to the SS *Birma*, the front page of the *New York Evening Journal*, and the 75-page report of the British Commission of Enquiry into the loss of the *Titanic*. All of the documents are printed on modern paper. Of particular interest are the letters of union leader Ben Tillett, who condemns the ship's owners for the abysmal loss of steerage passengers, the official death reports, and the letter of first-class passenger Alfred Omont, who states unreservedly that the notion of the lifeboats holding 60 people is "ridiculous" (even though some were filled to capacity). Stanley Lord's letter defending his own actions (or lack thereof), holds some interest, but his handwriting is nearly illegible. The collection is presented as a stepping stone for further independent learning and research into the *Titanic*, and the guide provides some useful information on how the average reader can find other official documents and government reports in libraries and public archives.

170 ***The Titanic Tragedy.*** B&B Audio (Buckingham Classics), 1987. Running time: Approx. 1 hour, 1 cassette. Narration: Dave Bodin.

Low-budget repackaging of the *Titanic* story as told in newspaper accounts of the day, and as a result, suffering from sensationalist tendencies. Interestingly, while the presentation includes the story of how Captain Smith rescued a baby before going under, it also throws a shadow on his reputation through the inclusion of incidents that happened to the *Olympic* under his command. The material taken from Harold Bride's account and his testimony deserves the most attention here; Bride discusses repairing the wireless set earlier in the day and also describes foiling the would-be lifevest thief.

171 Tyler, Sidney F. ***A Rainbow of Time and Space: Orphans of the Titanic.*** Tuscon, AZ: Aztex, 1981. Softcover, 94 pp.

Story of mysterious young French survivors Michel and Edmond Navratil, who traveled with their father under assumed names, as told by Tyler, who met the "orphans" as a boy when they stayed at his house in Philadelphia; they were reunited some 70 years later.

172 Vess, John. ***The Titan and the Titanic: The Life, Works, and Incredible Foresight of Morgan Robertson.*** Chapmansboro, TN: Pleasant Valley, 1990. Softcover, 130 pp.

Biography of Robertson, whose novel 1898 *Futility* (q.v.) bears some resemblance to the facts of the *Titanic*.

173 Wade, Wyn Craig. ***The Titanic: End of a Dream.*** New York: Rawson, Wade, 1979. Hardcover, 366 pp.

This thorough and often overlooked account of the disaster reconstructs events from the viewpoints of various survivor accounts, drawing most significantly from the U.S. Senate inquiry. By taking this investigative tack, Wade attempts to answer such questions as whether and why the ship was speeding through icy waters, why the *Titanic*'s calls for help apparently went unheeded, and why one-third of the survivors were crew members.

The author is a clinical psychologist and member of the *Titanic* Historical Society at the time of publication.

Other editions: Mass-market paperback (Penguin, 1980), 488 pp.; trade paperback (Penguin, 1986); Reissue paperback (Penguin, 1992), 358 pp.

174 Walker, John Bernard. ***An Unsinkable Titanic: Every Ship Its Own Lifeboat.*** New York: Dodd, Mead, July 1912. Illustrations: Include 37 line drawings and black-and-white plates. 185 pp. + xi.

In this early book, *Scientific American* editor J. Bernard Walker argues that the *Titanic* disaster was the inevitable result of the increasing mass of steamships coupled with the gradual relaxation of safety standards. Walker's thesis hinges on a comparison between the *Titanic*'s design and that of the *Great Eastern* 50 years before. According to Walker, the *Great Eastern*, which he calls the safest ocean liner ever built and a truly "unsinkable" ship, survived a collision even worse than the *Titanic*'s and still managed to arrive in port under its own steam. The safety standards present on the *Eastern*, including a double skin, longitudinal bulkheads (which increases the number of compartments), and watertight deck were conspicuously absent on the *Titanic*, Walker points out. Many of these features, Walker argues, could be added to future luxury liners by eliminating such expensive amenities as swimming pools. (In fact, the *Olympic* was refitted with a double skin and bulkheads that reached the watertight deck soon after the *Titanic* disaster.) The book presents a rational and technical argument at a time when most discussions centered on whether to blame the *Titanic*'s crew, the lack of lifeboats, or Captain Lord's supposed indifference. While not denying the importance of those factors, Walker poses a more immediate question: Why did the ship sink at all?

The book is dedicated to the memory of John Bell, chief engineer of the *Titanic*, and his 33 assistants.

175 Walker-Smith, Derek. ***Lord Reading and His Cases: The Study of a Great Career.*** New York: Macmillan, 1934. Clothbound, 400 pp.

This biography of Sir Rufus Issacs, the attorney general who represented the Board of Trade during the British *Titanic* investigation, includes a chapter on the hearing.

176 Warren, Mark D. ***Distinguished Liners from the* Shipbuilder, *1907–194, Vol. 1.*** New York: Blue Riband, 1995. Clothbound, 230 pp.

Anthology of *Shipbuilder* issues focusing on single liners, including a reprint of the *Titanic* issue as well as issues on the *Lusitania, Carmania, Avon, Storsdad, Adriatic,* and *Mauretania.*

177 Watson, Arnold. ***Titanic Crew List.*** Indian Orchard, MA: *Titanic* Enthusiasts of America, 1974. Softcover, 42 pp.

Earlier, small-run edition of below.

178 Watson, Arnold, and Betty Watson. ***Roster of Valor: The Titanic Halifax Legacy.*** Riverside, CT: 7 C's Press, 1984. Clothbound, 98 pp. + xiv.

Provides lists of *Titanic*'s crew and officers with home cities and ranks. Illustrated with black-and-white photographs. Arnold Watson died in the year of publication.

179 Wels, Susan. ***Titanic: The Exhibition.*** Time-Life Books/Tehabi Books, 1998. Softcover.

Companion book to the RMS *Titanic* exhibit.
Other editions: Revised softcover, 1999.

180 Wels, Susan. ***Titanic: Legacy of the World's Greatest Ocean Liner.*** Time-Life Books/Tehabi Books, 1997. Hardcover, 206 pp.

This coffee-table tome ostensibly chronicles R.M.S *Titanic* Inc.'s efforts to salvage artifacts and ship debris from the ocean floor. Those wishing to survey the catalog of materials recovered would do better to seek out Wels's other exhibition souvenir book, as this particular volume gives over at least half its pages to a standard recollection of historical events. Additional chapters focus on Ballard's discovery expedition and scientific efforts to better understand the technological aspects of the disaster, while a slim chapter directly relates the story of the French salvage expeditions.

Wels has also authored books on Pearl Harbor and the Olympics.

181 White, Alma. ***The Titanic Tragedy: God Speaking to the Nations.*** Bound Brook, NJ: Pentecostal Union, 1913. 214 pp.

Chapin describes this early book as a "religious interpretation of the disaster." Many were to follow in this vein.

182 ***The White Star Triple Screw Atlantic Liners Olympic and Titanic.*** Wellingborough: Patrick Stephens, 1970. Hardcover, 164 pp.

Reprint of the 1911 *Shipbuilder* issue focusing on the design and building of *Titanic* and her sister ship *Olympic*. Includes an epilogue by maritime historian John Maxtone-Graham.

183 Whyte, Frederic. ***The Life of W. T. Stead.*** New York: Houghton-Mifflin, 1925. Hardcover, 345 368 pp.

Biography of esteemed editor and *Titanic* victim Stead. Whyte also produced works on Mussolini and English theater.

Other editions: Reprint (New York: Garland, 1971), issued just a year before a new biography by Raymond Schults.

184 Winocour, Jack, ed. ***The Story of the Titanic as Told by Its Survivors.*** New York: Dover, 1960. Softcover, 320 pp. + xii.

This workmanlike and thrifty anthology collects the previously published first-hand accounts of survivors Lawrence Beesley, Archibald Gracie, Charles Lightoller, and Harold Bride. Some of the added illustrations, as the editor points out, are of the *Olympic* from the journal *Shipbuilder*.

Dover has built a business out of republishing classics inexpensively, with many editions selling for as little as $1.

185 Young, Filson. ***Titanic.*** London: Grant Richards, 1912. Hardcover, 204 pp.

This early effort by now-obscure Irish journalist and novelist Filson Young was termed a "documentary novel" by his biographer Silvester Mazzarella. The book reached bookstore shelves just 37 days after the sinking.

A prolific writer and raucous public figure, Wilson's most famous novel during his lifetime was the mildly scandalous *The Sands of Pleasure*. He also penned works on Christopher Columbus and the automobile and achieved additional fame through professional (and sometimes adversarial) relationships with James Joyce, Rudyard Kipling, and Arthur Conan Doyle.

2 Novels and Short Stories

186 Aspler, Tony. ***Titanic.*** Toronto: Doubleday, 1989. Hardcover, 312 pp.

In this mystery tale of robber barons and murderous greed, an English banker named Henry Blexill finds employment with a New York tycoon and quickly becomes enmeshed in a web of deceit and violence. He loses the job, but employer and employee are brought together again when Blexill takes a job aboard the *Titanic*.

Other editions: Mass market paperback (Bantam, 1990; 324 pp.); UK paperback, 1998.

187 Bainbridge, Beryl. ***Every Man for Himself.*** Carroll & Graf, 1996. 224 pp. Softcover, 224 pp.

In this breezy yet potent coming-of-age story, told in first person, 22-year-old Morgan embarks on a journey of self-discovery as he attempts to befriend and seduce rich and famous first-class passengers. Morgan swims to safety aboard the capsized collapsible lifeboat B.

The novel won the Whitbread Award for best novel of 1996, and was nominated for both the Booker Prize and the *Los Angeles Times* Book Prize. Bainbridge's previous novel, *The Birthday Boys,* fictionalized the Scott expedition to the South Pole.

Other editions: Paperback edition, 1997; audio, 1997.

188 Barnes, William. ***I Built the Titanic: Past-Life Memories of a Master Shipbuilder.*** Gillette, NJ: Edin Books, 1999. Audio (cassette, 4 hours).

The author, born 41 years after the sinking of the *Titanic*, learns that he was the shipbuilder Thomas Andrews in a past life. By probing the haunted memories of his past life, he is able to solve such mysteries as who scrapped the idea for more lifeboats and what thoughts went through the shipbuilder's mind during the dramatic last hours of the ship. The book was released by a publisher specializing in metaphysical and reincarnation themes.

189 Barnes, William. ***Thomas Andrews, Voyage Into History: Titanic Secrets Revealed Thru the Eyes of Her Builder.*** Gillette, NJ: Edin Books, 2000. Softcover, 188 pp.

Paperback companion to Barnes's audio conversations. The book is represented as a biography, but it is written more as a novel, with Barnes recreating conversations between "Tommie" and Captain Smith, Bruce Ismay, and others.

190 Barnes, William, and Frank Baranowski. ***A Past-Life Interview with Titanic's Designer.*** Gillette, NJ: Edin Books, 1999. Audio (cassette, 3 hours).

Thomas Andrews once again speaks from beyond the grave in this follow-up/companion to *I Built the Titanic*.

191 Bass, Cynthia. ***Maiden Voyage.*** Bantam Doubleday Dells, 1997. Softcover, 240 pp.

Coming-of-age novel centers on the adventures of 12-year-old Sumner, whose activist mother named him after the abolitionist senator Charles Sumner. On the *Titanic*, the young man seeking his identity comes under the influence of two passengers (presumably representing the divergent worlds of his parents): an American feminist named Ivy Earnshaw and an aviator named Pierce Andrews. The sinking of the ship provides an opportunity for the three friends to learn something about character and courage. The high production values and cover of this novel peg it as a "literary novel," although the prose is accessible and even light-hearted at times.

192 Baxter, Stephen. ***"The Twelfth Album."*** First published: *Interzone 130*, April 1998. Collected in: Hartwell, David G., ed. *Year's Best SF 4*. Harper, 1999. Paperback, 496 pp.

In this "alternate history" story, two friends find a mysterious phonograph album among their recently deceased friend's belongings. When they play the record, they discover it to be the nonexistent Beatles twelfth record. It is also revealed that the ship their friend was working on, an old liner dry-docked and operating as a hotel, is actually the *Titanic*.

The term SF is often used to distinguish literary or thoughtful science fiction (SF) from the superficially similar yet more juvenile "sci-fi" or fantasy, stories dealing with bug-eyed monsters and busty women on distant planets. Originally SF was an abbreviation for "speculative fiction"; the abbreviation only seemed to confuse matters.

193 Bodkin, M. McDonnell. *"The Ship's Run."* First collected in *The Quests of Paul Beck* (T. Fisher Unwin, 1908, Little, Brown, 1910). Reprinted in *Murder on Deck!: Shipboard and Shoreline Mystery Stories,* edited by Rosemary Herbert (Oxford University Press, 1998).

Although written and published four years before the *Titanic*'s maiden voyage, lawyer-turned-mystery writer Bodkin's tale of shipboard intrigue provides evidence that the buzz surrounding the *Titanic*'s construction was quickly spreading several years before she set sail. He describes the ship as the "largest and fastest passenger boat afloat." Of course, although speed contributed to the *Titanic*'s undoing, she was not the fastest ship afloat. Nonetheless, speed plays a key role in this detective story, which takes place just as the *Titanic* nears its New York harbor destination (making it one of the few *Titanic* stories in which the ship completes her voyage). The story centers on a few men who bet on the ship's daily run (against the policy of the White Star Line) and the detective who goes undercover to foil them. Although it was collected in *Murder on Deck!,* the simple detective story involves no grisly foul play.

Those looking for clues that the author foretold the disaster will likely be disappointed, although the storyline does involve one gambler sabotaging machinery (in order to win the pool), thereby bringing the ship to an eerie and abrupt halt and sending the passengers into a frenzy. But the reader is left to assume that a little oil will put the ship back in operation soon enough. A more humorous "clue" can be found in the author's description of a cherry cobbler as "crowned with small icebergs."

194 Bristow, Diana. ***Captain's Karma.*** 1st Books Library, 2001. Paperback, 220 pp.

Speculative fiction from the point of view of Captain Smith, originally self-published and reissued by the vanity publisher 1st Books.

195 Butler, Robert Olen. *"Titanic Survivor Found in Bermuda Triangle."* (1996) Collected in: Butler, Robert Olen. *Tabloid Dreams.* Henry Holt, 1996. Hardcover, 1996.

Tabloid Dreams is a collection of experimental fiction, with all the stories based on sensational tabloid headlines. Butler is perhaps better known for much-anthologized short story "A Good Scent from a Strange Mountain."

196 Butler, Robert Olen. *"Titanic Victim Speaks Through Waterbed."* (1996) See above.

The soul of a *Titanic* passenger is found to be residing in a couple's waterbed. The victim reveals himself to be an Englishman who urged his lover to board a lifeboat before perishing in the sinking. The woman recounts the same shipboard romance in Butler's final story in the same collection, "*Titanic* Survivor Found in Bermuda Triangle."

197 Carr, John Dickson. ***The Crooked Hinge.*** New York: Popular Library, 1938. Other editions: Macmillan, 1984; Softcover, 256 pp.

In the denouement to this Dr. Gideon Fell mystery, two men switch identities aboard the sinking liner. Most of the action of the novel takes place in England in the 1930s.

Carr, considered by some to be the "king of mystery fiction," was most well known for his contributions to the "locked room" subgenre, in which a corpse is found in a room locked from the inside. *The Crooked Hinge* has been reissued by several different publishers many times over the years.

198 Cather, Willa. ***"The Diamond Mine."*** (1920) First published: *Youth and the Bright Medusa.* Knopf, 1920. Also published in *Coming, Aphrodite!* (Penguin, 1998) and other anthologies.

In the final part of this four-part "remembrance" of fictional American socialite Cressida Garnet, it is revealed that the showy and independent opera singer perished aboard the *Titanic,* after leaving England a week after her companions so that she could travel on the "sea monster." She did not leave her modest cabin during the sinking, the narrator reveals, and was never seen on deck. Much of the rest of the story concerns the disposition of her estate as her survivors fight for a share of the inheritance.

Other editions: Reprints, Vintage, 1979; Random House, 1999.

199 Chalker, Jack. ***Dance Band on the Titanic.*** Ballatine Books, 1988. Paperback, 339 pp.

Science fiction short-story collection that has nothing to do with the *Titanic* but employs the band metaphor as convenient shorthand for institutional blindness in the face of looming disaster. *And the Played On,* a 1987 book and movie dealing with the AIDS epidemic, also used this metaphor in slightly different guise.

The title short story was first published in *Isaac Asimov's Science Fiction Magazine* in 1978.

200 Clarke, Arthur C. ***The Ghost from the Grand Banks.*** New York: Bantam, 1990. Hardcover, 274 pp.; Mass-market paperback, 1992, 274 pp.

One hundred years after the sinking of the *Titanic,* in 2012, two corporations compete to raise the sunken liner from the floor of the Atlantic. In true science-fiction fashion, the real heroes of the story are the competing technologies, which are explored in some detail.

An afternote reveals the history of Mr. Clarke's fascination with the *Titanic*, while an appendix contains a wonderfully confounding mathematical explanation of the Mandelbrot Set, a concept used in computer imaging.

201 Collins, Max Allan. ***The Titanic Murders.*** New York: Berkley Prime Crime Mystery Books (Penguin), 1999. Paperback, 258 pp.

Intriguing mass-market paperback forgoes the usual route of creating fictional characters with real-life passengers as extras, and instead fictionalizes the story of mystery writer Jacques Futrelle, one of the passengers who perished. Collins, a true-crime author, imagines Futrelle as an amateur detective who must solve the last mystery of his life.

202 Cussler, Clive. ***Raise the Titanic!*** New York: Viking Press, 1976. Hardcover, 312 pp. Paperback, 373 pp. Reprint edition: Buccanner Books, hardcover 1997.

Best-selling author Cussler sends his clever-yet-tough hero Dirk Pitt to the bottom of the Atlantic in this convoluted techno-thriller. Pitt's mission is to find a way to raise the wreck of the *Titanic* in order to recover a store of the rare element byzanium, needed to power a secret U.S. defense project.

203 Dann, Jack. ***"Going Under."*** First published *Omni* Magazine, July 1986. Collected in *Jubilee* (Tor Books, 2003).

Enigmatic science fiction story puts a spin on the standard time-traveling tale by casting the *Titanic* as a gigantic, futuristic death machine on which modern passengers can choose to meet their fate or experience the adventure of surviving. A dirigible cleverly named the *California* hovers overhead to pick up those passengers who have signed on to survive. The wish of the heroine, a young woman named Esme, to die aboard the ship becomes complicated when she falls in love with an optimistic yet impatient passenger named Stephen. What begins as a rather light-hearted sci-fi yarn, complete with a dead father resurrected as a robotic talking head, evolves into a poignant exploration of the meaning of human love in the face of inevitable death.

204 Duprey, Richard, and Brian O'Leary. ***Spaceship Titanic.*** New York: Dodd, Mead, 1983. Hardcover, 230 pp.

On the maiden voyage of *Titan*, the first space shuttle to carry civilian passengers, winners of a "Space Getaway Contest" soon find themselves in a desperate situation when one of the ship's engines fails to fire. As the ship begins to burn in orbit, the decision must be made to crash-land or attempt an unplanned rendezvous in space. Not so much a science-fiction story as a stock 1970s disaster story in which the limits of human compassion and heroism are tested.

Co-author Brian O'Leary served as an astronaut and scientist with NASA.

205 Ellison, Harlan. *"Escapegoat."* (1983) First published: *Omni*, Nov. 1983. Also published: Ellison, Harlan. *Angry Candy*. Houghton-Mifflin, 1988. Hardcover, 324 pp.

A trio of time-traveling commandos arrive on the bow of the *Titanic* at 11:27, April 14, just a few minutes before the expected collision. One of the commandos, surly Sgt. Ratliff, is charged with the dangerous duty of using explosives to ensure the wreck after the wheelman nearly steers the ship to safety.

The title of the *Angry Candy* collection comes from a line in e. e. cummings' poem "the Cambridge ladies who live in furnished souls": "above Cambridge if sometimes in its box of sky lavender and cornerless, the moon rattles like a fragment of angry candy." On the back cover of this collection, Ellison includes his own bit of verse using the angry candy metaphor, in which he imagines it as a solace for grief and sorrow.

As much as for his high-brow science fiction, Harlan Ellison is known for his outspoken manner and quirky persona. Disney once fired him for jokingly suggesting that the company make a pornographic film, and he became known in the late 1990s for his vocal efforts to protect his stories from Internet piracy.

206 *Fanfiction.*

Speculative fiction written by fans, or "fanfiction," boomed as a cultural phenomenon on the World Wide Web in the 1990s. Most fanfiction, whether written about the Hanson brothers, Star Trek, or Harry Potter, is the product of wish fulfillment, as amateur authors lead characters into unauthorized romantic relationships and other new directions. Some fanfiction, often written by young girls, even involves the authors themselves as characters in fantasy situations. *Titanic* fanfiction, nearly all of it generated in 1998 and built around the characters of Jack and Rose from James Cameron's *Titanic*, can still be found on the Internet on websites devoted to collecting such material. Most fanfiction stories are a few paragraphs long with plenty of dialogue; some are longer and are touted as "books," although even these generally don't run more than 20 pages. Many of the stories, created from this fantasy mindset, have Jack survive the disaster and build a new life with Rose in America. Others deal more extensively with providing more details to Jack and Rose's shipboard romance or tell the story of Rose's new life without Jack.

One of the most prolific Internet *Titanic* fanfiction authors, known on her site only as Jeanita, penned 10 "novel-length" stories and continued to update her site in 2003.

207 Finney, Jack. ***From Time to Time.*** New York: Simon and Schuster, 1995. Hardcover, 303 pages.

In this long-awaited sequel to the time-traveling mystery *Time and Again* (which was set in 1882), original time explorer Simon Morley and his supervisor Ruben Prien travel to 1912 New York in an attempt to prevent World War I. Unfortunately, the man who carries the papers that might help avert the war (none other than Archibald Butt) is traveling aboard the *Titanic*. The *Titanic* doesn't really appear in the storyline until the final few chapters, when Morley crosses the Atlantic aboard the *Mauretania* to catch the *Titanic* before she sails. As fans of *Titanic* time-traveling fantasies know, the course of history is rarely altered.

Many of the devoted fans of Finney's earlier novel were disappointed by this work.

Illustrated with photographs, sketches, and advertisements from the period.

Editions: Paperback, 1996; Audio (read by Campbell Scott), 1995.

Friedlaender, Robert *see* Prechtl

208 Fritscher, Jack. ***"Titanic!"*** (1984) Collected in Fritscher, Jack. *Titanic: Forbidden Stories Hollywood Forgot and Other Gay Canon Stories of Gay History, Queer Culture, Leather, Bearotica, and Gay Studies.* Palm Drive, 1999. 228 pp.

Gay-erotica novella focuses on the sexual lives of first-class passengers Michael and Edward. Molly Brown, "the stoker," and others figure in as minor characters. Although the anthology was not published until 1999, all the stories therein were written much earlier.

Fritscher, an outspoken gay-culture scholar, is perhaps best known for his memoir of photographer Robert Mapplethorpe, *Mapplethorpe: Assault with a Deadly Camera* (LPC Group, 1998).

209 Fullerton, Alexander. ***Wave Cry.*** London: Little, Brown, 1999. Hardcover, 428 pp.

After her husband and child perish on the *Titanic*, third-class Irish passenger Eileen Maguire sets out to exact revenge on Bruce Ismay.

Other editions: Paperback and audio.

210 Glasser, Perry. ***Singing on the Titanic.*** Urbana: University of Illinois Press, 1987.

Short-story collection that includes a title story that uses the *Titanic* as a metaphor, but nothing more. The title refers to the fact that passengers sang hymns as the ship was sinking.

211 Hansen, Eric Fosnes, and Joan Tate (translator). **Psalm at Journey's End: A Novel.** New York: Harvest Books, 1996. Originally published as *Salme ved reisens slutt* (J. W. Cappelens Forlag, Norway, 1990). Hardcover, 372 pp. Softcover, 372 pp.

This Norwegian literary novel centers on the lives of seven musicians on the *Titanic*'s maiden voyage. With life aboard the doomed ship serving as an evocative background, Hansen reveals the inner conflicts and background stories of the musicians as representatives of an odd sector of European culture and breeding. The fictional musicians are not based on the actual band musicians who perished in the sinking. The novel met with critical and popular success in continental Europe before being translated for English audiences.

A handful of chapter epigraphs include quotations from Shakespeare, Hesiod, and Dante.

The hardcover and softcover editions feature different cover illustrations.

212 Hine, Al. **The Unsinkable Molly Brown.** Greenwich, CT: Fawcett, 1964. Softcover, 144 pp.

Mass paperback novelization of the stageplay.

213 Hoch, Edward. *"The Adventure of a Dying Ship."* (1999) Collected in: *The Confidential Casebook of Sherlock Holmes* (Kaye, Marvin, ed. Griffin, 1999; 368 pp.)

In yet-another piece of Holmes-reinventing, the famous detective finds himself embroiled in a mystery aboard the *Titanic*, where he meets famed French mystery writer Jacques Futrelle. Holmes also finds a seat aboard a lifeboat, allowing him to escape the disaster.

Holmes is also placed on the *Titanic* in Williams Seil's mystery (q.v.).

214 Hoh, Diane. **Remembering the Titanic.** New York: Scholastic, 1998. Softcover, 268 pp.

Mass-market sequel to *Titanic: The Long Night*. The story begins one year after the ship's sinking and follows the characters from the first book as they establish careers in America and attempt to deal with the emotional fallout and "survivor guilt."

215 Hoh, Diane. **Titanic: The Long Night.** New York: Scholastic, 1998. Softcover, 371 pp.

Mass-market romance paperback, with the storylines revolving around fictional first-class passengers Elizabeth Farr and Max Whittaker and third-class passengers Brian Kelleher and Kathleen Mahoney. As the ship makes her way toward collision, the passengers spend much time talking about the various restaurants (including the Parisian sidewalk café, which a character notes does not have a sidewalk and is not outside), the food, and the fashions of the day. The book found an audience with young female fans of the Leonardo DiCaprio film, and a sequel followed (q.v.). Several standard *Titanic* accounts, including Walter Lord's *A Night to Remember* and Eaton and Haas's *Titanic: Triumph and Tragedy*, are listed as resources.

216 Jones, Terry. ***Douglas Adams' Starship Titanic.*** Harmony Books, 1997. Introduction by Douglas Adams. Hardcover, 246 pp.

Based on a story outline by quirky science fiction author Douglas Adams, this sci-fi adventure follows the action aboard a mysterious and spectacular starship launched to much fanfare and media attention. The starship shares more than a name with the fateful ship of 1912, however. The ship's architect, Leovinus, notices on the night before the launch that much of the work remains unfinished, and during the launch the starship undergoes Spontaneous Massive Existence Failure (a Douglas Adams phraseology if there ever was one). Leovinus is left to uncover the mystery of the doomed starship. The book's author was one of the founding writers of Monty Python's Flying Circus.

A computer game based on the book was released in 1998.

Other editions: Paperback, 1998. Audio, Simon and Schusters, 1997 (unabridged).

217 Kelly, D. F. ***Way Back When.*** Vantage Press, 1993.

After escaping from prison, hard-luck confidence man Jimmy Paige boards the *Titanic* with his mother-in-law and wife with plans to remarry aboard the ship. The two perish together but are reunited 78 years later in the reincarnated souls of David and Angeline Kelly.

Vantage Press is the most well known "vanity" publisher in the United States and is noted for the physical quality of the books it produces.

218 Kirch, Donald Allen. ***Still Waters.*** Commonwealth, 1997. Paperback, 328 pp.

An ancient mummy known as Ka-Re is smuggled aboard the *Titanic*, bringing about a series of mysterious murders and breathing new life into an old urban legend.

219 Kite, Janet. ***Death of Maiden.*** British *Titanic* Society, 1949. Reprint edition: Plus, 1999.

This short novel was originally published in pamphlet form. It is in essence a self-published book.

Lacey, Pat *see* entry in *Nonfiction*

220 Llywelyn, Morgan. ***1916: A Novel of the Irish Rebellion.*** Forge, 1998. Hardcover, 384 pp.

Fifteen-year-old Irish farmboy Ned Halloran survives the *Titanic* sinking to live through the Irish rebellion of 1916. Although the disaster only occupies a short part of the beginning of this historical novel, the fictional Halloran recalls the *Titanic* as a source of strength and perseverance.

Other editions: Paperback (St. Martin's Press), Audio (Brilliance Audio)

221 McCarver, Sam. ***The Case of Cabin 13.*** New York: Signet Books, 1999. Paperback, 246 pp.

Pulp mystery novel, promoted as the first in a series on detective John Darnell, the "world's first and only paranormal detective." Readers will thereby assume that the detective somehow survives his journey aboard the *Titanic*, as he attempts to discover why passengers have been dying in first-class cabins numbered 13 aboard other White Star ships, and whether an alleged ghost can be held responsible.

222 Mizner, Wilson. "You're Dead." (1936) Collected in: *Stories for Men*. Little, Brown, 1936.

Two gambling hustlers travel on the *Titanic*; one dies and the other is haunted by images of the disaster.

Mizner, a screenwriter, once earned money playing cards on Atlantic luxury liners. He is now primarily remembered for his Dorothy Parker–like witticisms (he described Hollywood as a "trip through a sewer on a glass-bottomed boat.").

223 Morris, Gilbert. ***The White Hunter.*** House of Winslow series. Minneapolis, MN: Bethany House, 1999. Hardcover, 322 pp.

A small part of this religious novel finds Annie Rogers, a missionary and member of the Winslow family, traveling aboard the *Titanic* after a whirlwind tour of Europe. The rest of novel narrates the lives of Rogers and other family members (including John Winslow, who travels to Africa and becomes a hunter) as they search for meaning and witness to other characters in the story.

224 O'Cork, Shannon. *Ice Fall.* New York: Harlequin, 1988. Softcover, 377 pp. Reprinted as *Titanic: A Love Story* (Mira Books, 1998).

Mass-market mystery romance set on the maiden voyage. Lurid storylines focus on a sex-obsessed and lustful Captain Smith, a homosexual Bruce Ismay, and two first-class twin girls (named, bizarrely, Swan and Smoke) who fall for the same man.

225 O'Hara-Keeton, Monica. *I Died on the Titanic: A Fascinating Investigation Through Hypnotic Regression.* Merseyside, UK: Countyvise, 1996. Softcover, 184 pp.

Although ostensibly a nonfiction account, *I Died on the Titanic* is here labeled a novel because it is essentially a narrative of the author's revisitation of the *Titanic* through the methods of hypnotic regression. The author claims to have died on the *Titanic* as Lucy Latymer (Latimer). As there is no record of a Lucy Latymer having traveled on the *Titanic*, the bulk of the book follows the author as she attempts to uncover the mystery of this personage, whom she eventually connects to chief steward Andrew Latimer. As the hypnotic sessions recount Ms. Latimer's interactions with historical figures on board the ship, this work as a whole must surely be labeled fiction. Includes a foreword by John P. Eaton.

226 Oldfield, Pamela. *Turn of the Tide.* London: Century Books, 1988. Hardback, 610 pp.

Nursemaid Grace Martin travels on the *Titanic* with her two young charges; romance and other unexpected events complicate matters.

Other editions: Paperback (Arrow Books, 1989); Large print (Thorndike, 1991); Audio (Soundings)

227 Orman, Kate. *The Left-Handed Hummingbird.* The New Doctor Who Adventures. Virgin, 1993. Paperback.

The time-traveling doctor from British children's television does battle with an Aztec god aboard the *Titanic*, among other places. The violence and mayhem in this book make it more suited to adult readers.

228 Pearson, John. *The Bellamy Saga.* New York: Praeger, 1976. Hardcover, 314 pp.

Novelization based on characters from the television series *Upstairs, Downstairs* (see Appendix B).

Other editions: Avon paperback.

229 Peck, Richard. ***Amanda/Miranda.*** New York: Viking Penguin, 1980. Hardcover, 544 pp.

Wealthy and devious Amanda and her look-alike handmaiden Miranda achieve mischief and confusion in their social dealings. Near the end of the novel, aboard the *Titanic*, Miranda discovers the opportunity to change her destiny forever.

Peck, known for his young adult novels, wrote the popular *Something for Joey*, later made into an even-more popular television movie.

Other editions: Paperback (Morrow, Avon, 1981); Young adult school binding (Dial Books, 1999); Young adult paperback, 169 pp. (Puffin, 2001).

230 Pemberton, Margaret. ***Some Distant Shore.*** New York: Gallen, 1981. Paperback, 392 pp.

Standard Harlequin-type romance follows the misadventures of wild and brash Christina. Following the death of her father and other life-turning events, Christina boards the *Titanic* with her blackmailing fiancé; the disaster presents an opportunity for Christina to assume a new life.

Other editions: Mass market paperback (Pocket Books, 1981).

231 Prechtl, Robert. ***Titanic.*** London: Martin Secker, 1938; New York: E. P. Dutton, 1940. Translated by Erna McArthur. Hardcover, 368 pp.

German novel that, after translation, met with some success in England and the United States. The novel is a fictionalized account of the disaster, with a handful of fictional characters interacting with real passengers and crew members.

The book is considered by many to be the first serious *Titanic* novel. Prechtl is the pseudonym of Robert Friedlaender (b. 1874).

232 Robertson, Morgan. ***Futility, or The Wreck of the Titan,*** M. F. Mansfield, 1898. Reprint Editions: 1912 reprint; Riverdale, CT: 7 C's Press, 1974 (with an introduction by William H. Tantum; Buccaneer Books, 1991; 100th Anniversary Facsimile Edition (including reproduction of original cover and inscription by Robertson, Los Angeles, CA: Virtual Ink, 1998.

Celebrated novella by early science-fiction writer centered on the sinking of a trans–Atlantic liner after a collision with an iceberg on her maiden voyage to New York. The book was published 14 years before the sinking of the *Titanic* and has been held up as evidence that the *Titanic* was a victim of preternatural, fatalistic events. Among the similarities between the *Titan* and the *Titanic*: The *Titan* was 800 feet, the *Titanic* 882.5 feet; the *Titan* and the

Titanic were both triple-screw liners with a passenger capacity of 3,000; both had watertight compartments; and both ships were at one point or another described as "unsinkable." Perhaps more remarkable is that Robertson describes the *Titan* as being outfitted with as few lifeboats as "required by law."

The description of the ship and the collision occur within the first 20 pages of the novel; most of the rest of the book, unlike subsequent *Titanic* stories, focuses on the aftermath and bureaucratic ramifications. Caught up in the hero-making tendency of *Titanic* myth, Robertson added a brief passage at the end of the 1912 edition to redeem the hapless hero of the book, a careless watchman named Rowland.

The 100th Anniversary Edition also includes the first chapter of Robertson's book *Beyond the Spectrum,* which has been described as correctly predicting events of World War II, including the Japanese attack on Pearl Harbor.

233 Seil, William. ***Sherlock Holmes and the Titanic Tragedy: A Case to Remember.*** London: Breese Books, 1996. Softcover, 253 pp.

The proliferation of fan fiction on the Internet owes its origins to such high-concept novels as this Sherlock Holmes adventure, which takes a beloved literary character into new (and equally familiar) territory. The result is likely to please or infuriate Holmes aficionados (of which there are quite a few), depending on what level of sacredness they attribute to the Edwardian detective. Nonetheless, the first-time author and avowed Holmes fan manages to hedge his bets by including a number of Holmes regulars, as well as a fine pastiche of Dr. Watson's understated description and wit.

234 Serling, Robert J. ***Something's Alive on the Titanic: A Novel.*** New York: St. Martin's Press, 1990. Hardcover, 400 pp.

Intriguing techno-thriller begins with the premise that Bob Ballard's expedition was not the first to discover or explore the *Titanic*'s wreck. Rather, an earlier salvage expedition had combed over the wreck in search of millions of dollars worth of gold. The novel follows a new team of explorers and scientists in 1993 as they dive to the wreck in search of the secrets of the earlier missions. *Titanic* aficionados will pick up on many well-researched historical and cultural references, including a mention of the myth of the Egyptian mummy carried on board the ship. The novel is dedicated to Bob Ballard.

Other editions: Paperback, 1993.

235 Smith, Dean Wesley. ***Laying the Music to Rest.*** Questar Science Fiction. New York: Warner, 1989. Paperback, 194 pp.

In this time-traveling genre novel, the hero dives into a haunted lake and finds an old mirror that carries him to a time-travel loop of the last six hours aboard the sinking *Titanic*.

The book was the first in a series that never fully materialized.

236 Smith, Dean Wesley. **"Two Roads, No Choices."** (1995) Collected in: Resnick, Mike and Martin H. Greenberg, eds. *Sherlock Holmes in Orbit*. DAW Books, 1995.

In this Sherlockian story, collected with other speculative and futuristic Sherlock Holmes stories, two scientists from 2014 travel back in time to meet with the famous detective and his assistant Watson to determine why the *Titanic* did not sink.

Smith also penned the speculative time-traveling novel *Laying the Music to Rest* (q.v.).

237 Stanwood, Donald A. **The Memory of Eva Ryker.** Coward, McCann and Geoghegan, 1978. Hardcover, 412 pp.

In 1962, a millionaire industrialist attempts to recover the wreck of the *Titanic* as a way of vanquishing the ghostly memory of his wife, who perished in the sinking. In the meantime, a frustrated Hawai'i detective discovers that an unsolved 1941 double murder and the survival of Eva Ryker, the industrialist's daughter, are somehow linked to a diamond-smuggling mystery.

The book was made into a television movie in 1980.

238 Steel, Danielle. **No Greater Love.** New York: Bantam Doubleday, 1991. Hardcover, 384 pp.

A young woman, Edwina Fairfield, becomes the sole caretaker for her siblings after their parents perish aboard the *Titanic*. The first 100 pages or so deal with the sinking; the rest of the novel takes place in America. Typical fare from the popular mass market romance novelist, the book was later made into a television movie (q.v.).

The cover illustration, dwindled by the title and author's name, depicts the sinking ship silhouetted against the iceberg.

The title is from a Bible verse: "Greater love hath no man than this, that a man lay down his life for his friends" (John 15:13).

Other editions: Dell Books, mass market paperback, 1992.

239 Swenson, Al. **Confessions of UB-One.** Chicago: Adams, 1986. Paperback.

Genre techno-thriller in which an early U-boat prototype has as its first mission to destroy the *Titanic*.

240 Trow, M. J. ***Lestrade and the Brother of Death.*** Washington DC: Regnery Gateway Editions, 1999. Hardcover, 224 pp.

In this seventh of a 16-book series, Arthur Conan Doyle's inept Inspector Lestrade finds his journey on the *Titanic* cut short after falling from an upper deck as she sets sail. Lestrade survives the ignoble fall with a broken leg and must solve a mystery of threatening letters as he recuperates at his fiancée's country home.

241 Walker, Bill. ***Titanic 2012.*** Baltimore: Cemetery Dance, 1998. Hardcover, 232 pp.

One of the many books to ride the coattails of the James Cameron film, this adventure novel is even more blatant in exploiting the connection. The book is dedicated to the blockbuster movie and characters are said to have been greatly influenced by the film. Early editions even included a sticker, "Inspired by the Academy Award-Winning Film."

The plot, as the title suggests, unfolds around a millionaire's attempt to recreate the *Titanic* and sail the ship on the hundredth anniversary of its forerunner. The millionaire, we learn, is the great-grandson of John Jacob Astor and wishes to honor those who died aboard the ship. Predictably, the protagonist (an old college friend of the millionaire's) soon discovers that all is not as it appears.

The title is presumably an homage to Clarke's famous novel.

242 Walker, James. ***Murder on the Titanic.*** Mysteries in Time series. Nashville: Broadman and Holman, 1998. Paperback, 488 pp.

Protagonist Morgan Fairfield (a fictional name) finds himself aboard the *Titanic* after a dying man entrusts him with a first-class ticket and a locked briefcase. His mission: to deliver a top-secret message to the American War Department. The usual string of love entanglements and suspenseful square-offs drive this murder-mystery genre novel. The book is dedicated to the "gallant men of the *Titanic*."

243 Walker, Jim. ***Voices from the Titanic.*** Mysteries in Time series. Nashville: Broadman and Holman, 1999. Softcover, 460 pp.

In this sequel to *Murder on the Titanic*, journalist Morgan Fairfield uncovers conspiracy and scandal as he attempts to bring to light the circumstances surrounding a murder he witnessed aboard the ship.

244 Ziavras, Charles E. ***Titanic Interlude.*** Lowell, MA: Ithaca Press, 1982. Hardcover, 359 pp.

Fictional working-class girl Jessica Traywick loses her wealthy groom on their honeymoon trip aboard the *Titanic*, even while she is picked out of the icy Atlantic by a lifeboat. After returning to England alone, she becomes involved with class struggles (including a 1912 textile strike) and the attitudes of her upper-class in-laws.

The book was also printed with Ziavras's last name changed to Jarvis.

Other editions: Paperback, Three Continents Press 1984.

3 Children's Books

The *Titanic* has proved to be a surprisingly rich source of stories and books for children of all ages. As the popular camp song "When the Great Ship Went Down" shows, the haunting, ironic legacy of the *Titanic* resonates in the imaginations of children and adults alike, and publishers continue to capitalize on the immediacy of the disaster in publishing readers and history texts.

245 Aaseng, Nathan. ***The Titanic.*** Building History series. San Diego, Lucent, 1999. 96 pp., with illustrations and maps.

Nonfiction account of the *Titanic*'s construction, maiden voyage, and sinking. Includes references and index.

246 Adams, Simon. ***Eyewitness Books: Titanic.*** New York: DK, 1999. Hardcover, 62 pp.

Picture-book encyclopedia issued as part of the familiar Eyewitness Books series, which, through the use of high-quality color reproduction and almost-tactile look-and-feel object photographs, appealed to adults as well as children. Sections of the book include a dissection of why the ship sank, how the wreck was discovered, and the ways in which the legend has lived on.

247 Archbold, Rick. ***Deep-sea Explorer: The Story of Robert Ballard, Discoverer of the Titanic.*** Ontario, Canada: Madison Press, 1994. Softcover, 166 pp.

Biography written for older elementary students. The second half focuses on Ballard's efforts to find and explore the *Titanic*; readers familiar with that story may find more interest in the stories of Ballard's youth, including the harrowing tale of a meat-cleaver-wielding cook aboard the research vessel *Orca*. The original edition includes black-and-white photographs, a glossary, and an index, and a later classroom edition includes a short play, *Destination Disaster*, by John Lipp.

Other editions: Houghton Mifflin, 1996 (classroom text edition).

248 Armstrong, Warren. ***Last Voyage: A Saga of Ships That Never Came Back.*** London: Muller, 1956. Hardcover, 240 pp.

Nonfiction anthology of shipwreck stories designed for the junior-high library set.

Other editions: American edition, 1958 (New York: John Day).

249 Avirom, Joel, and Jason Snyder (designers). ***James Cameron's Titanic Poster Book.*** New York: HarperCollins, 1998. Softcover, no page count. Photographs by Merie W. Walace.

This oversized "book," released at the height of the frenzy set off by James Cameron's film, includes no text. Rather, readers are encouraged to rip the book apart to reveal the 12 fold-out posters inside (the posters cannot be seen completely without tearing them from the book). Each poster, depicting a famous scene from the movie, measures 20-by-25 inches. Most of the scenes focus on the Leonardo DiCaprio/Kate Winslet love story, dubbed here as the "tragic romance of the century."

250 Ballard, Robert D. ***Explorer: A Pop-up Book.*** Atlanta: Turner, 1992. Illustrated by James Dietz. Designed by Jon Z. Haber. Paper engineering by Tor Lokvig and Dennis K. Meyer. Hardcover, 10 pp.

This three-dimensional pop-up book for beginning readers includes sections on six of Ballard's underwater explorations, including the *Titanic*.

251 Ballard, Robert D. ***Exploring the Titanic.*** A Time Quest Book. New York and Ontario: Scholastic and Madison Press Books, 1988. Softcover, 64 pp. Edited by Patrick Crean. With some editorial input by Shelley Tanaka (q.v.) and Hugh Brewster (q.v.). Illustrations by Ken Marschall and others.

This scientifically-skewed book for curious young readers (aimed at children ages 10–13) is heavily illustrated with numbered diagrams, underwater photographs, and many color illustrations (including a nice diagram that aptly illustrates the vast distance between Ballard's research vessel *Knorr* and the *Titanic*'s wreck). The emphasis is on the facts and numbers surrounding the *Titanic*'s construction, her sinking, and Bob Ballard's discovery mission. The book's back matter includes a glossary and timeline.

The first of Ballard's Madison Press books, *Exploring the Titanic*, remained popular with younger readers, having entered its 20th printing by 1997.

252 Ballard, Robert D., and Rick Archbold. ***Ghost Liners: Exploring the World's Greatest Lost Ships.*** New York and Ontario, Canada: Little, Brown and Madison Press Books, 1998. Hardcover, 64 pp. Illustrated by Ken Marschall. Also includes archival color and black-and-white photographs.

Another Madison Press/Bob Ballard teaming, *Ghost Liners* takes older-elementary readers on board sunken liners using shipwrecks as springboards to historical and personal accounts of such disasters as the *Empress of Ireland*, the *Lusitania*, the *Britannic*, and the *Andrea Doria*. The first chapter (and much of the book's packaging) focuses on the *Titanic*. Probably the best find here is the account of 11-year-old survivor Willie Coutt, in a sidebar titled "Nearly Lost Because of a Hat." Includes a short glossary and bibliography.

253 Ballard, Robert D., with Nan Froman. ***Finding the Titanic.*** Hello Reader! series. New York and Ontario: Scholastic and Madison Press Books, 1993. Softcover, 48 pp. Illustrated by Ken Marschall. Also includes archival photographs.

Elementary-school reader designed for students in grades 2–3. Chapter 1 presents a first-person account of Ballard's dream to find the wreck of the *Titanic*, and how he accomplished that goal with the help of the underwater sled *Argo*. Chapters 2–4 tell the story of first-class passenger Ruth Becker, who was 12 at the time of the disaster. (Becker is a celebrated survivor who has attended conventions and given many interviews for documentarians.) Chapters 5 and 6 return to Ballard's research vessel in 1985, as he and his crew journey to the bottom of the ocean aboard the submersible *Alvin*. An epilogue by Ballard criticizes efforts to salvage artifacts from the wreck.

254 Blos, Joan W. ***The Heroine of the Titanic: A Tale Both True and Otherwise of the Life of Molly Brown.*** New York: Morrow Junior Books, 1991. Hardcover, 40 pp. Illustrated by Tennessee Dixon.

Imaginative retelling of the life of Molly Brown, from her days as a rough-and-tumble wife to her "heroic" trip aboard the *Titanic*. In an epilogue, the authors admit that biographical information on Molly Brown is scant, and they choose to portray her as the mythical heroine of legend in the six pages that deal with the *Titanic*. "Move over sailor," she tells a terrified sailor in the lifeboat, "I was born in a cyclone on the Mississippi River, and I don't plan on drowning at sea." Short, chorus-like poems propel the narrative forward.

The fiery, red-haired woman of the book's illustrations favors the musical version of Molly (as portrayed by Debbie Reynolds) over the later Molly played by Kathy Bates.

255 Boning, Richard. *Titanic.* The Incredible Series. Baldwin, NY: Barnell Loft, 1974. Hardcover, 47 pp. Illustrated by Harry J. Schaare.

This grade-school level book retells the story of 16-year-old survivor Miss Katie Gilnagh, an Irish girl who traveled in third class. It is said that Gilnagh's parents did not believe she had survived the sinking until they received a photograph.

A library edition was published by Dexter and Westbrook in the same year.

256 Boyd, David. *The Danger Beneath.* Rubicon, 2002. Paperback, 120 pp.

One of a series of juvenile novels centering on the adventures of teenage detectives Wordsy and Jess, *The Danger Beneath* finds Wordsworth Doyle and Jessica Redd transported back in time to the *Titanic* through the malfunctioning of video equipment.

257 Brewster, Hugh, and Laurie Coulter. *888½ Amazing Answers to Your Questions About the Titanic.* Toronto, Ontario: Madison Press Books, 1998. Hardcover, 96 pp.

Engaging and thoughtful reference book aimed at young readers seeking more information after multiple viewings of James Cameron's *Titanic*. Among the inventive 888½ (representing the length of the ship) questions are "Was the *Titanic* the biggest ship ever built?"; "Why was the *Titanic* carrying dragon's blood?"; "Was there a real Jack Dawson?"; and "Where are the victims buried?" Unlike other *Titanic* trivia books, *Amazing Answers* is organized into sections and includes an index, making the bits of information more accessible and useful even to the adult reader. Sections include "The *Titanic*'s Passengers," "The Last Evening," "Launching the Lifeboats," and "The World Reacts." Two pages of questions are devoted to Cameron's film, while six focus on Robert Ballard's discovery and exploration of the wreck.

Besides Ken Marschall's famous paintings, the book is illustrated with many black-and-white photographs and diagrams. Other credits include text research by Greg Curtis and historical consultation by Don Lynch.

258 Brown, Muffet Laurie. *The Titanic Tale of the Unsinkable Molly Brown.* La Jolla, CA: Positive, 2000. Softcover, 32 pp.

Coloring and activity book for children, written and illustrated by the great-granddaughter of Molly Brown. The cover and several of the inside illustrations and activities deal with Brown's encounter with the *Titanic*. Privately published, *Titanic Tale* is offered for sale at the Molly Brown House Museum in Denver.

259 Bunting, Eve. ***SOS Titanic.*** San Diego: Harcourt Brace, 1996. Softcover, 246 pp.

Fictional account of 15-year-old first-class passenger Barry O'Neill, told in the style of and packaged like a young-adult novel. Barry meets and becomes smitten with an Irish steerage passenger named Pegeen, whose brother threatens to throw him overboard. Later, the boys forgive all when Barry becomes their only chance to escape steerage as the ship goes under.

At the beginning of the voyage, Barry encounters an older man who fears for the fate of the ship and quotes Morgan Robertson's novel *Futility* to back his feelings. Captain Smith and radio operator Jack Phillips also put in appearances.

A teacher's guide to using this book in the classroom was published in 1999.

260 Chipperfield, Joseph E. ***The Story of a Great Ship: The Birth and Death of the Steamship Titanic.*** NY: Roy, 1959. Hardcover. Illustrated by Charles King.

Describes the building and sinking of the ship through the point of view of a Harland and Wolff apprentice shipbuilder.

261 Cole, Michael D. ***The Titanic: Disaster at Sea.*** American Disasters series. New Jersey: Enslow, 2001. Hardcover, 48 pp.

Straightforward account of the disaster for preteen readers.

262 Conklin, Thomas. ***The Titanic Sinks!*** New York: Random House, 1997. Paperback, 128 pp.

Detailed nonfiction account for children ages 9–12. Includes archival black-and-white photographs as well as color photographs of the wreck site. Other editions: Library binding, 1999; reprint, 2000.

263 Cooke, Arthur Owens. ***A Day in a Shipyard.*** New York: Hodder and Stoughton, ca. 1911.

Children's picture book predating the *Titanic* disaster includes black-and-white photographs, diagrams, and color illustrations taken from the shipyards of Harland and Wolff as it constructed the *Titanic* and her sister ship *Olympic*.

264 Copeland, Peter F. ***The Titanic Coloring Book.*** Mineola, NY: Dover, 1997. Softcover, 32 pp.

Evocative cover gives way to a collection of typical, paper-doll-like coloring book illustrations. Some of the drawings (crewmembers running from the boilerrooms as water rushes in) are more intricate than others (Captain Smith and two officers standing on the bridge). The lengthy captions (perhaps meant to be read to younger readers) tell the story of *Titanic* and her sinking.

265 Cullimore, D. Roye. ***Colin Ore and Rebecca Rust's Adventures on the Titanic.*** Droycon Bioconcepts, 1999. Softcover, 84 pp.

One of the more interesting children's books dealing with the *Titanic*, this story by biologist Cullimore deals with flecks, mythical creatures who lived in the steel of the *Titanic*'s hull. The legend is that this book was written in three days after a colleague challenged Cullimore to write a *Titanic* book that had a happy ending.

266 Deady, Kathleen W. ***The Titanic: The Tragedy at Sea.*** Disaster! series. Capstone Press, 2002. Hardcover, 32 pp.

History for beginning grade school readers.

267 Donkin, Andrew. ***The Unsinkable Titanic.*** UK: Hodder Wayland, 1998. Hardcover and softcover, 44 pp.

Fact-based fictional story presents the events through the eyes of nine-year-old traveler Sarah Fisher.

268 Donnelly, Judy. ***The Titanic, Lost and Found.*** Step Into Reading: A Step 3 Book. New York: Random House, 1987. Illustrated by Keith Kohler. Softcover, 48 pp.

Reading primer for children in grades 2–3 moves quickly from a physical description of the ship (with a nice cutaway illustration) into the collision and its aftermath. Very few of the regular characters are mentioned by name, but the story does mention an old couple who refuse to separate; the story also pays close attention to the fate of the collapsible lifeboats and those few passengers who managed to survive by hanging on to flotsam. The final chapter (of a total of four) deals with Bob Ballard's efforts to find the wreck of the *Titanic*.

269 Dubowski, Mark. ***Titanic: The Disaster That Shocked the World.*** Eyewitness Readers series. New York: DK, 1998. London: Dorling Kindersley, 1998. Softcover, 48 pp.

Colorful nonfiction reader (for readers in grades 2–3) combines a basic history of the disaster with photographs, paint-by-numbers illustrations, and sketches (including a cutaway diagram of the ship). The final two chapters focus on Bob Ballard's discovery of the wreck and "Lessons Learned" from the *Titanic* (illustrated with a color photograph of an aged survivor talking to a reporter). A glossary at the end of the book assists young readers with terms like "davits" and "wireless."

270 Duey K., and K. A. Bale. ***Survival! Titanic.*** New York: Simon and Schuster (Aladin Paperbacks), 1998. Softcover, 175 pp.

In this first entry of the Survival! young adult series (which also includes stories involving earthquakes and blizzards), fictional young Irish crewmember Gavin Reilly works in the galley peeling potatoes to help earn his passage to America. Aboard the *Titanic*, he meets a young American girl, Karolina Green, who is traveling in third-class with her Aunt Rose. Karolina spends much of her time worrying about her family problems (her parents died in England), and she finds a friend in Gavin. In keeping with the theme of the series, both Gavin and Karolina survive (although Gavin has to take his chances on the capsized lifeboat with Officer Lightoller).

271 Gaines, Keith. ***Titanic Tragedy: Year 5: Danger Theme.*** Oxford Literacy Web Spiders series. UK: Oxford University Press, 2002. Paperback, 24 pp.

Yet another grade-school reader built around the history and impact of the *Titanic* tragedy.

272 Gormley, Beatrice. ***Back to the Titanic!*** Travelers Through Time #1. New York: Scholastic, 1994. Softcover, 132 pp.

Brother and sister Matt and Emily travel back in time to the *Titanic* with best friend Jonathan aboard a time machine invented by Matt and Emily's grandfather, who sailed on the *Titanic* as a young boy. Like the many other time travelers before them, Matt and Emily prove that nobody can prevent the sinking of the *Titanic*.

The book's one illustration is a blueprint-like diagram of the ship. Other books in this time-traveling series (designed to appeal to readers ages 8–12) include adventures involving Paul Revere and Abraham Lincoln's assassination.

273 Hamilton, Sue L. ***Royal Mail Steamship Titanic.*** The Day of the Disaster series. Bloomington, MN: Abdo & Daughters, 1988. Hardcover, 32 pp., with illustrations. Edited by John C. Hamilton.

A fictional account of the disaster as told from the point of view of one of the ship's officers. The book includes a list of reference sources.

274 Harmon, Daniel E. ***The Titanic.*** Great Disasters and Their Reforms series. Broomall, PA: Chelsea House, 2000. Hardcover, 128 pp.

Historical account from an educational nonfiction publisher.

275 Harrison, Cora. ***Titanic: Voyage from Drumshee.*** Dublin: Wolfhound Press, 1998. Niwot, CO: Irish American Book, 1998. Illustrations by Orla Roche. Softcover, 128 pp.

Fourteen-year-old orphan Kitty McMahon feels alone and misunderstood after her parents die and she is taken in by an uncle and aunt. Luckily, a local upper-class woman recognizes her potential and, very soon after meeting her, hires Kitty to be nanny to her niece and nephew on a voyage to America aboard the *Titanic*. Her grandmother strongly objects to Kitty's voyage and expresses premonitional fears that the child will not survive. The uncle fuels the grandmother's superstitious fears by giving Kitty an heirloom necklace that she says must never leave the family farm or "bad luck will follow." Kitty's lack of experience with children becomes somewhat obvious when the ship begins to sink and her two charges turn up missing. In her frantic search for the children, she nearly bumps into Captain Smith and Thomas Andrews and brazenly interrupts two men working in the Marconi room. The nanny and children miss the lifeboats, but survive in a improvised craft made from a lifejacket storage box (perhaps appealing to the inventive childlike mind that believes *some* random object could surely have been used to float to safety).

Voyage from Drumshee is the sixth book in a series of preteen historical novels loosely connected by a crumbling Irish fortress.

276 Heiligman, Deborah, and James Watling. ***The Story of the Titanic.*** New York: Random House, 1998. Softcover, 24 pp.

Targeting a *Titanic* book at the preschool set (this one is part of a "Please Read to Me" series) naturally creates the need for some oversimplification, resulting in such passages as, "But there was a big problem. There were only enough lifeboats to carry 1,100 people." Nonetheless, this book deals with the facts in responsible fashion, and its watercolor illustrations are more imaginative and skilled than most of the illustrations of books aimed at this age group.

277 Henkel, Virginia. ***Letters from the Past.*** Petone, New Zealand: Nelson Price Milburn, 1989; Steck-Vaughn Library Edition, 1991. 24pp. Illustrated by Bruce Luxford.

While visiting her great-grandmother, young Jessica discovers letters written many years ago by a pen pal who survived the *Titanic* disaster.

278 Hill, Christine M. ***Robert Ballard: Oceanographer Who Discovered the Titanic.*** People to Know series. New Jersey: Enslow, 1999. Hardcover, 128 pp.

A biography of Ballard written for junior-high school and young adult readers. The book begins with an account of the discovery of the *Titanic*'s wreck. Includes black-and-white photographs.

279 Hodges, John. ***Titanic.*** Vantage Press, 1999.

Young adult novel published from the point of view of a stowaway-teenage boy. Printed by a U.S.–based vanity publisher.

280 Hughes, Susan, and Steve Santini. ***The Titanic: Book and Submersible Model.*** Somerville House Books, 1999. Book: *The Science and Story of Titanic.* Softcover, 52 pp. Illustrated by Margo Davies Leclair.

Novelty boxed set pairs a slim softcover history book with a snap-together plastic model that floats—until you slide a switch on the bow of the ship's hull. At that point, the ship begins to take on water, sinks bow first, splits into two pieces, and plunges to the bottom of the bathtub.

The colorful book includes chapters on the specifications of the *Titanic*, her construction and launching, its layout and deck plans, and a timeline of the sinking. A final chapter explores the mystery of why an iceberg was able to sink an "unsinkable" ship. A glossary is also included.

281 Jenner, Caryn. ***Survivors: The Night the Titanic Sank.*** New York: DK, 2001. Softcover, 32 pp. Illustrated by John James.

"Level 2" reader (for children "beginning to read alone") tells the story of the *Titanic* from the point of view of young third-class passenger Will Tate and his family, who survive the sinking.

Breakout boxes throughout the book, many of them illustrated with authentic photographs, present factoids about life aboard the ship. A final page includes information on modern nautical safety innovations.

282 Keene, Carolyn. ***Operation Titanic: A Nancy Drew and Hardy Boys Super Mystery.*** New York: Simon and Schuster, 1998. Softcover, 215 pp.

In this better-than-average young adult yarn from the Stratmeyer Syndicate (producer of Hardy Boys and Nancy Drew books written by many different nameless authors over the years), teenage detective Nancy Drew investigates a radio-giveaway scam involving tickets for a promotional cruise to see the *Titanic* raised. The Hardy Boys are pulled into the mystery when they visit a friend at the Wedge Grove Oceanography Institute (which sounds suspiciously like the Woods Hole Oceanographic Institute), which is planning to film the raising of the *Titanic* and give the film away for free to sabotage the commercial potential of the project. Along the way, the amateur detectives encounter shady Gulf War arms deals and a mysterious billionaire who innocently romances the young Nancy. To appeal to more modern readers, the Hardy Boys utilize a wide range of high-tech gizmos, including the Internet, waterproof laptop computers, cellular telephones, and night-vision goggles. It is all mostly window-dressing, allowing the author to construct a modern tale around an 80-year-old shipwreck.

The novel naturally comes to a close as the three detectives and friends find themselves aboard the highly publicized cruise, where they are treated to a harrowingly realistic holographic presentation of the *Titanic* disaster. The plan to raise the *Titanic* itself involves using 5,000-gallon marine lift bags filled with diesel fuel.

283 Kent, Deborah. ***The Titanic.*** Cornerstones of Freedom series. Chicago: Grolier (Childrens Press), 1993. Softcover, 32 pp.

Thoughtful and coherent nonfiction history of the *Titanic* disaster touches on most of the important aspects of life aboard the ship, the details of the collision, and Bob Ballard's exploration missions. Illustrated with black-and-white and sepia photographs of the passengers, paintings, period advertisements, and diagrams.

The text is written for readers approximately 7–10 years old.

284 Kentley, Eric. ***Discover the Titanic.*** New York: DK, 2001. Hardcover, 32 pp. Illustrations by Hans Jenssen.

Explores the history of the *Titanic* from the point of view of exploring the wreck. The book is heavily illustrated and includes cut-out 3-D model and pull-out features. The author, Kentley, served as a curator of the National Maritime Museum and took part in a 1994 expedition to the wreck. Also published in Spanish.

285 Kentley, Eric. ***Story of the Titanic.*** New York: DK, 2001. Hardcover, 32 pp. Illustrations by Steve Noon.

Oversized and handsome history for older elementary readers. Follows the stories of actual passengers; inset text provides a chronology of events. Includes a glossary, index, and the intricate cutaway illustrations for which DK is known.

286 Kupperberg, Paul. ***Tragedy of the Titanic.*** When Disaster Strikes! series. New York: Rosen, 2003. Hardcover, 48 pp.

Basic history written for preteen readers and aimed at the library market.

287 Landau, Elaine. ***Heroine of the Titanic: The Real Unsinkable Molly Brown.*** Clarion, 2001. Hardcover, 132 pp.

Biography for preteen readers. Much of the book focuses on Brown's beginnings and her rise to Denver society; however, Landau also vividly describes Brown's experiences on the *Titanic* and her notorious behavior aboard the lifeboat. Includes black-and-white photographs.

288 Lawlor, Laurie. ***American Sisters: A Journey Across the Sea, 1912.*** New York: Simon and Schuster (Pocket Books), 1998. Hardcover, 202 pp.

In this intelligent and well-rendered story, Swedish sisters Alfreda (16) and Erna Anderson (10) reunite for a journey on the *Titanic* to join their father in Chicago. Although Lawlor's account is technically fictional, Erna and Alfreda were listed among the Swedish steerage passengers on the *Titanic*, and the author drew from historical sources and personal accounts as much as possible. Only Erna survived the voyage, and in Lawlor's story, the elder sister sacrifices herself to save her younger sister and newfound friend.

289 Leininger, Tracy. ***Nothing Can Separate Us: The Story of Nan Harper.*** San Antonio, TX: Vision Forum, ca. 2000s. Hardback, 62 pp.

This fictionalized account tells the story of *Titanic* passenger Nina Harper, daughter of the Rev. John Harper, from a Christian perspective. According to Leininger's story, Nina (here Nan) spent the rest of her life building on her father's legacy. (Harper did survive the sinking; she was six at the time.) The publisher, Vision Forum, is associated with the Christian Boys' and Men's *Titanic* Society.

290 Lindley, Sally. *Make Your Own Titanic.* Clifton, Bristol UK: Parragon, 1998. Softcover, 16 pp.

One of several cardboard-cutout, glue-together *Titanic* models marketed as a book, *Make Your Own Titanic* included nearly 10 pages of text on *Titanic*'s construction and shipboard life. (The page count does not include the rigid center tear-out pages. Curiously, even with the limited pages, the author concludes with a section on the famous shipwrecks *Lusitania, Atocha,* and *Mary Rose.*

291 Majoor, Mireille. *Titanic: Ghosts of the Abyss.* Hyperion, 2003. Hardcover, 48 pp.

Exploration of the wreck illustrated with 3-D images. The book serves as a companion to the IMAX 3-D film of the wreck by James Cameron.

292 Malam, John. *Titanic: Shipwrecks and Sunken Treasure.* DK Mega Bites series. UK: Dorling Kindersley, 2003. Softcover, 96 pp.

Part of a series designed for quick research for school projects, this little book includes accessible facts, figures, diagrams, and photographs. Also includes a list of top *Titanic* websites.

Other editions: Published in the United States as part of DK's Secret World series (2003).

293 Marsh, Carole. *Gigantic Titanic Trivia for Kids! Titanic* for Kids series. Peachtree City, GA: Gallopade, 1998. Paperback, 40 pp.

Trivia book for grade-school students from an educational publisher. Marsh is an executive with the publishing company. This is the only title in the proposed series.

Other editions: Hardcover, 1999.

294 Marschall, Ken, and Hugh Brewster. *Inside the Titanic: A Giant Cut-Away Book.* Boston and Ontario: Little, Brown and Madison Press Books, 1997. Hardcover, 32 pp.

Oversized and nearly flat, *Inside the Titanic* surely rates as one of the most attractive children's *Titanic* books ever produced. With detailed cutaway illustrations of the ship's design and operation, this book provides the kind of rainy-day escapism likely to keep an imaginative young reader enthralled for hours. Topics covered include the *Titanic*'s first day at sail, the dining rooms, class accommodations, Sunday activities, the iceberg collision, the lifeboat loading, the sinking, and the rescue. A center cutaway foldout, remarkable both for its comprehensiveness and precision, gives an illustrative overview of the *Titanic*'s entire bow-to-stern layout.

295 Martin, Les. ***Young Indiana Jones and the Titanic Adventure.*** New York: Random House, 1993. Softcover, 140 pp.

Henry Jones, Jr., or "Indy" (who later becomes the world-famous archeologist Indiana Jones) journeys to America aboard the *Titanic* after traveling to London to meet Sherlock Holmes author Sir Arthur Conan Doyle. On the voyage, Indy is charged with protecting his former tutor, Miss Seymour. His journey is also complicated by a young Irish stowaway named Molly and his overhearing a plan to blow up the *Titanic*. The story is populated by mostly fictional characters, although J. J. Astor and others are mentioned by name. The narrative closes with an homage to Walter Lord's book: "In the history of the sea, this would be a night to remember. But for young Indiana Jones, the rest of it would be a night to forget." A short epilogue recaps some of the historical footnotes mentioned in the narrative, and a brief bibliography is also included.

The Young Indiana Jones books were inspired by the television series "The Young Indiana Jones Chronicles," a semi-educational prime-time series that alternated storylines between a preteen and adolescent Indiana Jones. This series was in turn inspired by the *Raiders of the Lost Ark* movies starring Harrison Ford.

296 McKeown, Arthur. ***Titanic.*** Dublin: Poolbeg Press, 1996. New York: Simon and Schuster (Aladdin Paperbacks), Ready-to-Read series, 1998. Illustrations by Peter Hogan. Softcover, 48 pp.

Yet another elementary-school reader (this one aimed at students ages 5–7) to employ the story of the *Titanic*. The story of a young first-class passenger, Mary, who is traveling to America to visit her aunt and uncle in New York, is intertwined with passages that describe the ship's construction, life aboard the ship, and a short biography of Captain Smith. In the book's brief 48-page narrative, McKeown manages to pack in many unsubstantiated myths: Thomas Andrews declares that the "ship can't sink," Captain Smith is seen rescuing a small child before going down with the ship, and the first-class passengers enjoy dancing in the ballroom on the night of the collision (the *Titanic* had no ballroom).

297 Navratil, Elizabeth. ***Survivors: A True-Life Titanic Story.*** Panda series. Dublin: O'Brien Press, 1999. Paperback, 221 pp. Translated by Joan de Sola Pinto.

In this grade-school nonfiction reader, two French boys, Michel and Edmond Navratil, are kidnapped by their father and taken to America. They must begin life anew when their father does not survive the sinking.

The father of the boys, Michel Navratil, traveled in second class under the name of Hoffman. Before he handed his sons to another passenger to be saved, he told them that he had intended to reunite the family. After being taken in by first-class passenger Margaret Hays, the boys were returned to their mother in Nice.

Survivors was originally published in French as *Enfants du Titanic*.

298 Osborne, Mary Pope. ***Tonight on the Titanic.*** Magic Tree House #17. New York: Random House, 1999. Hardcover, softcover, 74 pp. Illustrated by Sal Murdocca.

Eight-year-old Jack and his seven-year-old sister Annie journey back to the *Titanic* in their time-traveling treehouse. The siblings manage to escape in time, but the ship still sinks. The final two pages of the book give young readers seven basic facts about the *Titanic*.

The magic treehouse is filled with books owned by Morgan le Fay, a "magic librarian" from King Arthur's time; in Arthurian legend, she was actually Arthur's half-sister and is sometimes identified as a fairy, sometimes as a witch. Other books in the Tree House series involve dinosaurs, mummies, and pirates.

299 Osborne, Will, and Mary Pope Osborne. ***A Nonfiction Companion to Tonight on the Titanic.*** Magic Tree House Research Guide. New York: Random House, 2002. Hardcover, softcover, 128 pp. Illustrated by Sal Murdocca.

This nonfiction companion provides information and details of shipboard life, the sinking, survivors and passengers, and the shipwreck.

300 Palazzo-Craig, Janet. ***Titanic Book of Fascinating Facts.*** Memphis, TN: Troll Books, 1999. Softcover, 32 pp.

This half-size book from a classroom book-club publisher covers a range of issues in page-long summaries, from the fate of passengers to new theories about the failure of the rivets. Includes black-and-white photographs and sketch illustrations.

301 Peck, Richard. ***Ghosts I Have Been.*** New York: Viking Penguin, 1977. Hardcover, 224 pp.

Young teen Blossom Culp, the dark and resourceful outcast of Bluff City, discovers that she is gifted with extrasensory perception and finds herself onboard the *Titanic* in a harrowing psychic encounter.

This young adult novel follows in a long tradition of connecting the *Titanic* to things supernatural, and it also profits from the appeal ghost stories (especially unsavory stories that might not be approved by parents) hold for young teens and preteens. *Ghosts I Have Been* stands out from other young adult *Titanic* books through its fresh approach and lyrical prose. Blossom Culp appears in several other similar books, including *The Dreadful Future of Blossom Culp* and *The Ghost Belonged to Me*.

Paperback edition: Puffin Books (Penguin), 2001.

302 Petty, Ouita. ***Titanic Troubles.*** Time Capsule series. Alberta, Canada: Polywogs & Wolypops Press, 1994. Illustrated by Carol McCallum.

This historical adventure intended for early grade-school classroom use is part of Petty's Time Capsule series, each of which followed the time-traveling adventures of five children (including Tubs, Microchip) and a dog named Quasar. As the story begins, the friends find that their time capsule has settled in a lifeboat aboard the *Titanic*. The last chapter of *Titanic Troubles* includes factual information and a removable wall chart of the ship.

303 Poole, Lynn, and Gray Poole. ***Danger! Icebergs Ahead!*** New York: Random House, 1961. Hardcover, 82 pp.

Nonfiction book designed for elementary school libraries.

304 Potter, Michael. ***Titanic Story.*** UK: Dorling Kindersley, 2000. Softcover, 32 pp.

Grade-school *Titanic* reader.

305 Ransom, Candice. ***Nicole.*** Sunfire series. Scholastic, 1986.

Young adult romance in which Nicole, traveling on the *Titanic*, must decide between two suitors, the handsome immigrant Karl and the adventurous Price. Ransom peppers her story with nonfiction details of the disaster, so that the romantic novel serves as an introduction to the history of the event.

306 Renner, Traci A. ***Emma's Nightmare.*** Prince Frederick, MD: Recorded Books, 1996. Softcover, 28 pp. + Audio (1 cassette) + Teacher's guide (14 pp.)

Fourteen-year-old Emma Phillips, a passenger on the "unsinkable" *Titanic*, fears something may be wrong when she feels a strange jolt in her cabin one night.

The "talking book" is designed to be used as a read-along classroom activity.

307 Rawlinson, Jonathan. ***Discovering the Titanic.*** Great Adventure series. Vero Beach, Florida: Rourke Enterprises, 1988. 32 pp. With illustrations.

Describes Robert Ballard's search for and discovery of the *Titanic*'s wreck 2 miles beneath the surface of the Atlantic. Includes index.

308 Regan, Ellen. ***The Titanic and the Mystery Ship.*** Ireland: Mercier Press, 1999.

The story of the *Titanic* is retold from the point of view of Sarah Kelly, a maid to the de Vray family, and by Oliver, a sailor on the *Californian*. In Regan's version of the story, however, the *Californian* comes to the rescue of the *Titanic* as she sinks, making this book perhaps the only suitable *Titanic* bedtime story.

The Kelly and de Vray names appear to be a creation of the author, although Irish women by the names of Kelly and Devaney sailed in third class. Ellen Regan is the pseudonym of novelist and poet William Wall.

309 Ruffin, Frances E. ***"Unsinkable" Molly Brown.*** American Legends series. New York: Powerkids Press, 2002. Softcover, 24 pp.

Library biography for young grade-school readers.

310 Ryan, Bernard Jr. ***Tyler's Titanic.*** Oakland, CA: RDR Books, 2001. Softcover, 60 pp.

In this early-grade school reader, young Tyler's dog Spoofer digs a hole in the sand one day as they walk along the beach. The ocean pours into the hole, and the shoreline recedes beyond the horizon. The boy and his dog are able to walk along the floor of the Atlantic Ocean until they reach the wreck of the *Titanic*. There the encounter the ghosts of the crew, who tell them the true story behind the sinking.

311 Senauth, Frank. ***To Save the Titanic from Disaster.*** Dorrance, 1999. Paperback, 96 pp.

Time-traveling juvenile novel printed by subsidy publisher.

312 Senauth, Frank. ***To Save the Titanic from Disaster—II.*** Trafford, 2000. Softcover, 170 pp.

Subsidy-published juvenile novel recounts the further adventures of a time-traveling young girl who attempts to save the *Titanic* (and its replica) from disaster. The storyline revolves around a legend that the ghost of Captain Smith will be freed if the replica ship safely reaches port.

313 Sherrow, Victoria, and Thomas Stacey. ***The Titanic.*** World History series. San Diego: Greenhaven, 1999. Hardcover and paperback, 112 pp.

Revised and updated edition of Stacey's earlier book, with additional material and sidebars that sketch the lives of those involved.

314 Shipton, Paul. ***Titanic.*** Penguin Readers series. UK: Longman Group, 2001. Softcover, 48 pp.

Nonfiction reader for preteen ages.

315 Slater, Timothy, and Michael Hulse, trans. ***Complete Guide to Building the Titanic.*** Germany: Taschen, 1993. Illustrated by Thomas Siwek. Softcover, 58 pp.

Heavy-paper fold-together model of the *Titanic* is here packaged as a book, with only five pages devoted to historical information and photographs of the ship. Both the history and the model instructions are printed in English, French, and German, with Slater and Hulse providing the English translations. The resulting 1:200 model is 53 inches long and would keep an adult model-builder busy for hours.

316 Sloan, Frank. ***Titanic.*** New York: F. Watts, 1987. Hardcover, 95 pp. With illustrations.

This book, aimed at preteen readers, offers a description of life aboard the *Titanic* and a history of the events that led up to the sinking and rescue efforts. Sloan also retells the story of Robert Ballard's discovery of the *Titanic*'s wreck. Additional material in the 1999 edition describe subsequent voyages to the wreck, new theories on the sinking, and the impact of James Cameron's film.

Revised edition: Raintree/Steck Vaughn, 1999. Library binding, 128 pp.

317 Spedden, Daisy Corning Stone. ***Polar the Titanic Bear.*** Boston: Little, Brown, 1994. Illustrated by Laurie McGaw; introduction and epilogue by Leighton H. Coleman III. Hardback, 64 pp.

Titanic first-class passenger Spedden first presented this "true" story about her son Douglas and his stuffed bear as a Christmas present to Douglas in 1913. Most of the story, told from the perspective of the bear, takes place before the family boards the *Titanic* and touches on their travels around the globe and Douglas' battle with measles. The harrowing details of the actual disaster are kept to a minimum (more easily done since Douglas, his parents, and his nanny all survived)—the only real moment of anxiety comes when

Polar is nearly forgotten onboard the lifeboat. An epilogue recounts the life of Daisy Spedden and provides a window into life in Edwardian class society.

Douglas is known to many as the young boy pictured spinning his top on the deck of the *Titanic* in Father Browne's famous photograph. Tragically, after surviving both the measles and the *Titanic*, Douglas (the Spedden's only child) died in an automobile accident three years later.

318 Stacey, Thomas. ***The Titanic.*** World Disaster series. San Diego: Lucent Books, 1989. Hardcover, 64 pp. Illustrated by Chris Miller.

Nonfiction account of the disaster, providing a basic chronology of the events. The book also includes a recounting of Ballard's search and exploration efforts.

319 Staiano, Andrew. ***Draw the Titanic.*** New York: Scholastic, 1998. Softcover, 64 pp. Illustrated by Jason Pederson.

More of a general drawing book for preteens and young teens, *Draw the Titanic* uses the *Titanic* as a source for practice illustrations for beginning artists. Exercises include drawing a boarding first-class female passenger, a lifeboat, the submarine *Alvin*, and Captain Smith. The exercise covering the ship itself runs four pages. More tangential exercises ask the reader to draw a swordfish, a tiger shark, and a 1911 Delage automobile.

The book includes a handful of informational breakout boxes throughout the book, a 12-page introduction on the voyage of the *Titanic*, black-and-white photographs, and a glossary.

320 Stewart, David. ***You Wouldn't Want to Sail on the Titanic!: One Voyage You'd Rather Not Make.*** Brighton, UK: Salariya, 2001. Danbury, CT: Franklin Watts, 2001. Softcover, 32 pp. Illustrated by David Antram.

Whimsically if inappropriately titled book invites preteen readers to put themselves in the positions of passengers aboard the doomed ocean liner. The heavily illustrated book takes an irreverent approach, with lampoonish cartoon illustrations (an illustration of a manservant resembles David Warner in 1997's *Titanic*), "fun" typography, and factoids presented as "handy hints" (e.g., "Note where the lifeboats are stored—there aren't enough for everyone on board"). Nonetheless, many of the facts presented are not typically found in children's books of similar quality, including that third-class only had two bathtubs and that Captain Smith's salary would today equal $73,000.

The book is part of a series of "You Wouldn't Want to..." titles created by David Salariya. Other titles include *You Wouldn't Want to Be a Roman Gladiator* and *You Wouldn't Want to Be a Slave in Ancient Greece*.

Other editions: Published in the UK as *Avoid Sailing on the Titanic!* (Book House, 2002).

321 Sullivan, George. ***To the Bottom of the Sea: The Exploration of Exotic Life, the Titanic, and Other Secrets of the Oceans.*** CT: Twenty First Century Books, 1999. Hardcover, 80 pp.

This nonfiction book for preteen readers traces the history of underwater exploration and shipwreck discovery from the 19th century forward.

322 Tanaka, Shelley. ***On Board the Titanic: What It Was Like When the Great Liner Sank.*** I Was There series. New York: Hyperion/Madison Press, 1996. Hardcover, 48 pp. Illus. by Ken Marschall.

Attractive and informational book aimed at grade schoolers. Among the more intriguing illustrations are Marschall's toy-like renderings of people and life onboard the ship, since Marschall usually focuses on the ship itself. Marschall's paintings are supplemented with many photographs and scientific diagrams, while the text relies on the narrative power of Jack Thayer and Harold Bride's first-person accounts. A brief glossary is included.

Other editions: Paperback Edition: Hyperion Press, 1998.

323 ***Touched by Titanic.*** Privately published, 2002.

A compilation of 50 stories, poems, and drawings submitted by students from elementary schools in Belfast, Ireland (where the *Titanic* was built), Cobh, Ireland (her last port of call), and Halifax, Nova Scotia (where many of the victims were buried). The book was published as part of the *Titanic* Made in Belfast celebration.

324 Trumbore, Cindy. ***Discovering the Titanic.*** Starburst series. South Melbourne, Australia: Pearson Education, 2000.

Heavily illustrated nonfiction reader, with particular focus on the wreck site.

325 Vance, Marguerite. ***Courage at Sea.*** New York: E. P. Dutton, 1963. Hardcover, 86 pp.

Juvenile novel focused on the heroics of a young male passenger.

326 Wallace, Jim. ***Choose Your Own Adventure: Terror on the Titanic.*** Bantam Books, 1997. Illustrated by Frank Bolle. Softcover, 118 pp.

The reader, after spending time studying classical piano in London, is set aboard the *Titanic* in this adventure story. The story has several different possible endings, depending on which choices the reader makes regarding his actions aboard the *Titanic*. At least one of the endings, in which the crew cannot hear the reader's warnings of icebergs ahead, results in the *Titanic* not sinking. (This ending would be based on the presumption that the ship would not have sunk but simply have been disabled had she hit the iceberg head on.) Illustrated with black-and-white comic-book-like sketches. *Terror on the Titanic* was No. 169 in this popular series.

327 White, Ellen Emerson. ***Voyage on the Great Titanic: The Diary of Margaret Ann Brady, RMS Titanic, 1912.*** Dear America series. New York: Scholastic Trade, 1998. Hardcover, 197 pp.

A mannered 13-year-old British orphan is hired as a traveling companion for a crass American woman traveling aboard the *Titanic*, enabling her to gain inexpensive passage to join her brother in the United States. The book is written in diary form in the verbose, articulate style peculiar to fictional preteen girls (especially well-educated Edwardian girls) with an aim to pleasing just such an audience. The text is riddled with such faux–Victorian phrases as "the most delicious mutton chops" that would sound stilted in other contexts; here they serve as evidence that the author is unwilling to insult the intelligence of her young readers. At any rate, the book's sentimental tendencies are redeemed by an attention to history and detail. In particular, the heroine spends much of her time describing the customs and accouterments aboard the ship. *Titanic* stock characters who make cameo appearances include Thomas Andrews, the Strauses, J. J. Astor, and Molly Brown. An epilogue provides a straightforward presentation of the facts surrounding the disaster, supplemented by a timeline, illustrations, and photographs.

Other books in the popular "Dear America" series chronicled the lives of girls during the Great Depression, aboard the *Mayflower*, and toiling on the prairies of frontier America.

The book is designed to look like a real diary, complete with a ribbon bookmarker.

Other editions: Released in the UK as a paperback under Scholastic's My Story series.

328 Williams, Barbara. ***Making Waves.*** New York: Scholastic, 2000. Softcover, 215 pp.

Sequel to *Titanic Crossing*. Having survived the sinking of the *Titanic*, 12-year-old Emily Brewer lives in Baltimore where she encounters the early Industrial Age problems of child labor, sweatshops, and the labor union struggles. Emily befriends Albert onboard the *Titanic* in Williams' first novel. In *Making Waves*, Emily and Albert continue to correspond.

329 Williams, Barbara. ***Titanic Crossing.*** New York: Scholastic, 1997. Softcover, 168 pp.

Returning home to America aboard the *Titanic*, young Albert is faced with difficult decisions when the ship goes down. Onboard the ship, Albert encounters such characters as theatre producer Harry Gordon. In the author's postscript, Williams says she was inspired to write this engaging young-adult novel by the tale of the 13-year-old boy who was at first refused a seat in a lifeboat.

330 Wormser, Richard. ***The Titanic.*** Explorer Books series. New York: Trumpet Club, 1994. Hardcover, 58 pp.

Unremarkable juvenile nonfiction account by author known for ready-made school library histories.

Other editions: Scholastic, softcover.

4 Narrative Films

331 *Atlantic* (1929). British International Pictures Ltd. and Süd Film (Germany/UK). Black and white, Approx. 90 min.
Director: Ewald André (E. A.) Dupont
Screenplay: E. A. Dupont, Victor Kendall, and Pierre Maudru, from the play *The Berg* by Ernest Raymond (q.v.)
Music: John Reynders and the British International Dance Orchestra
Sound: RCA Photo-Phone System
British/Silent Cast:

> Franklin Dyall . . . . *John Rool*
> Madeleine Carroll . . . . *Monica*
> John Stuart . . . . *Lawrence*
> Ellaline Terriss . . . . *Alice Rool*
> Monty Banks . . . . *Dandy*
> Donald Calthrop . . . . *Pointer*
> John Longden . . . . *Lanchester*
> Syd Crossley . . . . *Telegraph Operator*

Also: Maxime Desjardins, Alice Field, Constant Rémy, Arthur Hardy, Helen Haye, D. A. Clarke-Smith, Joan Barry, Francis Lister, Sydney Lynn, and Dino Galvani.
German Cast:

> Fritz Kortner . . . . *Heinrich Thomas*
> Elsa Wagner . . . . *Anna Thomas*
> Julia Serda . . . . *Clara von Schroeder*
> Heinrich Schroth . . . . *Harry von Schroeder*
> Philipp Manning . . . . *Captain von Oldenburg*
> Georg August Koch . . . . *First Officer Lersner*
> Syd Crossley . . . . *Telegraph Operator*

Also: Elfriede Borodin, Lucie Mannheim, Francis Lederer, Willi Forst, Hermann Vallentin, Theodor Loos, Georg John.

The first full-length narrative film of the *Titanic* story is an early "talkie" film and very much a relic of its era — from the flapper hairdos and glamorous cigarette holders to the unrelenting background period music. The inconsequential dialogue serves mainly to break the monotony of long periods of music and primitive, grating sound effects. The fictional storylines the film sets against the backdrop of the *Titanic* include the sentimental story of a wheelchair-bound passenger who must decide whether to board the lifeboats with the women and children. The passengers join in singing "Nearer My God to Thee" as the ship sinks.

Although there is no mention of the *Titanic* specifically (and none of the usual cast of characters), the film nonetheless provoked a letter from several White Star Line managers, who criticized the portrayal of the company and the shipping industry in general. Specifically, White Star managers seemed dismayed that a British film company would turn against patriotic loyalty to exploit the tragedy. Compared to subsequent films, though, the film's portrayal of the sinking is relatively tame, closing with a strange and sentimental final-frame fadeout of a cloudy sunrise.

Three versions of the film were released: A German-language version, released in 1929 and starring a completely different set of German-speaking actors, became the first German "talkie." The English-language film, shot using the same sets, was released in 1930 and was co-directed by Jean Kemm. A silent version, released in 1929, incorporated footage from both films.

Available: British version released on video as *Titanic: Disaster in the Atlantic,* Bennu Multimedia, in the U.S. in 1999. The video version includes a videotaped introduction by David McCallum, who played Harold Bride in *A Night to Remember* and has narrated several *Titanic* documentaries.

332 *Atlantis* (1913). Nordisk Film (Denmark). Black-and-white, silent, 113 min.

Director: August Blom
Screenplay: Gerhart Hauptmann (from novel)
Cast: Michael Curtiz, Ida Orlov, Ebba Thomsen, Frederik Jacobsen, Carl Lauritzen, et al.

Tale of ocean liner crossing focuses on the romantic story of a doctor who is torn between a third-class passenger and a first-class society woman. The film, perhaps inspired by the events of the *Titanic* (the name of the ship is evocatively similar), was a success due to its realistic effects for the time, including footage of an actual, smaller ship sinking. It was restored in 1993 by the Danish Filmmuseum. An alternate, "unhappy" ending was filmed for Russian audiences.

Available: Video, Image Entertainment

333 *Chambermaid on the Titanic* (1997) (aka *La Femme de chambre du Titanic*). UGC YM La Sept Cinema, France 2 Cinema, Rodeo Drive Mate Productions, Tornasol Films, and Westdeutscher Rundfunk (France and Spain). Distributed in the United States by Samuel Goldwyn. Color, 101 min.

Director: Bigas Luna
Screenplay: Cuca Canals, Jean-Louis Benoit, and Bigas Luna, from the novel by Didier Decoin
Producers: Yves Marmion and Daniel Toscan Du Plantier
Music: Alberto Iglesias
Cast:

Olivier Martinez	Horty
Romane Bohringer	Zoe
Aitana Sánchez-Gijón	Marie
Didier Bezace	Simeon
Aldo Maccione	Zeppe
Jean-Marie Juan	Pascal

Also: Arno Chevrier, Marianne Groves, Didier Bénureau, Alberto Cassadie, Giorgio Gobbi, Yves Verhoeven, Vincenzo De Caro, Salvador Madrid, and Barbara Lerici.

In this mock-romantic fantasy, a French foundry worker (Martinez) wins the chance to travel to England to see the launching of the *Titanic* on her maiden voyage. The night before the launching, he spends the night in a luxury hotel. A woman claiming to be a chambermaid on the *Titanic* knocks on his hotel room door and asks to share his room, as she cannot find lodging in the city. He allows her to stay, but the arrangements are strictly platonic. He sees her off at the dock and manages to get a photograph of her before she leaves. The rest of this playful and visually appealing film has Horty recounting to his countrymen, in humorous and increasingly elaborate detail, his sexual encounters with the chambermaid.

The film (with English subtitles added) was given an art-house run in the United States after the success of James Cameron's film in 1998 and was advertised under the slogan "There Was More than One Love Story on the *Titanic*."

Available: U.S. video release set for October 1999.

334 *In Night and Ice* (1912). (*In Nacht und Eis*). Continental-Kunstfilm (Germany). Black and white, silent, Approx. 30 min. *Working Title: Titanic.*

Director: Mime Misu

After being considered a lost film for many years, a copy of this film turned up in a private collection in Berlin in 1998. It was shown at the British Film Institute in April 1999. The radio operators figure prominently in the storyline. The film, released in August 1912, was originally advertised as being the first film to be based on "authentic reports," to distinguish it from the earlier Dorothy Gibson effort.

335 *The Memory of Eva Ryker* (1980-TV) Irwin Allen/CBS. Color, 144 min.

Director: Walter Grauman
Screenplay: Donald A. Stanwood
Cast:

Jean-Pierre Aumont	*Inspector Laurier*
Ralph Bellamy	*William E. Ryker*
Tonya Crowe	*Young Eva*
Bradford Dillman	*Jason Eddington*
Morgan Fairchild	*Lisa*
Mel Ferrer	*Dr. Sanford*
Robert Foxworth	*Norman Hall*
Peter Graves	*Rogers*
Robert Hogan	*J. H. Martin*
Roddy McDowall	*MacFarland*
Natalie Wood	*Eva/Claire Ryker*

Television movie version of the novel by Donald Standwood (q.v.). References to the *Titanic* have been eliminated in favor of a similar disaster set 20 years later.

336 *A Night to Remember* (1956-TV) *Kraft Television Theatre.* Kinescope, 60 min. (Live). Originally aired March 28, 1956, NBC; repeat performance May 2, 1956.

Director: George Roy Hill
Teleplay: George Roy Hill and John Whedon from the book by Walter Lord
Makeup: Bob O'Bradovich
Costumes: Robert Mackintosh
Art Director: Duane McKinney
Technical Director: Bob Hanna
Music: Wladimir Selinsky
Cast: Claude Rains (narrator)
Crew: Clarence Derweat, Don Marlow, Eric Micklewood, David Cole, Frank Leslie, Roger Evan Boxill, John Wayne Evans, Victor Thorley, Leonard Stone, Richard Newton, William Becker, Peter Forster, Roger Hamilton, Neil North, et al. *First-class passengers:* Millette Alexander, Peter Pagan, Anthony

Kemble Cooper, Edgar Sichli, Cavada Humphrey, Joanna Roos, Clifford David, Jerome Kilty, Roger Plowden, Hugh Dunne, et al. *Steerage passengers:* Walter Burke, Sandy Ackland, Dan Morgan, Helena Carroll, et al. *Stewards:* Victor Wood, Drew Thompson, John Mackwood, George Cathrey, et al.

Remarkably watchable and dynamic teleplay based on *A Night to Remember,* setting the stage for the feature film two years later.

The narrator/host sets up the performance with a discussion of the similarities between Morgan Robertson's novel and the *Titanic* disaster, in keeping with the format of Lord's book. The pacing and scenes are not unlike the later film, with more narration to describe the action (as was the trend in early live television, since talent and producers had cut their teeth on radio drama). The band does not play "Nearer My God to Thee."

This live television production was considered one of the most elaborate of its day, with 107 actors in the cast. The usual limitations of live television are barely noticeable, except in the small detail that the ship is never shown in her entirety.

337 *A Night to Remember* (1958) Rank Organisation (UK) Black-and-white, 123 min.

Director: Roy Baker
Screenplay: Eric Ambler, from book by Walter Lord
Art Direction: Alex Vetchinsky
Director of Photography: Geoffrey Unsworth
Producer: William MacQuitty
Executive Producer: Earl St. John
Music: William Alwyn
Special Effects: Bill Warrington
Cast:

Kenneth More	*Second Officer Charles Lightoller*
Ronald Allen	*Mr. Clarke*
Robert Ayres	*Major Arthur Peuchen*
Honor Blackman	*Mrs. Liz Lucas*
Anthony Bushell	*Captain Arthur Rostron*
John Cairney	*Murphy*
Jill Dixon	*Mrs. Clarke*
Jane Downs	*Mrs. Sylvia Lightoller*
James Dyrenforth	*Colonel Archibald Gracie*
Michael Goodliffe	*Thomas Andrews*
Kenneth Griffith	*Jack Phillips*
Harriette Johns	*Lady Richards*
Frank Lawton	*Chairman*

Richard Leech	*First Officer William Murdoch*
David McCallum	*Harold Bride*
Alex McCowen	*Sparks Cottam*
Tucker McGuire	*Molly Brown*
Laurence Naismith	*Captain E. J. Smith*
Russell Napier	*Captain Stanley Lord*
Jack Watling	*Joseph Boxhall*
Gerald Harper	*Thomas Andrews*
Bernard Fox	*Frederick Fleet*
Norman Rossington	*Steward*

Also: John Merivale, Ralph Michael, Redmond Phillips, George Rose, Joseph Tomelty, Patrick Waddington, Meier Tzelniker, Helen Misener, Thomas Heathcote, Michael Bryan, Philip Ray, Tim Turner, et al.

Critics often misleadingly term this classic British screen adaptation of the *Titanic* disaster a "documentary drama" or "docudrama." Although the film is based on actual events and contains all the familiar factual elements, its emphasis of the disaster's more mythical moments (the heroic diligence of the wireless operators and the orchestra's final rendition of "Nearer My God to Thee," for instance) places it squarely in the tradition of British romanticism. In fairness, the film's sentimentality sometimes seems more a function of form than feeling, as the traditional romantic elements are balanced by the plight of steerage passengers and other unseemly truths. All in all, the film is good cinema, to be enjoyed as much for its emotional impact as for its reliance on Lord's hard facts.

The director integrates newsreel footage (without sound) into the film, perhaps contributing to the overall docudrama feel. But the grainy footage, combined with the use of scale models, leaves the film far from seamless in the technical/special effects arena. The soothing effect of the crisp black-and-white cinematography helps make such problems less obvious, while the emphasis on factual events and interior shots is refreshing in light of latter-day *Titanic* special-effects bonanzas. Grim comic relief is provided by the chief baker, who, when realizing he will almost certainly perish, drinks himself into a stupor and starts throwing deck chairs to drowning passengers.

Although *ANTR* is often touted as the most historically accurate *Titanic* film, it is not without its now-famous gaffes. Newsreel footage at the beginning of the movie shows a ship being christened; in fact, the White Star Line never christened its ships. The footage was actually taken during the launching of the *Queen Elizabeth*.

The screen credits include acknowledgments of Captain Grattidge, ex-commodore of the Cunard Line and Commander Boxhall, 4th officer of the *Titanic*.

Available: Hallmark Home Entertainment video, letterbox format. Sometimes sold in "double feature" package with *Titanic* (1953).

338 *No Greater Love* (1996-TV) The Cramer Company, NBC (USA) 120 min. with commercials.

Director: Richard T. Heffron
Screenplay: Carmen Culver from the novel by Danielle Steel
Executive Producer: Douglas S. Cramer
Producers: Dennis Hammer and Christopher Morgan
Music: Billy Goldenberg
Cast:

Kelly Rutherford	*Edwina Winfield*
Chris Sarandon	*Sam Horowitz*
Nicholas Campbell	*Malcolm Stone*
Daniel Hugh-Kelly	*Ben Jones*
Michael Landes	*George Winfield*
Gina Philips	*Alexis Winfield*
Susan Hogan	*Kate Winfield*
Daniel Pilon	*Bert Winfield*

Also: Simon MacCorkindale, Christopher Fuller, Sarah Freeman, Hayden Christensen, and Polly Shannon.

Soapy television movie version of Danielle Steel's novel (q.v.) about a young woman (Rutherford) who must raise her siblings alone after losing her lover and parents aboard the *Titanic*. The *Titanic* scenes are rather sterile and perfunctory, with the gleaming passengers looking as if they almost expect the ship to sink. Portraying the ship accurately is not one of the goals of this film (which includes an elaborate ballroom scene), although the band does manage to squeeze in a rendition of "Nearer My God to Thee" before it's all done. The story becomes more palatable when it moves to dry land, as the self-sacrificing Edwina Winfield deals with the trials and tribulations of raising a family on her own.

339 *Raise the Titanic!* (1980) Lord Grade Productions (USA) Color, 122 min. Directed by Jerry Jameson. Music by John Barry.

Production Design: John F. Decuir
Executive Producer: Martin Starger
Screenplay by Adam Kennedy from the novel by Clive Cussler
Adaptation by Eric Hughes
Produced by William Frye
Cast: Jason Robards, Richard Jordan, David Selby, Anne Archer, Alec Guiness, Bo Brundin, M. Emmet Walsh, J. D. Cannon
Also: Norman Bartold, Elva Baskin, Dirk Blocker, Robert Broyles, Paul Carr, Michael G. Gwynne, Harvey Lewis, Charles Macaulay, Stewart Moss, Michael Pataki, Marvin Silbersher, Mark L. Taylor, Maurice Kowalewski,

Nancy Nevinson, Trent Dolan, Paul Tuerpe, Sander Vanocur, Ken Place, Michael Ensign, and Craig Shreeve.

Muddled, dialogue-heavy adaptation of Clive Cussler's novel (q.v.) begins with five minutes of historical still photographs of the *Titanic*'s building and launching, with a focus on dramatic shots that emphasize the liner's size and grandeur. From there, it moves into a shaky plot, set in modern times, of international Cold War intrigue. Visually, the movie resembles many of the adventure-disaster movies of the period (such as the *King Kong* remake). Unlike James Cameron, these filmmakers had no real wreck to reference or film for the ocean-floor sequences; when the salvage operation locates the wreck, she is in one piece and remarkably pristine. In a sentimental touch to an otherwise cynical story, Dirk Pitt raises the White Star flag on the ship's deck and the ship is pulled into its harbor of destination, 70 years overdue.

Alec Guiness receives special billing for his role as surviving crewmember "Bigelow," who helps adventurer Dirk Pitt pinpoint the location of some missing valuable ore aboard the ship. His few scenes as the contemplative old sailor are the best reasons to watch this film.

The film became famous for its excessive budget and failure at the box office; it cost $40 million to make and took in only $7 million.

Available: Originally released on VHS by Magnetic Video in association with ITC Entertainment.

Released on laser disc by CBS Fox in 1989.

340 *Saved from the Titanic* (May 1912) Eclair Moving Picture Company (USA) Silent, Black and White, Approx. 10 min.

Director: Étienne Arnaud
Producer: Harry Raver
Cast:

> Dorothy Gibson . . . . *Miss Dorothy*
> Alex Francis . . . . *Father*
> Miss Stuart . . . . *Mother*
> Jack Adolfi . . . . *Ensign Jack*

Also: William Dunn, Guy Oliver

This short silent film, released a month to the day after the *Titanic* disaster, starred (and was spearheaded by) movie actress and *Titanic* survivor Dorothy Gibson. Although all prints of the film were subsequently lost (as is common for films of the period), the trade periodical *Moving Picture World* summarized the plot of the film in its May 11, 1912, issue.

Dorothy embarks on the *Titanic,* on her way home to be married to U.S. Naval Officer Ensign Jack. Impatient for news of her arrival, Jack travels to the wireless office, where he learns that the *Titanic* has struck an iceberg. An anguished Jack informs Dorothy's parents of the news. Later, the audience learns that Dorothy was in fact among the saved. She vividly recounts the details of the disaster to her parents and her betrothed, and is so overcome with emotion that she faints. The next day, Dorothy's mother insists that Jack resign from the Navy, as the sea is too full of perils. He thinks it over, and decides that his loyalty must lie with his service to his flag and country. Dorothy's father, impressed with the young man's patriotism, gives him his daughter's hand in marriage.

According to Frank Thompson, who devotes a chapter to the film in his book *Lost Films* (Citadel Press, 1996), Dorothy Gibson wore the same clothes during filming that she had worn the night of the shipwreck.

341 *S.O.S. Titanic* (1979-TV) Roger Gimbel Productions, Argonaut Films, EMI Television (USA) Color, 105 min. (Orig. 180 min. with commercials)

Originally aired: ABC, Sept. 23, 1979
Director: William Hale
Executive Producers: William S. Gilmore and Roger Gimbel
Screenplay: James Costigan
Producer: Lou Morheim
Music: Howard Blake
Cinematography: Christopher Challis
Special Effects: Martin Gutteridge and Wally Veevers (supervisors)
Art Direction: Tim Hutchinson
Set Decoration: Martin Atkinson
Cast:

Harry Andrews	*Captain E. J. Smith*
David Battley	*S. Stebbing*
Ed Bishop	*Henry Harris*
Tony Caunter	*Chief Officer Henry Wilde*
Nicholas Davies	*Alfie King*
Matthew Guiness	*Father Byles*
Jerry Houser	*Dan Marvin*
David Janssen	*John Jacob Astor*
Cloris Leachman	*Molly Brown*
Susan Saint James	*Leigh Goodwin*
David Warner	*Laurence Beesley*
Madge Ryan	*Violet Jessop*
Malcolm Stoddard	*Charles Lightoller*
Michele O'Connor	*Kate Mullins*
Victor Langley	*Wallace Hartley*
Gerard McSorley	*Martin Gallagher*

John Moffatt	*Benjamin Guggenheim*
Nancy Nevinson	*Ida Straus*
Gordon Whiting	*Isidor Straus*
Paul Young	*William Murdoch*
Peter Bourke	*Harold Bride*
Warren Clarke	*Joseph G. Boxhall*
Ian Holm	*J. Bruce Ismay*
Geoffrey Whitehead	*Thomas Andrews*

Also: Aubrey Morris, Martin Murphy, Philip O'Sullivan, Robert Pugh, Norman Rossington, Shevaun Briars, Nick Brimble, Jacob Brooke, Lise Hilboldt, Kate Howard, Karl Howman, Beverly Ross, Alec Sabin, and Philip Stone.

This made-for-television movie ushered in the modern era of *Titanic* filmmaking as the first color, relatively big-budget film based on the disaster. The opening titles state that the script is based on factual research and the characters drawn from real life, but its emphasis on personal drama (typical of television movies) separates it from the docudrama style of *A Night to Remember*. The period costumes and sets are well done, and the actors effectively evoke the mannerisms and style of Edwardian society. Laurence Beesley (whose storyline helps mesh the *Titanic* story with true romance for the first time) and Thomas Andrews move to the forefront as significant characters, as do John Jacob Astor and his young bride. One story thread centers on the filmmaking efforts of Dan Marvin; Daniel Marvin was in fact a first-class passenger on the *Titanic*, and his father was the president of the Biograph Film Company, but the movie camera on board the *Titanic* belonged to Noel Malachard, a cameraman for a newsreel company. One oddity: in a running gag, the Molly Brown character (played for the second time by Cloris Leachman) insists on other passengers calling her "Molly," and not Maggie. Overall, an enjoyable film that manages to tell a familiar story from many different angles and keeps its ambition in check.

On the myths: "Nearer My God to Thee" is absent from this film. Bruce Ismay is made out to be a coward for boarding a lifeboat, but he expresses remorse for his actions. The film's most memorable line is delivered by Astor's wife when a passenger offers her sandwiches and coffee aboard the *Carpathia*: "No coffee. No God either." The ship sinks in one piece, as was the prevailing belief at the time.

The *Titanic* Historical Society is given credit for research on this film.

Available: Thorn EMI Video

342 *Thumbtanic* (1999) Image Entertainment (DVD) Color, 27 min.

Writer/Director: Steve Oedekerk

This spoof of *Titanic* (1997), which uses human-thumb puppets as characters in its story, originally garnered a cult following on the Internet in 1998. It was expanded and released for its release as a budget DVD; the marketing insert proclaims the film to be "historically inaccurate." The romantic leads in the story are Jake and Geranium. The DVD also includes optional audio commentary by the director.

343 *Titanic* (1943) Universum Film Aktiengesellschaft (UFA, Germany) Black and white, in German, 85 min.

Director: Werner Klingler, Herbert Selpin
Producer: Willy Reiber
Original Music: Werner Eisbrenner
Screenplay: Herbert Selpin, Walter Zerlett-Olfenius (from story by Harald Bratt)
Cinematography: Friedl Behn-Grund
Cast:

> Sybille Schmitz .... *Sigrid Olinsky*
> Hans Nielsen .... *First Officer Petersen*
> Kirsten Heiberg .... *Gloria*
> Ernst Fritz Fürbringer .... *Bruce Ismay*
> Karl Schönböck .... *John Jacob Astor*
> Otto Wernicke .... *Captain Edward J. Smith*
> Franz Schafheitlin .... *Henderson*

Also: Claude Farell, Sepp Rist (Jan)), Charlotte Thiele (Madeleine), Hermann Brix, Liselotte Klinger (Anne), Theodor Loos (Bergmann), Werner Scharf (Christobal Mendoz), and Theo Schall (Murdock).

From the scrawled, ominous opening titles to the pointy beard and shadowy features of Captain Smith, this Nazi propaganda film makes no pretenses to a sentimental view of the *Titanic* disaster. The *Titanic* becomes a metaphor for the evils of capitalism, as embodied in the many shots of the pumping crankshafts that restate the impersonal nature of capitalism as a machine indifferent to the lives of common men. Predictably, the main targets here are Bruce Ismay and the White Star Line, which seeks to increase its stock value (the ultimate distasteful symbol of capitalism) by beating the trans–Atlantic speed record. Compared to the other, more genteel retellings of the disaster, which have almost always romanticized the trappings of Edwardian society, this film takes the usual conventions of the story and turns them inside-out. First Officer Petersen is a last-minute German replacement aboard the ship, and he becomes the story's hero, the man who predicts the disaster and stands up to Ismay. The crew and passengers all speak German, of course, and the drab, inaccurate interiors and costumes scarcely resemble the lavish sets of other films. Soon after the ship strikes the iceberg, the crewmember finds

Captain Smith enjoying himself in the nonexistent ballroom. The band *does* play "Nearer My God to Thee" as the ship sinks, however.

Although prints and videotapes of this film have circulated for years, no official English dubbed or subtitled version has been released. The shorter and more common video version of the film ends with the ship's sinking amidst the chaos of drowning passengers attempting to climb on to overfilled lifeboats. The full-length version of the film ends with a trial in New York blaming Captain Smith for the ship's sinking.

Because of the scenes of mass panic, the film was deemed inappropriate for release in Germany during the war. It premiered in Paris in 1943, and was eventually shown in Germany beginning in 1949.

Available: German Language Video Center, Indianapolis, Indiana.

344 *Titanic* (1953) 20th Century–Fox (USA) Black and White, 97 min.

Director: Jean Negulesco
Producers: Charles Brackett and Jean Negulesco
Script: Charles Brackett, Walter Reisch, and Richard Breen (Academy Award)
Music: Sol Kaplan
Cinematography: Joseph MacDonald
Set Decoration: Stuart A. Reiss
Costume Design: Dorothy Jeakins
Special Photographic Effects: Ray Kellogg
Cast:

Clifton Webb	*Richard Ward Sturges*
Barbara Stanwyck	*Julia Sturges*
Robert Wagner	*Giff Rogers*
Richard Basehart	*George Headley*
Audrey Dalton	*Annette Sturges*
Thelma Ritter	*Mrs. Young*
Brian Aherne	*Captain Smith*
Allyn Joslyn	*Earl Meeker*
James Todd	*Sandy Comstock*
Frances Bergen	*Madeleine Astor*
William Johnstone	*John Jacob Astor*
Barry Bernard	*First Officer Murdoch*
Charles B. Fitzsimmons	*Chief Officer Wilde*
Edmund Purdom	*Officer Lightoller*
Roy Gordon	*Isidor Straus*
Michael Rennie	*Narrator*
Helen Van Tuyl	*Mrs. Straus*

Also: Patrick Aherne, Harper Carter, Donald Chaffin, William Cottrell, Anthony Eustrel, Michael Ferris, Ashley Cowan, Camillo Guercio, Melinda Markey, Robin Hughes, Ron Hagherty, David Thursby, et al.

The first major American film based explicitly on the *Titanic* disaster brims over with Hollywood clichés and Edwardian sentimentality. As such, it is a genuine product of the Hollywood studio system. The film emphasizes the human drama of the disaster and includes a random sprinkling of standard legends, including the antics of the irreverent and remonstrative Molly Brown, a man masquerading as a woman to get aboard a lifeboat, and the ship owners pushing for a speed record. Noticeably absent from the story is the ship's designer, Thomas Andrews. The fictional stories of the aristocratic first-class passengers take center stage; in fact, most of the film takes place before the wreck. By the time we have witnessed the melodramatic marital woes of the fictional Sturges and a bizarre song-and-dance number ("Navajo Ray") by Robert Wagner, the wreck comes almost as a cleansing, Diluvian relief. The redemptive nature of the shipwreck is symbolized in the personal transformation of the jaded Richard Sturges (played by Clifton Webb), who in death regains the love of his son. The filmmakers gloss over some of the more unseemly aspects of the lifeboat-loading fiasco, but if the Glamour Factory cannot sentimentalize the *Titanic* disaster, who can?

The video version of the film, released in simulated stereo, includes original promotional trailer.

345 *Titanic* (1996-TV) American Zoetrope (USA) *Originally aired:* CBS, November 17–18, 1996. Miniseries, 173 min., broadcast in Surround Sound.

Director: Robert Lieberman
Screenplay: Ross LaManna and Joyce Eliason
Exec. Producers: Fred Fuchs, Jeff Kleeman, Frank Konigsberg, Larry Sanitsky
Producers: Rocky Lang, Harold Tichenor
Music: Lennie Niehaus
Cinematography: David Hennings
Art Direction: Eric Norlin
Historical Photographs: Ken Marschall (for supplying photographs)
Visual Effects: Janet Muswell (supervisor)
Cast:

      Peter Gallagher . . . . *Wynn Park*
      George C. Scott . . . . *Captain Edward J. Smith*
      Catherine Zeta Jones . . . . *Isabella Paradine*
      Eva Marie Saint . . . . *Hazel Foley*
      Tim Curry . . . . *Simon Doonan*
      Roger Rees . . . . *J. Bruce Ismay*

Harley Jane Kozak	*Bess Allison*
Marilu Henner	*Molly Brown*
Malcolm Stewart	*First Officer Murdoch*
Kevin McNulty	*Second Officer Lightoller*
Scott Hylands	*John Jacob Astor*
Barry Pepper	*Harold Bride*
Matt Hill	*Phillips*
Matthew Walker	*Stanley Lord*
Gerard Plunkett	*Fourth Officer Boxhall*
Janie Woods-Morris	*Ida Straus*
Peter Haworth	*Isidor Straus*

Also: Sonseeahray Flöthmann, Felicity Waterman, Kavan Smith, Terence Kelly, Tamsin Kelsey, Eric Keenleyside, Kevin Conway, Devon Hoholuk, Crystal Verge, Byron Lucas, and Don MacKay.

Picturesque but ultimately humorless and uninspired television miniseries that attracted a lot of attention because of the impending release of James Cameron's heavily publicized movie. Ironically, some wondered if the cookie-cutter miniseries would steal the thunder from Cameron's gargantuan effort. However, this star-studded television movie (the second inspired by the disaster) quickly faded from memory.

More than any other film ever made about the disaster, this film portrays Bruce Ismay as the clear-cut villain who oversteps his bounds in absurd ways to ensure that the *Titanic* breaks the Atlantic-crossing speed record (one scene even places him in the boiler room, ordering the stokers to light two more boilers). Scott seems an obvious choice to play Captain Smith, and he turns the usually mysterious Captain Smith into a gruff commander with a poetic bent (he quotes Samuel Johnson without crediting him). In the absence of a Thomas Andrews character, Smith becomes the one who must inform the crew that the ship will certainly sink. He even upbraids the crew for not hitting the iceberg head-on, although there is no evidence that this possibility for saving the ship was introduced until long after the fact.

Other dubious myths about the disaster take center stage in this film, including the supposed suicide of Murdoch and the passenger who takes a seat aboard a lifeboat by dressing like a woman (in this version, the scoundrel is given a complete storyline as a thieving crewmember). Other stories include a deranged governess who foresees the disaster in her nightmares, a young ne'er-do-well and would-be movie actor who steals a ticket from a drunken acquaintance, and a young married woman who is reacquainted with the love of her life (Gallagher), a dashing, dark-haired first-class passenger who conveniently drowns, thereby sparing his lover the pain of a divorce. Molly Brown, as portrayed by the miscast Marilu Henner, is given more screen time than usual, as are John Jacob Astor and his young bride. Fictional characters and storylines are thrown into the mix to little effect.

The ship itself, when pictured as a whole, is not badly realized, but overall the movie relies heavily on interior scenes, giving the film a claustrophobic feel that is not easily balanced by slow-motion, portentous shots of ocean waves.

The opening credits run over still photographs of the *Titanic* during its building and launching. Part 1 of the miniseries ends with the iceberg collision, a rhythm that will be familiar to those who have seen the Broadway musical.

Available: Evergreen Entertainment (video; 165 min.)

346 *Titanic* (1997) 20th Century–Fox, Paramount (USA) Color, 194 min., Rated PG-13.

Director: James Cameron
Screenplay: James Cameron
Producer: James Cameron, Jon Landau
Co-producers: Al Giddings, Grant Hill, Sharon Mann
Executive Producer: Rae Sanchini
Music: James Horner
Additional Music: Mozart
Cinematography: Russell Carpenter
Art Direction: Martin Laing, Bill Rea
Set Decoration: Michael Ford
Costume Design: Deborah Lynn Scott
Cast:

Leonardo DiCaprio	*Jack Dawson*
Kate Winslet	*Rose DeWitt Bukater*
Billy Zane	*Cal Hockley*
Kathy Bates	*Molly Brown*
Frances Fisher	*Ruth DeWitt Bukater*
Gloria Stuart	*Rose Dawson Calvert*
Bill Paxton	*Brock Lovett*
Bernard Hill	*Captain E. J. Smith*
David Warner	*Spicer Lovejoy*
Victor Garber	*Thomas Andrews*
Jonathan Hyde	*J. Bruce Ismay*
Suzy Amis	*Lizzy Calvert*
Lewis Abernathy	*Lewis Bodine*
Nicholas Cascone	*Bobby Buell*
Anatoly M. Sagalevitch	*Anatoly Milkailavich*
Danny Nucci	*Fabrizio De Rossi*

Also: Ewan Stewart (Murdoch), Ioan Gruffudd (Lowe), Jonathan Phillips (Lightoller), Mark Lindsay Chapman (Wilde), Richard Graham (Rowe),

Paul Brightwell (Hichens), Ron Donachie (Master-at-Arms), Eric Braeden (Astor), Charlotte Chatton (Madeleine Astor), Bernard Fox (Gracie), Michael Ensign (Guggenheim), Martin Jarvis (Cosmo Duff Gordon), Rosalind Ayres (Lady Duff Gordon), Jonathan Evans-Jones (Wallace Hartley), Simon Crane (Boxhall), Scott G. Anderson (Fleet), Craig Kelly (Bride), Gregory Cooke (Phillips), Elsa Raven (Ida Straus), Lew Palter (Isidor Straus), et al.

James Cameron pushed his grand and sweeping vision of the *Titanic* disaster to the financial limits of filmmaking and was rewarded beyond expectations for his tenacity and excess. While the film's enormous success made it, its wonder-boy star Leonardo DiCaprio, and James Cameron easy targets for parody and derision during most of 1998, the film survives as a stunning tribute to old-fashioned, overblown movie-making and as a valentine to the architectural beauty of the ship. It is easy to forget that *Titanic* began its run in December 1997 with a large shadow of potential failure hanging over it. The film was under-hyped and over-budget, and, at three-and-a-half hours long, much longer than the supposed attention span of modern movie-goers. Articles written about the film during production compared the film to Kevin Costner's spectacular failure *Waterworld,* and journalists seemed smug in the knowledge that the out-of-control budget would doom the film at the box office.

But audiences succumbed to Cameron's romantic vision and ensured the film's success.

The film's strengths lie in Cameron's obvious passion for the ship and her legend, which resulted in his much-publicized obsessive agonizing over the smallest details of the set design and editing. Cameron built a full-scale replica of the ship (shortened by 10 percent) and went to extreme lengths to ensure that furnishings and props matched the originals (down to the White Star logo embossed on each cup and saucer). The computer-generated shots of the ship (complete with "cyber-extras") at sea are remarkable, and no money was spared in littering this film with authentic reproductions of *Titanic* deck chairs, lifeboats, ashtrays, and dishes. The evidence of the most expensive set ever can be seen in the fact that many of the props were later sold through the J. Peterman catalog, known for its exotic selection of one-of-a-kind clothing and personal items (one of the film's lifeboats, labeled as "not seaworthy," sold for roughly $25,000).

Many *Titanic* buffs were bothered by the ambitious film's lightweight treatment of the facts and myths surrounding the disaster. That Cameron chose to center his film around a fictional romance between fictional passengers perhaps makes his superficial reliance on old myths more suspect to serious fans. The film's heroes are mostly third-class scamps, while many of the first-class passengers and crew are portrayed as boorish and cowardly. All this unseemly tension sets the stage for a melodramatic clash between the classes while giving the heroes in steerage plenty of opportunity to cold-cock obnoxious stewards. In addition, Cameron chooses to play up several undocumented myths, including the suicide of Officer Murdoch (spurring a lawsuit from Murdoch's descendants). The overall credibility of the movie is not helped by more than a few lines of groan-inducing dialogue, including Molly Brown's mock-awed declaration as the ship goes down: "Now there's something you don't see every day."

As legend has it, Cameron originally intended his film to be a big-budget remake of *A Night to Remember,* an ironic notion given that the biggest backlash against the film came from *ANTR* loyalists. In fact, discounting the love story, the two movies probably have more in common than any other two *Titanic* films in terms of devotion to a factual timeline and serious intent on recreating historical events as they happened.

In spite of the film's critics, the film became the most successful film of all time, affirming that public fascination with the disaster had not waned after nearly 90 years. After more than nine months in theaters, *Titanic* had grossed nearly $2 billion worldwide, making it the most profitable movie of all time. Souvenir books, soundtrack CDs, posters, and other merchandise pulled in additional millions in cash for the studios and stars. DiCaprio became the heartthrob of choice for preteen girls across the country, while the theme song "My Heart Will Go On" played endlessly on Top 40 radio stations.

Backlash against the film's astonishing success and notoriously egomaniacal director grew with the box-office receipts: In May 1998, for instance, *New York* magazine questioned Cameron's assertion that he drew the charcoal drawings in Jack Dawson's sketchbook. The magazine claimed that three of the sketches were based on famous photographs by modern photographers such as Sally Mann. The backlash reached its apex when James Cameron declared himself "king of the world" on national television after his film garnered 11 Academy Awards.

Some points of trivia worth noting: Scenes of the *Californian*'s role in the disaster were filmed but cut from the final film. Cameron makes a brief appearance during the steerage dance scene. Historians and experts who consulted on the film include Ken Marschall and Don Lynch (who also played a bit part).

Available: Paramount Home Video (two-tape VHS widescreen and pan-and-scan editions available); DVD, 1999.

347 *TITanic 2000* (1999) Seduction Cinema (USA) 85 min., Color.

Directors: John Paul Fedele, Claney Fitz Simmons
Starring: Michael R. Thomas, Jacob Bogert, Tina Krause, Elizabeth Cintron (as Molly Black), Lenore Tammy (as Vladimina), William Hellfire, Zachary Winston, et al.

This straight-to-video B-grade parody gained attention for being notably bad. The plot centers around Vladimina, a lesbian vampire who sets sail on the *Titanic 2000* to Europe in order to continue her search for a queen. Unfortunately, it is soon discovered that half of the ship is made of aluminum foil because the captain demanded a steering wheel of solid gold. *TITanic 2000* (as it is spelled in marketing materials) is a throwback to the sexploitation films of the 1960s and 1970s, but it is also representative of the kinds of movies that have made their way to DVD, thanks to relatively cheap production costs. The computer-generated graphics are especially amateurish.

The DVD (the film was also released on VHS) includes an unrelated bonus feature on the reverse side, *Suzie's Bad Day*.

348 *Titanic Orgy* (1995) Pepper Productions/CDI Entertainment Group (USA) Approx. 1 hr., 50 minutes, Color.

Screenplay: Jack Stephen
Producer: Jack Stephen
Director: Mitchell Spinelli
Starring: Nicole London, Jordan Lee, Tina Tyler, Nikki Sinn, Frank Towers, et al.

Distasteful, hard-core pornography video set on the modern day cruise ship *SS Titanic II*. Although the plot ostensibly revolves around a shortage of life preservers as an ocean liner heads toward a collision with an iceberg, the cruise-ship setting (vaguely hinted at through sailor uniforms and fake portholes painted on wood-paneled walls) is of little consequence here. Like most films of its ilk, this film largely misses the opportunity for imaginative lowbrow humor. The only real attempts at humor and satire are found near the beginning of the film (as a male passenger complains to the ship doctor that every time he approaches his wife, his manhood "sinks like the *Titanic*") and on the video's packaging, redesigned in 1997 after the success of Cameron's film. Here the video is billed as "an epic tale worthy of 11 Academy Awards." Those looking for special effects (a demographic that would be hard to imagine) will be disappointed to find that the sinking of the ship is not depicted, and the ship's lifeboats are yellow inflatable rafts.

349 *The Unsinkable Molly Brown* (1964) Color (Metrocolor), 128 min. MGM, Not rated.

Director: Charles Walters
Screenplay: Helen Deutsch from the musical play by Richard Morris and Meredith Wilson
Musical Director: Robert Armbruster
Cinematography: Daniel L. Fapp

Choreography: Peter Gennaro
Cast:

>   Debbie Reynolds .... *Molly Brown*
>   John J. Brown .... *Harve Presnell*
>   Ed Begley .... *Shamus Tobin*

Also: Jack Krischen, Hermione Baddeley, Vassili Lambrinos, Fred Essler, Harvey Lembeck, Lauren Gilbert, Kathryn Card, George Mitchell, Harry Holcombe, and Martita Hunt.

This film version of the hit musical based on the life of *Titanic* survivor Margaret Brown is typical of the boisterous Western movie musical comedies of the time (*Seven Brides for Seven Brothers, Hello Dolly!*) and suffers from the same kind of suspended sense of time and logic. Debbie Reynolds gives the contractual over-the-top performance as the brassy, hot-tempered gold digger Molly Brown, whose fortunes lead her to marry a gold prospector and become one of the most famous of the *Titanic's* passengers. As a whole, the Molly Brown character as presented here seems to be a product of another era; she is singularly motivated by a need to acquire more money and prove her worth with Denver society. Modern audiences may find her wholly unlikable (as compared to the earthy, tongue-in-cheek Molly as portrayed by Kathy Bates). The scenes involving *Titanic* are brief but serve as a key turning point in the story; as Molly decides to rededicate herself to her husband, she grabs an oar aboard the lifeboat and makes a symbolic return to her former, rough-and-ready self. The effects and props used to recreate the *Titanic* are effective but not memorable.

Harve Presnell brings some depth to the character of John Brown, who did not make the journey on the *Titanic* with his wife.

Available: MGM/UA Home Video (1996)

5 Television Episodes/Anthologies

See separate chapters for documentaries and films that originally aired on television.

350 *Futurama* (1999). "A Flight to Remember." Color, 30 min. Episode first aired September 26, 1999, FOX.

Series Creator: Matt Groening
Director: Peter Avanzino
Writer: Eric Horsted
Voices: Billy West (Phillip J. Fry/Zapp Brannigan/Prof. Hubert J. Fansworth/Dr. Zoidberg), Katey Sagal (Leela), John DiMaggio (Bender), Dawnn Lewis (LaBarbara), Phil LaMarr (Hermes), Lauren Tom (Amy)

Parody of James Cameron's movie (coming about a year too late) has Fry and gang vacation on a space cruise, only to have the spaceship sucked into the grasp of a black hole. In the midst of the chaos, love blossoms between the show's lazy, alcoholic robot (Bender) and a rich female robot.

The animated series was brought to television by Simpsons creator Groening. The premise of the show was simple: a 25-year-old pizza delivery boy named Fry accidentally freezes himself in a cryogenics lab and awakens in the year 3000. The rest of the show centered on the misadventures of Fry and a few other misfits as they traveled through space on daring missions.

Kraft Television Theatre see ***A Night to Remember*** in *Narrative Films*

351 *NewsRadio* (1998). "Sinking Ship" (Episode #75). Color, 30 min. Episode first aired May 12, 1998, NBC.

Series Creator: Paul Simms

Co-Executive Producers: Joe Furey and Josh Lieb
Producer: Kent Zbornak
Teleplay: Joe Furey, Brian Kelley, Josh Lieb, and Sam Johnson
Director: Tom Cherones
Cast: Dave Foley (Dave Nelson), Maura Tierney (Lisa Miller), Phil Hartman (Bill McNeal), Andy Dick (Matthew), Joe Rogan (Joe), Stephen Root (Jimmy James).

This sharp parody of the 1998 *Titanic* craze poses the question, "What if WNYZ wasn't a radio station at all, but a massive luxury liner called the *Titanic*?" The cast sets out to answer just that question "with a budget of over $200." The office restroom serves as the boiler room, the ship's "carpenter" tries to patch the leak with a roll of duct tape, and the hapless lookout Matthew whines, "Dave, what is your obsession with these so-called icebergs?"

This was the final episode of *NewsRadio* to feature comic actor Phil Hartman, who was killed by his wife in an apparent murder-suicide in 1998. His character and the resident half-wit Matthew were the only two characters who didn't meet their doom in the *Titanic* episode, which some critics speculated was written as a tongue-in-cheek series finale. However, the series aired an additional year without Hartman.

352 *One Step Beyond* (1959). "Night of April 14." B&W, 30 min. Originally aired January 27, 1959 (series originally titled *Alcoa Presents*).

Director: John Newland
Producer: Collier Young
Teleplay: Larry Marcus
Series Creator: Merwin Gerard
Host: John Newland
Cast: Barbara Lord, Isobel Elsom, Patrick MacNee
Also: Gavin Gordon, Jeanne Bates, Marjorie Eaton, John Craven, Gil Stuart, and Gavin Muir

One of the first television shows to capitalize on the supernatural appeal of the disaster, this episode of "One Step Beyond" centers on the story of a commercial artist who surprises his new bride with tickets on the maiden voyage of the *Titanic*. The young woman agrees to go, although she has experienced ominous, terrifying nightmares of her own drowning. Once aboard the ship, the couple's extrasensory connection to the impending disaster continues as the husband finds himself compelled to sketch a macabre scene of the *Titanic*'s demise (taken from an early illustration, "Sinking of the *Titanic*," included in J. Henry Mowbray's 1912 book), complete with screaming passengers flailing about in the water in the foreground of the sketch. When the premonitions are realized, the husband declares, "If you ever have a bad dream again, I'll listen to you." The host closes out the teleplay with what will become a familiar frame for television retellings of the disaster: a rundown of the similarities between the *Titanic* and Morgan Robertson's *Titan*.

Although an important entry in the history of *Titanic* lore — showing the potential for one of the first times for the ship to be used as a plot device in a fictional account — modern viewers are likely to find this melodrama to be a bit claustrophobic and dated.

353 *Rod Serling's Night Gallery* (1971). "Lone Survivor." Technicolor, 30 min. Episode originally aired January 13, 1971.

Producer: Jack Laird
Host: Rod Serling
Teleplay: Rod Serling
Music: Robert Prince
Director: Gene Levitt
Cast: John Colicos, Torin Thatcher, Hedley Mattingly
Also: Charles Davis (Officer of Watch), Brendan Dillon (Quartermaster), William Beckley (Richards), Terence Pushman (Helmsman), Edward Colmans, Pierre Jalbert, Carl Milletaire

In this provocative episode from the popular Rod Serling anthology series, an ocean liner picks up a lone survivor in a drifting lifeboat, only to discover that the lifeboat belongs to the *Titanic*. The viewer soon discovers (via the name of the ship on the life buoy, a familiar device for such discoveries) that the drifting survivor has been rescued by the similarly ill-fated *Lusitania*, three years after the sinking of the *Titanic*.

Touching on one of the familiar *Titanic* myths, the lone survivor is found dressed in women's clothing. This is one of the few *Titanic* stories in which none of the action takes place on the ship; as a result, the actors are left to shoulder the burden of retelling the disaster without the aid of the usual clichés and myths. This proves to be a liberating restriction.

Serling introduces the episode by pondering the mystery of an evocative sketch called "Lone Survivor."

The idea of a *Titanic* survivor who unaccountably survives for many years has been touched on by a number of different authors. Serling improves on the idea with one of his classic twists: the survivor realizes he is a "Flying Dutchman," doomed to drift in lifeboats from one doomed ship to another.

354 *Telephone Time* "The Unsinkable Mrs. Brown" (1957). Black and white, 30 min. Originally aired: CBS, February 24, 1957.

Producer: Jerry Stagg
Host: John Nesbitt
Teleplay: John Nesbitt
Cast: Cloris Leachman (Mrs. Brown), *et al.*

Leachman, a former contestant in the Miss America contest, was only 30 when she appeared as Molly Brown in this teleplay; she would play her again more than 20 years later in the made-for-television movie *S.O.S. Titanic*. Only a segment of the episode deals with the *Titanic*.

355 *Tickets for the Titanic* (1987). UK.

Now-obscure television anthology that presented stories of paranoia and intrigue with an overlayer of black humor. Besides the title, the series had nothing to do with the *Titanic*.

356 *The Time Tunnel* (1966). "Rendezvous with Yesterday." (Debut) Irwin Allen Productions/Twentieth Century–Fox. Color, 60 min. Episode first aired September 9, 1966, ABC. Series Created and Produced by Irwin Allen.

Teleplay: Harold Jack Bloom and Shimon Wincelberg
Story by Irwin Allen, Shimon Wincelberg, and Harold Jack Bloom
Director: Irwin Allen
Music: Johnny Williams
Cast: James Darren and Robert Colbert
Also: Lee Meriwether (Dr. Ann MacGregor), Whit Bissel (General Heywood Kirk), and John Zaremba (Dr. Raymond Swain).
Guest Stars: Michael Rennie (Capt. Smith), Susan Hampshire (Althea Hall), Gary Merrill (Senator Clark)

This 1960s science-fiction series centered on the adventures of two scientists, Tony Newman (Darren) and Doug Phillips (Colbert), lost in the ravages of time after the time machine they have been working on malfunctions. Each week, the two scientists find themselves in the midst of an important historical event, as their colleagues back home work to bring the men back to the present.

In the debut episode, Dr. Newman goes through the time tunnel after a touring Senator (a modern-day Ismay) badgers them into testing the machine prematurely. Newman is dropped onto the decks of the *Titanic* on its maiden voyage. Once aboard the ship, Newman tries to convince the captain that he is from the future and attempts to warn him of the fate of his ship. As reward for his efforts, he is placed under ship arrest as a stowaway (in a forward cabin that his fellow scientists believe will be "slashed open" when the *Titanic* hits the iceberg). When the scientists back home learn of Newman's predicament, Dr. Phillips dons appropriate period dress, grabs a newspaper with news of the *Titanic*'s sinking, and jumps through the time machine in an attempt to save him. Their colleagues manage to pull them off the ship just in time, although they are unable to control their next destination in time (thus setting the series in motion).

The sets and special effects involving the *Titanic* are adequate if somewhat spartan. Scenes from *Titanic* (1953) were used for additional visuals.

This imaginative and visually appealing series, with its polyester uniforms and blinking gadgets, has much in common with others of the era (*Star Trek*), but the phony sets and dated special effects add to the charm of the series as a prime nostalgic example of sci-fi as it was conceived in the 1960s. The fact that the series' writers chose the *Titanic* as the first destination for their time travelers speaks to the immediacy of the disaster as an image of imminent and unavoidable peril. Even time travelers cannot change the fate of the *Titanic*.

Note: The time travelers warn the captain that his lifeboats will only hold about 750 passengers. This is roughly the number of passengers who were *saved* on the lifeboats, which were filled well below their full capacity. They make no attempt to tell the captain to instruct his crew to fill the boats more carefully.

357 *Voyagers* (1983). "Voyagers of the *Titanic*." First aired NBC, Feb. 27, 1983. 60 min.

Director: Paul Stanley
Cast:

> Jon-Erik Hexum .... *Phineas Bogg*
> Meeno Peluce .... *Jeffrey Jones*

Also: Tracy Brooks Swope (Olivia Dunn), Will Kuluva, Lee de Broux

The *Titanic* became the destination of choice for time travelers yet again in this short-lived sci-fi series, in which two time travelers each week found themselves in the midst of a historic moment in human history. Traveling back to the decks of the *Titanic* is a stock storyline in such series, of course, and seems to feed off the collective desire both to experience the majestic aura of the ship and to prevent the tragedy that, in hindsight, seems so preventable.

In this episode, Bogg and Jones land on the *Titanic* the night that she is destined to collide with the iceberg. They try to warn the captain but, like their *Time Tunnel* colleagues, are thrown in the brig for their troubles. The time travelers meet up with a fellow passenger, Olivia Dunn, who is also a Voyager, and they are able to escape soon after the ship hits the iceberg. While off the *Titanic*, they help Louis Pasteur perfect his rabies vaccine. They then return to the ship to help Olivia with her Voyager assignment to recover the stolen *Mona Lisa* from the *Titanic*. Leonardo's masterpiece was not traveling on the *Titanic*.

6 Documentary Films and Videos

Includes films as well as those documentaries originally broadcast on television and produced for the direct-to-video market.

358 ***The Battle for Titanic*** (1999) (Television). John Gau Productions, Channel 4 Television Corporation, and Public Broadcasting Service. 60 min.
Executive Producer: John Gau
Producers: John Gau and Chris Powell
Director: Chris Powell
Script: John Gau
Cinematography: Christopher Hall
Narrator: John Roberts

  PBS television documentary traces the controversy over the ownership and salvage rights of the *Titanic*'s wreck.

359 ***Beyond Titanic*** (1998-Television). Van Ness Films, in Association with FoxStar Productions, Fox Television Studios, and the A&E Network. Originally aired Sept. 6, 1998, A&E Cable Network. 100 min.
Executive Producer: Kevin Burns
Producer: Larayne Decouer
Script: Jerry Decker, Tom Jennings
Narrator: Victor Garber

  Engaging and thoughtful documentary traces the importance of the *Titanic* as a cultural icon in mass media through the 20th century. The producers seem to have gotten much of their inspiration from the work of *Titanic* cultural historian Stephen Biel (q.v.), who provides on-camera analysis along with fellow authors Paul Heyer (q.v.) and Daniel Allen Butler (q.v.). Although the documentary touches on the many myths surrounding the disaster, as well as news coverage, music, books, sermons, and editorials, it is by and large a history of the *Titanic* in the movies (and understandably so, as this allows for the use of dramatic cuts from the various *Titanic* movies). Featured scenes include those taken from such early films as *In Night and Ice* and *Atlantis*. The documentary moves into the present with a look at the newfound interest in the *Titanic* as manifested in tourism, the Broadway musical, and a never-ending stream of books. A more touching segment focuses on the story behind the popular children's book *Polar the Titanic Bear* (q.v.).

Available: A&E Home Video

360 *Deep Inside the Titanic* (1998-television). Discovery Channel/Classic Worldwide Productions. Approx. 60 min.

Producers: Steve Burns, Bob Anderson
Writer: Jeff Holland
Animation: Cyberflix
Original Music: Michael Whalen
Narrator: Dave Corey

One in a series of Discovery Channel documentaries that uses diving footage from the wreck as its centerpiece. Supplementary material includes computer animation and interviews with survivors Edith Russell, Eva Hart, and, from archival footage, Charles Lightoller. Perhaps the film's most valuable contribution is the story of the Black Gang, the coal shovelers who worked to keep power on the sinking ship. Promotional tags for Discovery's Internet site prove especially distracting.

361 *Ghosts of the Abyss* (2002). Earthship Productions, Walden Media, and Walt Disney Pictures. 3-D IMAX, 59 min.

Director: James Cameron
Producers: James Cameron, Chuck Comisky, et al.
Exec. Producer: Giedra Rackauskas
Original Music: Joel McNeely
Creative Producer: Ed Marsh
Narrator: Bill Paxton

"You leave the *Titanic*, but it doesn't leave you," Bill Paxton says as he leads the viewer into another journey below the surface of the Atlantic, fairly summing up James Cameron's own fascination with the event that has once again taken him to the sight of the wreck. Taking advantage of 3-D IMAX technology and new robotic cameras, *Ghosts of the Abyss* follows Paxton's real-life first-time voyage to the *Titanic* wreck at the invitation of his former director. While some may wonder if Cameron has anything left to wring from the *Titanic*'s ghost, the film succeeds with Cameron's usual blend of pathos, drama, and humor. In a surprisingly emotional scene, for instance, Cameron demonstrates his passion for the technology as he nearly loses the robotic cameras. Similarly, perhaps more than any other director who has touched on this subject, Cameron is particularly adept at connecting the *Titanic*'s tragic past to the wreck's ghostly presence.

Experts and others featured in the film include Don Lynch, Charles Pellegrino, Ken Marschall, Mike Cameron, and Lewis Abernathy (Paxton's unkempt sidekick in *Titanic*).

362 *In Search of... the Titanic* (1981). Alan Landsburg Productions. Produced for syndicated television, 30 min.

Series Producer: Andy White
Executive Producer: Alan Landsburg
Narrator: Leonard Nimoy

In this installation of the popular late 1970s television series (which typically examined "controversial" mysteries of the occult and other unexplained phenomena such as UFOs), the producers turned their cameras on a more realistic topic, namely the many mysteries surrounding the *Titanic* and, more specifically, its final resting place (which was not known before 1985). While the episode does bring up many of the old mysteries (Why were ice warnings ignored? Why were there so few lifeboats?), the bulk of the documentary consists of old movie footage with voiceovers recounting the events of that night. Also follows the failed efforts of the Jack Grimm expedition, and includes interviews and voiceovers by such *Titanic* experts as Louis Gorman and Peter Padfield.

Available: Reeves Entertainment Co. (Out-of-Print)

363 *It's the Titanic* (1998). Approx. 40 min.

Children's educational video (designed for ages 6–12) includes survivor interviews and a smattering of information on how the *Titanic* was built, what life aboard the ship was like, and how the ship met her end. "Fun" packaging serves as yet another reminder of how little connection the myth of the disaster has to grim reality.

364 *Lost Film from the Titanic* (1998). Tapeworm Productions.

Newsreel and documentary footage compilation showcases shots of the *Titanic* in her final stages of construction at Belfast, as well as footage of the *Carpathia* and *Olympic*.

365 *The Making of "A Night to Remember"* (1993). Ray Johnson Productions. 60 min.
Producer: Ray Johnson
Director: Ray Johnson
Music: Peter Young
Narrator: Ray Johnson

Stylish and thoughtful documentary is more than a behind-the-scenes glimpse at the "biggest film in British history." Much of the first half of the film is devoted to interviews with William MacQuitty and Walter Lord and their lifelong obsessions with the ship. Particularly inspiring is Lord's story about how he came up with one of publishing's most memorable titles. The behind-the-scenes footage spotlights the film's many innovative and sophisticated touches, including the meticulous recreation of costumes and shipboard accoutrements (proving that James Cameron was not the first to approach the *Titanic* in this manner). The CD-ROM version also includes the British theatrical trailer for the original release of the movie.

Available: Included as bonus CD in multimedia package Total *Titanic: A Night to Remember*.

366 *The Making of "Titanic"* (1997). HBO, 30 min. Rated TV-PG.
Producer and Director: Ed W. Marsh
Director of Photography: Anders Falk
Executive Producers: Jon Landau, Rae Sanchini
Music: James Horner (from the film)
Additional Music: Gaelic Storm, I Solonisti
Archival Images: Ken Marschall, George Behe, Ulster Folk and Transport Museum

Certainly designed to promote the movie, with the self-congratulatory actors and director waxing poetic on how the film was conceived and how the filmmakers worked to capture the emotional immediacy of the disaster, but worth watching nonetheless. Those interested in the technical aspects of the special effects would do better to find a copy of the special *Cinefex* issue (q.v.) dealing with *Titanic*. This documentary does remind one of how meticulous the set and costume design for *Titanic* really was (down to the White Star stamp on each piece of cutlery), as well as the difficult physical maneuvering involved in filming the flooding and sinking sequences.

Behind-the-scenes footage is complemented with on-camera interviews with Don Lynch, Ken Marschall, Bill Paxton, Leonardo DiCaprio, Kate Winslet (who really does speak with an English accent), and the unintentionally abrasive James Cameron ("It's like a great novel that really happened").

367 *Memories of the Titanic: 11 Survivors Recall the Tragedy* (1991). *Titanic* Historical Society/Robert Video Productions. Approx. 90 min. (Video).

Producers: Karen and Edward Kamuda
Editor: Robert Barnes
Videography: Walter L. Childs
Studio Production: Robert Barnes

Conceived and filmed at the April 1988 *Titanic* Historical Society Convention, this video includes interviews with eleven *Titanic* survivors, ranging in age at the time of filming from 76 to 100. Low-grade production values do not undercut the archival importance of this video, and do not diminish the fact that the THS had the foresight to document the remembrances of these survivors while it was still possible. The documentary includes casual vignettes from survivors as recited at the convention (with all the attendant audio problems), as well as lengthier monologues from the omnipresent Eva Hart and Ruth Becker Blanchard (who died in 1990). Blanchard's lively, detailed account of traveling on the *Titanic* as the daughter of a missionary provides the documentary's most compelling narrative. Author and long-time THS member George Behe provides the introduction. Tedious 10-minute transitional sequence consists of computer wipes of archival photographs set against organ music.

Survivors who contribute stories and memories include Beatrice Sandstrom, Millvina Dean, Eileen Schefer, Elanor Johnson Shuman, Michael Navratil, and Frank Aks, who was eight months old at the time of the sinking.

368 *The Mystery of the Titanic* (1996). Martin Productions/Madacy Entertainment. Made for video. Color/Black and white, Approx. 30 min.

Executive Producers: Philip Nugus and Jonathan Martin
Music: De Wolfe
Graphics: Wil Mobberley
Researcher: Amanda Burrell
Scriptwriter and Historical Advisor: Robin Cross

Serviceable, low-budget documentary relies heavily on still photographs, computer animation, and stock footage as the narrator ponders the many mysteries surrounding the ship's building and subsequent sinking—i.e., how did an "unsinkable ship" falter and why were there not enough lifeboats aboard? One unexpected benefit of a documentary made noticeably on the cheap is that the producers focus on the "known" facts and numbers of the disaster, including the absurdity of the comfort provisions (e.g., 20,000 bottles of beer) and the chronology of the collision and sinking. The standard tools of *Titanic* documentary-making — survivor interviews and footage of ghostly underwater wreckage — have been well utilized elsewhere and are not missed here. (Eva Hart does put in an appearance, however.)

Computerized background music and computer video effects, as well as an abrupt ending, add to the "homemade" feel of this documentary.

Available: Madacy Entertainment, VHS video (1998). The film was paired with a very brief documentary on the crash of the *Hindenburg* and released as "Vol. 3" of Madacy's *Mysteries and Myths of the Twentieth Century* series.

Return to the Titanic (1981) see **Search for the Titanic**

369 ***Return to the Titanic — Live!*** (1987). Westgate Entertainment Corporation. Color, 92 min.

First broadcast: October 1987
Director: Louis J. Horvitz
Producer: Michael B. Seligman
Host: Telly Savalas

Live-television event from Paris promised to bedazzle viewers with the opening of a valise carried on the *Titanic*. Although the valise was found to contain documents, money, and jewelry, some claimed that it was packed with authentic-looking replicas beforehand. (A live television event produced by the same company in the same era, in which Geraldo Rivera promised to reveal the secrets of Al Capone's secret lost vault, similarly disappointed viewers with its failure to deliver.)

370 ***Search for the Titanic*** (1981). *Titanic* 1981 Inc. Bridgestone Group Video.

Dismal two-pack video set is the most easily available way to view the documentary films that were produced as a result of Jack Grimm's futile expeditions to find the wreck of the *Titanic*. Funded by Grimm himself, the films are oddly upbeat and optimistic.

Executive Producer: Jack Grimm
Producer/Director: Mike Harris
Music: Dale Schacker

Part 1: Search for the Titanic (1980). Written by Karen C. O'Malley. 109 min.
Narrator: Orson Welles

This film documents millionaire Jack Grimm's first failed effort to find the wreck of the *Titanic*, with the assistance of a deep-sea submersible named *Aluminant*, a full six years before Bob Ballard would succeed in locating the wreck. Unfortunately, without the climax of actually finding the wreck, the documentary footage will be of interest only to those with an interest in the way the undersea exploration technology (including deep-sea submersibles and magnetometry) developed along the way. The presence of Orson Welles helps, even if this film only provides more evidence that Welles was not very discriminating when it came to choosing his final projects. Perhaps because Welles had come to be identified with another time, his narration was removed from the later DVD version of this film.

To fill the space, the film includes scenes from *A Night to Remember,* a interview with Frank Goldsmith, who was a nine-year-old steerage passenger at the time of disaster, a frivolous interview with the cook aboard Grimm's research vessel *The Fay,* footage of the crew relaxing in Bermuda, and a supposed close encounter with a Cold-War Russian submarine. Most amusing to *Titanic* lore collectors, perhaps, will be the bizarre original song "Ballad of the *Titanic*" (written and performed by Kenny Star) that turns on the refrain, "We'll Find the *Titanic.*" The song was understandably cut from the DVD version. Another mysterious anecdote centers on a note supposedly found in a bottle thrown from the *Titanic* by a steward.

Welles closes the documentary of the failed effort on an optimistic and poetic note as he muses, "She lives seductively just beyond our grasp."

Part 2: Return to the Titanic (1981). Written by James Drury. 53 min.

Narrator: James Drury
Animation: Ken Marschall

Overwrought and unnecessary film documents the second Grimm/Harris expedition in search of the *Titanic* wreck. Like the first film, this documentary plods its way through a lot of mushy ground in ungraceful fashion. It begins with a stale comparison of the *Titanic* to modern cargo ships in the Port of Houston (where Grimm was based), drawn out with pointless and ponderous narrative meditations on the nature of technology and the challenges of human adventure. Mock-dramatic narrator James Drury, who also wrote the script, spends most of his screen time waxing poetic on the *Titanic* and the philosophical implications of finding the wreck. The "climax" of the search comes when Grimm (who believes the hull of the *Titanic* will be found intact) and colleagues spot the shadowy shape of what they believe to be a propeller from the ship.

The second search is conducted from the *Gyre,* a Texas A&M research vessel.

Available: Bridgestone Multimedia

371 *Secrets of the Titanic* (1986). National Geographic Society. Approx. 60 min. (Special Edition 70 min.)

Exec. Producer: Dennis B. Kane
Producer and Director: Nicolas Noxon
Directors: Robert Ballard and Graham Hurley
Writer: Nicolas Noxon
Music: Craig Safan
Cover Art: Ken Marschall

"Last Hours" Segment
Producer: Stephen Burns
Music: Fred Karns
Narration: Martin Sheen

  This above-average documentary chronicles Bob Ballard's discovery of the *Titanic*'s wreck two miles below the surface of the Atlantic. It begins with a concise and thoughtful summary of the *Titanic*'s construction and maiden voyage, framed in the social/cultural context of Edwardian class society. Visuals in the first part of the documentary were thankfully chosen to break the mold of the standard *Titanic* documentary, and include Francis Browne's eerie shipboard photographs, newsreel footage both of the news of the wreck and of Edwardian society at work and play, and excerpts from *Atlantic* (q.v.). The film then moves deftly into the story of Bob Ballard's discovery mission. Although the shots of the actual wreck are not as attractive or as lively as those in *Titanica* (q.v.) and other films, and the videography is static in the way that mid–1980s video tends to be, this film has the distinction of being the original. As such, it gives a much better feel for emotional climate aboard the ship and for the impact that the discovery had on society at large at the time. Particularly moving is the way that Ballard deals directly and honestly with his own mild depression and reticence brought on by the discovery. The film undoubtedly served as a source of inspiration and information for James Cameron's 1997 epic. In particular, the documentary touches on many motifs and images central to the Cameron film, including the Brown photographs, the role the discovery of the wreck played in filling in gaps of the public imagination, and the possible final moments of Captain Smith (in Cameron's film, he wanders off to the bridge to die alone). Consultants on the film include the ubiquitous historians Eaton and Haas.

  A final segment, called "Last Hours of the *Titanic*," is available on a "special edition" video version of the film. The additional segment includes an additional interview with Bob Ballard, spliced with animation sequences, explaining how the search was conducted. Although fairly out of joint with the look and feel of the rest of the video, this segment adds a good deal to the story behind the discovery of the wreck.

  Available: Warner Brothers Home Video, Special Edition (1997)

372 *Secrets of the Unknown: The Titanic* (1987). ABC Enterprises/MPI Video. Approx. 30 min.

Exec. Producer: Craig Haffner
Series Producer: Erik Nelson
Producer: Sue Perry
Writer: Erik Nelson
Narrator: Edward Mulhare

Supernaturally tinged, exploitative direct-to-video documentary opens with the standard invocation of the *Futility* coincidence and offers nothing new thereafter. Old footage and stills accompany pseudo-ominous retellings of how the *Titanic* was doomed by not being christened and how Frederick Fleet took his own life. Poorly executed reenactments and amateurish production tricks (including heavy use of digital wipes and green "sci-fi" titles) seem par for the course for this series, which has also explored the mysteries of Stonehenge and UFOs.

Available: MPI Video

373 *Special Effects: Titanic and Beyond* (1998-Television). First aired Nov. 3, 1998, PBS (U.S.).

Written and Directed by: Bill Lattanzi
Producer: Bill Lattanzi
Narration: Edward Herrmann and Susanne Simpson

An installment in PBS's *NOVA* series, this program traces the evolution of movie special effects from the silent era onward. Much of the show focuses on modern, big-budget films; films discussed include *Jurassic Park, Twister, The X Files, Flubber,* and *Terminator 2. King Kong* and *Earth Vs. the Flying Saucers* are among the earlier films examined. The segments on the history of special effects and special-effects masters are excellent, as are the explanations of how the brain "perceives" and interprets special effects. James Cameron's film receives its due attention, and the film's explanation of the miniature submarine shots and how designers made extras appear aboard the 45-foot model are fascinating, even if the narrator's claim that the "computer-generated extras pass by without notice" is exaggerated.

374 *Terror on the Titanic: The Shocking Truth Behind the Disaster* (1997). UAV Entertainment. *Times of Terror* series, Pantheon Productions. Made for Video, 45 min.

Written and Directed by: Jean-Pierre Isbouts
Co-producer: Cathie Labrador
Creative Design: Kiran Lovejoy
Producer: William A. Schwartz

Executive Producer: Jerry Pettus, Jr.
Narration: Ralph Votrian, Anthony Longman, Mike Galanis

Straightforward, simplistic documentary doesn't quite live up to its salacious title, except with its weak assertion that the *Titanic* was speeding to get to New York because of a fire in the coal bins (in all likelihood, the coal fire, a rather routine event, was already smoldering before *Titanic* left her final port of departure). The broad scope of the film leaves little time for in-depth discussion of the "controversies" at hand — namely, six mysteries (enumerated at the beginning of the film) ranging from "How did the ship sink so fast?" to "Why did so many third-class children die?" Strangely, the film indicts Officer Lightoller for not knowing the full weight capacity of the lifeboats. Includes much retread footage and unremarkable computer simulations of the sinking. The film is made more watchable by the cohesive narration and even pacing.

375 The Titanic (1986-Television). *Nightline* episode. *First aired:* July 18, 1986. ABC News/ABC Video. Approx. 23 min.

Host: Ted Koppel

This television news documentary produced in the wake of the discovery of the *Titanic*'s wreck was one of the first quality programs to take advantage of the new footage courtesy of Bob Ballard, and it was also the first opportunity many had to view those startling images. The video serves well as an introduction to the activities of Ballard and *Alvin*. Among those interviewed are Ruth Becker (Blanchard), author Charles Haas, and Dr. Dana Yoerger of Woods Hole. Scenes from the movies *A Night to Remember* and *Raise the Titanic!* accompany Koppel's pseudo-literary voiceovers, as he wonders aloud about the location of such cargo as the 12 cases of opium to be used in patent medicine.

Available on video: MPI Home Video (1990)

376 Titanic (1994). Arts & Entertainment Network/Greystone Communications. Approx. 200 min. (4 cassettes).

Exec. Producers: Craig Haffner and Donna E. Lusitana
Producer, Writer and Director: Melissa Peltier
Music: Christopher L. Stone
Narrator: David McCallum

Seamless and well-regarded four-part documentary interplays still photograph fades with narrations by *Titanic* survivors and experts, in much the style of A&E's Biography series.

Volume 1: "Death of a Dream." Approx. 50 min.

The first segment explores the impact the wreck of the *Titanic* had on society, both in a practical and a metaphorical sense, and attempts to answer the question of whether the sinking destroyed man's faith in progress and technology. The construction and appointments are covered in some detail, as is the life of Bruce Ismay, who is portrayed as a cold and aloof competitive businessman.

Those interviewed on the first tape include survivors Millvina Dean, Edith Brown Haisman, and Ruth Becker, as well as authors Wyn Wade and Walter Lord.

Volume 2: "Death of a Dream, Part II." Approx. 50 min.

This segment includes the story of the actual wreck, what factors may have contributed to the wreck, and the confusion that led to disaster in the loading of the lifeboats. Author George Behe, who has made a specialty of the lifeboat-loading debacle, provides insights.

Volume 3: "Legend Lives On"

Presents more details on the disposition of the lifeboats as well as the story of the arrival of the *Carpathia* in New York.

Volume 4: "Legend Lives On, Part 2"

The last segment shows how the White Star Company dealt with the insurance payoffs, hearings and trials, and bad publicity that naturally followed the disaster. The segment ends with Bob Ballard's discovery of the wreck and uses this footage to particularly good effect.

As the credits note, interior shots of the *Olympic* were used throughout the series for illustrative purposes.

Available: A&E Home Video; also released as 3-hour single video

377 *Titanic* (1998-DVD). Approx. 90 min. Red Rock Management Services/Simitar.

Executive Producer: Jesse Weatherby
Producer: Dick Artlett
Script: Linda Cooper
Music: Jeff Lass
Narration: Bill Wilson
Source Material: ABC Archives, Bass Museum, Bloomburg New Service, British News Service, Conus News, RMS *Titanic* Inc., National Archives.

Cut-rate DVD documentary pieces together still photographs, familiar and tedious footage from old *Titanic* conventions and survivor interviews (much of which has appeared in earlier documentaries such as *Titanic: A*

Question of Murder), a séance in which survivor Eva Hart attempts to contact her father, and model simulations set against computer-generated music. The producers have nothing new to offer, except the novelty of the DVD format (which allows for skipping easily between the eight sections of the video) and a relatively inexpensive price for this emerging technology.

Available: Simitar Entertainment; released on two-part, 63 min. video cassette set in 1996 (with the two parts titled "The *Titanic* Documentary" and "*Titanic* Survivors").

378 *Titanic* (1998-DVD). 3-part DVD: "The Search," "The Discovery," and "Remembered." Madacy Entertainment Group.

This attractively packaged DVD set consists mostly of older *Titanic* documentaries dressed up in the slick style of the DVD format. This allows for some new interactive features—including biographies and a trivia game on each disk in which correct and incorrect answers lead to appropriate scenes from *A Night to Remember*—but mostly this set is superfluous. "Nearer My God to Thee" plays during the menu. Each video is approx. 50 min.

"The Search"

Part 1 covers the failed search for the *Titanic* under the direction of millionaire Jack Grimm. The documentary is a virtual duplicate of *Search for the Titanic (1980)* (q.v.), sans Orson Welles (whose presence the producers may have feared would have dated the film).

"The Discovery"

Part 2 repackages the material from *Return to the Titanic (1981)* with few changes.

"Remembered." Ray Johnson Productions (1992)

Narrator: Ray Johnson
Music: Neil Young, Peter Young
Producer: Ray Johnson

Slapdash documentary includes the same familiar footage from *Titanic* conventions and interviews with minor *Titanic* historians and experts from the British and American *Titanic* societies. This video is also included in the *Titanic Collection*.

379 *The Titanic Chronicles* (1999). Bennu Multimedia, Arrow Video. UK, Color, Approx. 55 min.

Host: David McCallum
Featuring: Eric Braeden, Tim Curry, Marilu Henner, Bernard Hill, Gloria Stuart, Cloris Leachman, et al.

Direct-to-video documentary in which actors from various *Titanic* films give voice to witnesses in the 1912 Senate hearings. The testimony is read in voiceover as various still images and illustrations play out on screen.

At one point, the video was released as a package with *Titanic: Disaster in the Atlantic,* also hosted by McCallum.

380 *The Titanic Collection* (Four video boxed collection). Madacy Entertainment. Approx. 4 hours.

Producer: Ray Johnson
Host: Ray Johnson
Includes:

Vol. 1: "*Titanic* Remembered" (1992). 55 min.

Straightforward review of the *Titanic*'s impact, myths, and legends, with narration accompanied by still photographs, art, and other public domain documents. Those interviewed include Philip Croucher and Richard Pryor of the *Titanic* Historical Society and survivors Eva Hart, Edith Haisman, and Betty Walker (who was supposedly conceived on board). Johnson also reviews some of the films made about the sinking and tours a Southhampton *Titanic* museum.

Vol. 2: "Echoes of *Titanic*" (1995). 55 min.

Not-bad documentary overlayers ominous music with dramatic art, photographs, and newspaper fronts. Among the topics touched on are the numerous songs and memorials, Walter Lord and his musical pig, and the ethics of the R.M.S. *Titanic* exhibition. The video includes a good deal of footage from *Atlantic* (q.v.) and also includes a montage of newsreel footage strangely set to the folk song "When the Great Ship Went Down."

Vol. 3: "*Titanic*: End of an Era" (1998). 55 min.

Exploration of how the sinking of the *Titanic* led to the end of the Victorian-Edwardian age of optimism in the realms of exploration and technology. The weakest entry of Johnson's collection, this video rehashes much familiar information about the building and outfitting of the ship, its cargo, and the inquiries that followed the wreck. Johnson rounds it out to nearly an hour with much stock footage, narration, and low-quality music. William MacQuitty, the producer of *A Night to Remember,* is interviewed.

Vol. 4: "Edward J. Smith: Captain of the *Titanic*"

Co-host: Richard Howells

Disjointed and aurally inferior video looks at the life and work of Capt. Smith. The droning tone of the narrator does not help; nor does the constant interruption of Eva Hart's onscreen musings. One clip of Smith inspecting the *Titanic* is particularly overused.

Available: Madacy Entertainment (video). Also packaged as a two-part series, *Titanic: Tragedy at Sea.*

381 *Titanic in a Tub: The Golden Age of Toy Boats* (1981). USA, Seven Seas Cinema. Produced for PBS. 28 min.

Director: Tim Forbes
Producer: Tim Forbes
Executive Producer: Robert Forbes
Script: Tony Stewart, Tim Forbes, R. Forbes
Director of Photography: Michael E. Smith
Music: Jacob Stern
Narrator: Rex Harrison
Cast (Recreations): John Vennema, Jonathan Ward, John Watson, Knowl Johnson, Michael Pearlman et al.

Odd but not unlikable documentary on the history of toy boats, especially at the trend's peak from 1890s–1930s. The film draws some interesting parallels between the dramatic advances in the real-life ship industry and the toy craze they inspired. Includes a brief overview of the *Titanic* disaster and its negligible effect on the sales of toy liners. The film was inspired by and built around the Forbes Magazine Collection of Toy Boats.

Available: Direct Cinema (Performance Video)

382 *Titanic Memories: A Video Scrapbook* (1996). Hollywood's Attic. Approx. 95 min.

Research: Public Record Office, British Science Reference Library, *Titanic* Historical Society

Piecemeal video collection of newsreels and survivor interviews offers little in the way of cohesion, with no transitions between the different films and interviews, but a few nice rewards along the way. Sections include "*Titanic* Survivors," which features the familiar Eva Hart séance and other footage that is virtually identical to that offered on "*Titanic*" (1996-DVD) and other, older *Titanic* documentaries. Those with the patience to endure these interviews yet again will find the silent *Titanic* newsreels of the day more intriguing. Some of these quick-and-dirty newsreels use footage of *Titanic* sister ships, but they are nonetheless valuable as relics of their time. Perhaps even more valuable are the extensive clips from the little-seen *Telephone Time* episode featuring Cloris Leachman as Molly Brown. Scenes from *A Night to Remember,* as well as its trailer, are also featured. The video closes out with a section called "The Last Great Human Adventure," which is really just selected scenes from an earlier *Titanic* documentary (*Titanic: The Adventure Continues*) hosted by Doug Llewelyn that draws an analogy between Jack Grimm's search for the *Titanic* with the making of *Raise the Titanic*.

Available: Hollywood's Attic Video

383 *Titanic* Newsreels

Soon after the *Titanic* disaster in 1912, film production companies rushed to supply the movie-going public with newsreels describing the details of the wreck and the fate of her passengers. With limited distribution channels in place, many theater owners simply pieced together their own slideshows and animation features (such as 1912's *Titanic Wreck*) of varying quality. Although the discovery of a 1912 newsreel print made news in 1998, many of these newsreels contained little if any footage of the actual *Titanic*. For the most part, filmmakers had to make do with the little existing film clips of the *Titanic* supplemented with footage from other White Star Line ships.

During the height of the popularity of James Cameron's film, several stories surfaced about private citizens coming forward with "rare" prints of *Titanic* newsreels. Some of these prints were duplicates of newsreels that were already in circulation, so that while they might have value as antique collectibles, they yielded no new information. The origin of other "rare" finds, including a 35-mm newsreel film showing footage of *Titanic* survivors arriving in New York, which was unearthed in the garden shed of a London projectionist's widow in 1998, remains less certain.

A 13-minute *Titanic* newsreel produced by Murnan is available in 16mm format from Blackhawk Films. Other compilations of the newsreels produced by Gaumont and other companies include *Lost Films from the Titanic* and *Titanic Memories*.

384 *Titanic Phenomenon* (1999). Chip Taylor Communications. 50 min.

Low-budget video documentary on *Titanic* fanaticism and collecting.

385 *The Titanic Tragedy: The Complete Documentary* (1998). Twilight Works Presents/Brentwood Home Video. Approx. 30 min.

Producer: Bud Bruntsman
Director: Geoff Chadwick
Script: Chad Moltman
Paintings: Ken Marschall
Narrator: Leonard Kildare

Ambitiously titled video documentary presents a good description of the *Titanic*'s specifications and luxurious interior appointments, with an overuse of visuals from old films, particularly *Titanic* (1953) and *Atlantic* (1929). The classical musical score and relative straightforwardness of the film make it palatable.

386 *Titanic: Anatomy of a Disaster* (1997-Television). Discovery Channel/Stardust Visual. Approx. 60 min.

First aired: April 13, 1997, Discovery Channel
Exec. Producer: Gregory Andorfer
Producers: Gary Hines, David Elisco
Writer: David Elisco
Music: Michael Whalen
Narrator: Martin Sheen

Compelling, workmanlike documentary of an "unprecedented expedition" to solve the mysteries and many secrets of the *Titanic* by exploring her wreck. Unfortunately chosen somber music and sequences from the *Adventure Out of Time* game lead into documentary footage of the research vessels *Nadir* and *Ocean Voyager*. The more interesting segments focus on the scientific questions, including a biologist's efforts to determine whether microorganisms are destroying the wreck and a seismic imaging expert's search for the mud-covered wound in the bow. Concludes with a dramatic raising of a piece of the *Titanic*'s hull.

Those interviewed include authors Charles Haas and John P. Eaton, who attempt to explain how the ship was done in by the shearing of rivets made brittle by the cold Atlantic water.

387 *Titanic: Answers from the Abyss* (1999-Television). Discovery Channel. Approx. 120 min.

First aired: April 25, 1999, Discovery Channel
Exec. Producer: Jonathan Pryce
Producers: Gary Hines and David Elisco
Writer: David Elisco
Animation: Home Run Pictures
Music: David Michael Fraser and Neil Goldberg
Narrator: Jonathan Pryce

In this companion and follow-up to *Anatomy of a Disaster*, the filmmakers attempt to solve many of the mysteries surrounding the *Titanic* by examining evidence from the wreck. Much of the discussion centers on the question of whether the sinking was caused by one long gash, a series of punctures, or a separation of steel plates due to rivet-shearing. Other highlights include a search for the boiler units to determine if they exploded on their journey to the bottom of the ocean and a computerized simulation to determine why the hull broke in two. Finally, the filmmakers tackle the question of why the bow remained fairly intact while the stern exploded. Quality, well-focused documentary which wisely steers clears of the well-treaded historical material. Recommended especially for those interested in naval architectural issues who do not need further historical or human-interest background.

The original broadcast was intercut with rather intrusive banner ads for Discovery Channel's website on the *Titanic*.

388 *Titanic: Breaking New Ground* (1998-Television). Zaloom-Mayfield Productions (U.S.). First aired: Feb. 13, 1998, FOX Network. Color, Approx. 60 min.

Exec. Producers: Chris Cowan, Jean-Michel Michenaud, George Zaloom
Producer: Jeffrey D. Cvengros
Director: Doug McCallie
Script: Doug McCallie and Yann Debonne
Director of Photography: Anders Falk
Narrator: Peter Coyote

This Fox special, built around and probably meant to promote James Cameron's film, relies heavily on clips and music from the movie. The program is not without its strong points, including good behind-the-scenes footage of the two Russian submersibles Cameron hired to film the wreck and revealing narration on how those shots were planned. Those interviewed include Cameron, Eva Hart, Ken Marschall, and historian Don Lynch.

Quotes from the documentary most likely to inspire derision from Cameron critics include "history is a collective hallucination" and "I didn't let the *Titanic* talk to me." Fans of the movie may be inclined to search for the shots included in this documentary that did not make the final cut.

A special credit is given to Ed Marsh for behind-the-scenes footage.

389 *Titanic: The Final Chapter—The Truth Behind the Legend* (1993). Ray Johnson Productions/Castle Communications. Color/Black and White. 55 min.

Narrator: Robert Powell
Executive Producer: Terry Shand
Director: Ray Johnson
Script: Ray Johnson
Music: Peter Young
Based on the book *RMS Titanic—A Modern Legend,* by David Hutchings

Excellent straightforward documentary weaves the story of the *Titanic* in steady, even-handed strokes, beginning with the story of how the ship was conceived by the White Star Line as an answer to the quicker ships of other lines. As the documentary rightly points out, the ship and her sisters were designed to set new standards in size, luxury, and safety, not speed. The rest of the documentary proceeds steadily through the well-worn facts of the disaster, attempting to show how many different events and factors combined to create the disaster. The writers carefully note the myths of the disaster (such as the last song played and the final fate of Captain Smith) that remain controversial. The documentary comes full circle in analyzing the press coverage after the disaster, in which the values of heroism and valour were said to have been upheld, and closes with footage of Bob Ballard's discovery of the rusty wreck. A scrolling footnote at the end of the film notes that new information has been uncovered that disputes that long-held notion that the *Titanic* fell victim to a single, 300-foot gash in her hull.

Relying on low-key narration voiced over documentary footage, photograph stills, and artwork (and only rarely lapsing into the overdone interviews with aging survivors), documentaries such as this one serve to point out that the drama and astonishing facts of the *Titanic* need no embellishment.

Occasionally shown on PBS affiliates as simply *Titanic: The Truth Behind the Legend.*

Available: Polygram Video (1997)

390 *Titanic: Live* (1998-Television). Discovery Channel. Approx. 120 min.

Exec. Producer: Maureen Lemura
Producer: Gary Hines
Writer: Laurie McCall

Live program attempted to capitalize on the runaway success of the movie by broadcasting an expedition to the wreck (aboard the French submersible *Nautile*) as it happened. Historian Charles Haas provides commentary for the live images, while the program is padded with clips from the computer game *Titanic: Adventure Out of Time* and historical images. Although the program was reportedly 10 months in the making, no real new information comes to the fore.

391 *Titanic: The Nightmare and the Dream* (1986). TVS International Productions. Color with black-and-white footage, 53 minutes.

Executive Producer: Peter Williams
Producer: Graham Hurley
Director: Graham Hurley
Music: Ray Swinfield
Program Consultant: Robert Ballard
Narrator: Peter Williams

Above-average British television documentary focuses on Bob Ballard's exploration efforts, from his role in developing *Jason*'s "telepresence" technology to the discovery of the *Titanic* wreck. The extensive on-camera narration by Ballard, as well as the footage aboard the research vessel *Atlantis II*, may seem redundant to those familiar with the National Geographic's *Secrets of the Titanic*. But the film has much to recommend about it, including Ballard's musings on the emotional impact of discovering the wreck, as well as his wistful and, given the later efforts of R.M.S. *Titanic* Inc., sad reflection that "nobody owns the ship." The documentary will also be of value to those with an in-depth interest in the deep-sea technology that allowed Ballard's team to succeed where others had failed, as the scientific team works to overcome various technological hurdles and historical unknowns. Nostalgia buffs will enjoy the giddy clips from television news shows of the day reporting on the first eerie transmissions of the *Titanic*'s wreck. Fine musical score helps.

Available: Video, MTM Enterprises/Public Media Incorporated, 1995. Packaged as "Program 2" with *Titanic: A Question of Murder*.

392 *Titanic: A Question of Murder* (1983). TVS International. Color with Black-and-white footage, 56 min.

Executive Producer: Peter Williams
Director: Alan Ravenscroft
Narrator: Peter Williams

This British documentary begins with a séance in which survivor Eva Hart attempts to contact her father, a scene that will be familiar to viewers of many later *Titanic* documentaries. The rest of the film is for the most part a patchwork of interviews with other survivors, most of them conducted at a meeting of the *Titanic* Historical Society. The footage has been re-edited and repackaged (often with different narration) for many other *Titanic* documentaries (e.g., the two DVD documentaries released in 1998). This earlier effort sets itself apart with its coherent editing and narration and through the inclusion of older, black-and-white interviews with long-dead survivors and shipbuilders.

The titillating title refers to the second part of the film, which examines "irrefutable evidence" that the shipowners failed to heed Harland and Wolff's advice to supply lifeboat capacity for all passengers. The filmmakers here present one of the most comprehensive, in-depth examinations of the state of lifeboat technology and shipping regulations at the time of the *Titanic* sinking that has ever been assembled (thanks to the efforts of a technical writer, John B. Francey).

The final, third part of the film further indicts the White Star Line officials using quaint "artist's rendering" sequences of British hearings, with actors supplying the voices for still color sketches of Bruce Ismay, White Star director Harold Sanderson, and others.

Available: Video: MTM Enterprises/Public Media Inc., 1995 (Packaged as "Program 1" with *Titanic*: The Nightmare and the Dream). 16 mm film: Wombat Film & Video, 1986

393 *Titanic: The Real Jack Dawson* (2001-Television). BBC Productions/Discovery Channel/Discovery Channel Video. Approx. 52 min.

Exec. Producer: Jean-Claude Bragard
Producer: Amanda Hancox
Director: Zab Chughtai
Narrator: Kate Harper

Unnecessary documentary explores the life of J. Dawson, a *Titanic* crewmember whose grave attracted hordes of young visitors to Halifax in 1998. Despite the misleading title, the film's producers admit that James Cameron had no idea of the existence of a real J. Dawson before he created his romantic hero, Jack Dawson.

Unfortunately, despite the producers' claims to present "new groundbreaking evidence and testimony," the biography of a nearly unknown crew member does not really add up to much. With scant evidence of the life of this infrequent White Star crew member (even his first name is in question), the film becomes more of a scavenger hunt following the efforts of researchers as they hunt Dawson's ghost. The clues include photographs of crumbling houses, a few crew records, and the cut-off photograph of a woman's hat. The spaces are filled with reenactments, some (but not enough) discussion of the hard lives of crew members, and speculations on Dawson's love life and even how he might have died. James Cameron's film is mentioned at regular beats, as the producers needlessly note coincidences such as the fact that the real J. Dawson was 23, which would be close to the age of Jack Dawson.

The film does manage to present a side of the *Titanic* story that is rarely touched upon — the grim work of the undertakers who recovered 205 bodies from the Atlantic and also presents some information that J. Dawson may have in fact been Joseph Dawson, of whom also little is known.

Discovery documentaries have been criticized for stretching bits of information into hour-long documentaries through so much speculation and poetic waxing, and this documentary certainly does little to disprove that notion.

394 *Titanic: Secrets Revealed* (1998-Television). Tribune Entertainment (USA). Originally aired: April 4, 1998 (Syndicated). Approx. 120 min.

Exec. Producer: John Joslyn
Co-Exec. Producer: John Tindall

Writer: Lou DeCosta
Narrator/Host: Bernard Hill

Standard, well-done documentary of the "real story" in the context of the 1997 movie, with the tagline, "her majesty would end, her mystery would end." The "mysteries" of the *Titanic* that are explored include the lack of lifeboats, whether the sinking was a hoax, the near-collision with the *New York*, the premonitions of passengers, the story of *Futility*, the coal bunker fire, and the question of whether the ship represented a dangerous combination of hubris and untried technology. Ghostly superimpositions of the film are intertwined with interviews with the likes of Eva Hart, Edith Haisman, *Titanic* exhibit organizer Jon Thompson, Harland and Wolff naval architect John Bedford, film producer William MacQuitty, authors D. E. Bristow and Don Lynch, and Muffet Brown, the great-granddaughter of Molly Brown. Cites the not-often recounted fact that Captain Smith had earlier been implicated in the collision of the *Olympic* with a Navy cruiser. Ismay is criticized for his desire to "rule the waves," although it is also pointed out that he financially helped several passengers after the disaster. Other myths touched on in this wide-reaching telecast include Robin Gardiner's theory of the *Olympic-Titanic* switch, the story of a baby who was snatched and recovered, and the passenger who declared "what a night" before disappearing. Much of the second half focuses on the French expedition of the submersible *Nautile* to recover artifacts from the wreck and an interesting experiment with a ship model to test the popular theory that flooding other watertight compartments would have helped more passengers to avoid drowning. Clips from the popular computer interactive game *Titanic: Adventure Out of Time* add an oddly futuristic dimension to the graphics.

395 ***Titanic: Ship of Dreams*** (1998). *Nightline* special. ABC News Productions. First aired March 20, 1998 (ABC). Transcript/Video available through ABC.

At the peak of James Cameron's *Titanic*, *Nightline* devoted an entire episode to exploring the man and myth behind the film's success. Unfortunately, this half-hour has little new to offer, and, at worst, ends up being a mouthpiece for Cameron's publicity machine. A monologue-type interview with Cameron (rather bizarrely sitting in a chair that appears to be floating in an Atlantic icefield) provides the main structure for the show, which also features some footage from the making of the film. The elaborate set is enough to make one wonder about the motivation behind such a special; even more egregious is that Cameron himself appears to have had a heavy hand in the editorial direction of the show, with much of the "interview" consisting of little more than his poetic musings on inspiration and the enduring legend of the *Titanic*. A low point, reminiscent of when Cameron declared himself "king of the world" at the 1998 Oscars, comes when the director describes seeing a white rainbow above the Atlantic as he ponders the wreck below.

396 *Titanic: Survivors* (1998). Front Row Entertainment. 41 min.
Exec. Producer: Peter Williams
Director: Alan Ravenscroft

Repackaged footage of *Titanic* conventions and interviews with survivors which has been included in other documentaries. Those interviewed include Eva Hart and Ruth Becker Blanchard. "Bonus" footage features Nickelodeon film set against tinny piano accompaniment.

397 *Titanic:* **Treasure of the Deep** (1992-Television). Columbia Pictures Television. Approx. 47 min.
Director/Executive Producer: Al Giddings
Producers: Terry Thompson, Sam Shore
Script: Sam Shore, Al Giddings
Director of Photography: Al Giddings
Paintings: Ken Marschall
Host: Walter Cronkite
Narrator: Peter Scott

Follows a 1991 joint U.S., Canadian, and Russian expedition to explore the wreck aboard a Russian submarine, in search of an answer to the question of whether "treasures" could be found among the ruins. Thankfully, the documentary does not spend too much time rehashing the well-known bits of history, although some scenes from *A Night to Remember* are included. Highlights include some nice shots of the Russian research vessel *Keldish* silhouetted against the Atlantic and behind-the-scenes footage of *Titanica* (q.v.) being filmed.
Available: Columbia Tristar Home Video (1998)

398 *Titanic: Untold Stories* (1998). Discovery Channel.
Executive Producer: Gregory Andorfer
Producer: David Elisco
Writer: David Elisco
Music: Michael Whalen
Narrator: Linda Hunt

Documents the French exploration and exploitation of the *Titanic* wreck while building a case for the use of these artifacts as way to preserve and document history. Colorful, dramatic footage and animation sequences are complemented with readings from actual passenger letters and ineffectual, dream-like dramatizations. The filmmakers balance the salvage angle with the more noble objective of bringing to light the lives of the oft-neglected steerage passengers and crew (including the always-poignant story of the postal workers' efforts to save 3,500 bags of mail).

399 *Titanica* (1992). IMAX Corporation (U.S.). IMAX format, Approx. 90 min.

Director: Stephen Low
Executive Producers: Joseph MacInnis, André Picard
Producers: Pietro L. Serapiglia, Stephen Low
Film Editing: James Lahti
Lighting: Christopher Nicholoson
Music: Eldon Rathburn
Narrators: Cedric Smith, Leonard Nimoy (video only)

This engaging and ambitious documentary represented a milestone in the art of IMAX filmmaking, and became one of the three *Titanic* theatrical powerhouses (along with the Broadway musical and James Cameron's film) released in the 1990s.

Originally planned and filmed for the six-story-high IMAX screens, *Titanica* loses much of its majestic appeal in its translation to video. The film chronicles the journey of American scientists aboard the Russian research vessel *Akademik Mstislav Keldysh* and to the depths of the Atlantic aboard a deepwater submergible. The deep-water footage is captivating, thanks to the first full-scale effort to light the wreck for commercial filmmaking. More than most modern-day documentaries, *Titanica* also gives heavy play to the work of marine biologists studying the strange lifeforms that live 2 miles beneath the surface of the Atlantic.

Titanica was released in three different versions: The original, approximately 90-minute film shown primarily at IMAX film festivals in 1993; a cut, theatrical version (approx. 45 min.) released for general audiences; and the video version, which contains some additional footage of interviews with survivors and other experts and runs 75 min. As of this printing, laser disc and DVD versions of the full-length film were unavailable.

Many of the film's most humorous moments, mostly involving personality clashes among the quirky scientists (such as a scene where a humanities professor shows off his full-dress White Star officer's uniform) were cut for the mass-release film. Inexplicably, Leonard Nimoy's narration was added to the video version (inviting comparisons to the earlier *In Search Of* episode).

Available: Video, Miramax Home Entertainment.

400 *Treasures of the Titanic* (1998). National Geographic Explorer. Syndicated Program. Approx. 60 min.

Exec. Producer: Michael Rosenfeld

Producer: Chris Powell
Writer: Robert Goldberg
Senior Writer: Jon Goodman
Narrator: Boyd Matson

This episode of National Geographic's *Explorer* syndicated program presents footage of the expeditions of R.M.S. *Titanic* Inc. to recover artifacts from the wreck for its worldwide exhibition. George Tulloch, the founder of R.M.S. *Titanic*, is presented as something of a shyster and former car dealer who formed the company at of pure self-interest. Nonetheless, the visuals of the relics themselves make it difficult to believe these expeditions had no immediate historical value. Among the 4,000 relics recovered included Captain Smith's bathtub and masses of coal, later sold to the public in lumps. In a special "Outro" segment, Robert Ballard makes the case for leaving the ship alone.

"Outro" segment
Producer and Writer: Robert Goldberg
Narrator: Stanley Anderson

Against images showing him at work salvaging Roman and Greek artifacts from ships in the Mediterranean, Bob Ballard presents his arguments against the retrieval of relics from the *Titanic*, which he believes is not old enough to be considered an archaeological site. It is a segment tinged with cynical disbelief: Ballard passed up first salvage rights to the *Titanic* wreck, thereby giving up the chance to oversee a recovery operation in his own way, because he believed others would respect his and the survivors' desire to leave the ship untouched.

401 *The "Unsinkable" RMS Titanic.* Whamo Entertainment/Red Rock Management. Made for Video, Approx. 75 min. Color/Black and white.

Executive Producer: Jesse Weatherby
Producer: Les Brown Jr.
Director: Les Brown Jr.
Script: Linda Cooper, Don Lynch, Les Brown Jr., and Randy Jones
Research: Don Lynch, Ken Marshcall, Jesse Weatherby, Jan Silverstein
Original music: Jeff Lass
Narrator: Les Brown Jr.

Overly long, ineffectual documentary has the sleepy look and feel of a documentary made for classroom viewing, complete with a cast of droning narrators enumerating the facts of the disaster against a background of seemingly endless still photographs, Ken Marschall paintings, and stock footage. The video is clearly a product of Cameron-*Titanic* mania, and features a few shots of the Broadway musical and more blatant plugs for the Cameron "opus."

The monotony is broken only briefly by on-camera interviews with author Don Lynch (q.v.) and survivor Ruth Becker Blanchard (as well as documentary stalwart Eva Hart). The documentary also features "behind the scenes" footage of the Cameron film, which doubtless proved invaluable in promoting this video before the highly-anticipated movie was released. Scenes from (movie) and Bob Ballard's explorations of the wreck provide additional window-dressing. Computerized background music and muddled sound do not help.

A note in the credits points out that photographs of the *Olympic* are used in the documentary to illustrate the *Titanic*.

Available: Video Treasures/Anchor Bay Entertainment, VHS format (1997).

7 Plays

402 *The Berg* (1929). By Ernest Raymond. First produced: London's Q Theatre, March 5, 1929.

One of only two plays by the popular and prolific British novelist Ernest Raymond, *The Berg* was a fictionalized and lurid dramatization of the last two and a half hours aboard the *Titanic*. The play was divided into three acts. The play enjoyed a brief run and was thereafter regularly picked up by repertory companies for a time. *The Berg* served as the basis for *Atlantic* (1929; q.v.), an early talkie film produced in the same year.

Of one of Raymond's novels, George Orwell said: "I think it gains a great deal from the fact that the author only partly grasps the pathetic vulgarity of the people he is writing about, and therefore does not despise them."

403 *Cavalcade* (1931). By Noël Coward.

See Appendix B.

404 *The Great American Disaster Musical, or The Titanic Goes Hawaiian.* By Sam Abel (book) and Narcissa Campion (music and lyrics). Published: Dover, MA: Charles River Creative Arts Press, 1984.

The playwright is involved in an organization that uses theater as a tool to curb youth violence; little else is known about this obscure play.

Contact: Aurora at Freelance Players—children's theater group.

A side note: The phrase "*Titanic* Goes Hawaiian" was later applied as a sobriquet to the blockbuster film *Pearl Harbor*.

405 *The Iceberg* (1974). By Stewart Parker.

Radio drama first broadcast on BBC.

406 *Scotland Road* (1992). By Jeffrey Hatcher. Published: New York: Dramatists Play Service, 1996, 48 pp. First Performed: Cincinnati Playhouse, 1992.

A doctor and skeptical *Titanic* expert attempt to unravel the mystery of a woman, wearing 1912 clothing and suffering from dehydration, found drifting on an iceberg in the North Atlantic in 1992. The woman remains in silence throughout most of the first act, uttering only the single word, "*Titanic.*" Is the woman an actual survivor somehow transported to the present or is she the instigator of a bizarre hoax? Encounters with an actual survivor and the great-grandson of John Jacob Astor (the skeptical expert) provide complications and clues to the psychological mystery.

The phrase "Scotland Road" refers to a nickname for a passageway connecting first-class and third-class quarters.

Scotland Road met with much success beginning in 1997 and the play opened across the country in small theaters.

407 *The Ship: A Play in Three Acts* (1922). By St. John Ervine. Published: New York: Macmillan, 1922.

Belfast ship designer John Thurlow creates the *Magnificent*, an oil-driven super-liner that meets a similar fate as the *Titanic* (which is mentioned in the play). Ervine was a native of Belfast.

408 *Titanic* (1974). By Christopher Durang. First produced: New Haven, CT, 1974. Published: Dramatists Play Service, 1983, 42 pp.; also included in *Christopher Durang: 27 Short Plays,* 1995

This one-act sexual farce focuses on a first-class American family, the Tammurais, as they travel aboard the *Titanic*. The passengers eagerly await *Titanic* to hit the iceberg, and when she is unable to find it, the play devolves into a series of sexual revelations and identity transformations. When the ship finally hits the iceberg, it turns out to be a record played by the captain's wife as a joke. The humor of the passengers wanting the ship to find the iceberg, as well as the irony of the collision not occurring when they expect it to, places this play somewhere in the murky genre of Theater of the Absurd in spite of its reliance on sexual farce. Durang toys with the notion that every *Titanic* story sails toward the same conclusion and purposefully twists these preconceptions while shocking his audience with decidedly non–Edwardian outlandish sexual fetishes (one seemingly innocent girl reveals that she used to enjoy keeping a mammal in her vagina). No real events or characters are represented; Durang instead seems concerned with examining the nature of the family against a backdrop of sexual repression.

Sigourney Weaver starred as "Lidia," the captain's daughter, in the off-

off–Broadway New York premiere of the play in 1976. The play later made it to off–Broadway, where it received howling reviews.

409 ***Titanic: Destination Disaster*** (1992). By John L. Lipp.
Characters: Murdoch, Mary Sloan, Edith Russell, John Jacob Astor, Captain Smith, Hitchens, Lawrence Beesley, etc.

Short (17 pp.) play designed for classroom use. Originally published *in Plays: The Drama Magazine for Young People*, April 1992. Reprinted in Archbold, Rick, *Deep-Sea Explorer* (q.v.).

410 ***Titanic: A New Musical*** (1997). Originally produced on Broadway at Lunt-Fontanne Theatre, April 23, 1997. Original Broadway run: April 23, 1997, to March 28, 1999.

Story: Peter Stone
Music and Lyrics: Music and Lyrics
Original Broadway Run: Lunt-Fontanne Theatre, 1997–1999
Director: Richard Jones
Choreography: Lynne Taylor-Corbett
Scenic and Costume Design: Stewart Laing
Lighting Design: Paul Gallo
Sound Design: Steve Canyon Kennedy
Orchestrations: Jonathan Tunick
Music Supervision: Kevin Stites
Music Coordinator: John Miller
Casting: Julie Hughes and Barry Moss
Production Stage Manager: Susan Green

Cast:
Officers and Crew:

John Cunningham .... *Captain E. J. Smith*
David Costabile .... *First Officer William Murdoch*
Ivan Rutherford .... *Second Officer Charles Lightoller*
Matthew Bennett .... *Third Officer Herbert J. Pitman*
Brian d'Arcy James .... *Frederick Barrett, Stoker*
Martin Moran .... *Harold Bride*
Henry Stram .... *Henry Etches, First Class steward*
David Elder .... *Frederick Fleet*
David Rossmer .... *Quartermaster Robert Hichens,*
.... *Bandsman Bricoux*
Sean McCourt .... *Fourth Officer Joseph Boxhall,*
.... *Bandsman Taylor*

Matthew R. Jones .... *Chief Engineer Joseph Bell,*
.... *Wallace Hartley*
Michele Ragusa .... *Stewardess Robinson*
Stephanie Park .... *Stewardess Hutchinson*
Pippa Pearthree .... *Bellboy*

First-class Passengers:

David Garrison .... *J. Bruce Ismay*
Michael Cerveris .... *Thomas Andrews*
Larry Keith .... *Isidor Straus*
Alma Cuervo .... *Ida Straus*
William Youmans .... *J. J. Astor*
Lisa Datz .... *Madeleine Astor*
Joseph Kolinski .... *Benjamin Guggenheim*
Kimberly Hester .... *Mme. Aubert*
Michael Mulheren .... *John B. Thayer*
Robin Irwin .... *Jack Thayer*
Scott Burkell .... *George Widener*
Jody Gelb .... *Eleanor Widener*
Caitlin Clarke .... *Charlotte Cardoza*
Sean McCourt .... *J. H. Rogers*
Matthew Bennett .... *The Major*
Mindy Cooper .... *Edith Corse Evans*

Also: David Elder, Emily Loesser, Kate Suber, Jennifer Piech, and Clarke Thorell

Second-class Passengers:

Don Stephenson .... *Charles Clarke*
Judith Blazer .... *Caroline Neville*
Bill Buell .... *Edgar Beane*
Victoria Clark .... *Alice Beane*

Also: Ivan Rutherford, Mindy Cooper, David Costabile, and David Elder

Third-class Passengers:

Jennifer Piech .... *Kate McGowen*
Kate Suber .... *Kate Murphey*
Emily Loesser .... *Kate Mullins*
Clarke Thorell .... *Jim Farrell*

Also: David Rossmer, Caitlin Clarke, Matthew Bennett, Mindy Cooper, Alma Cuervo, Lisa Datz, Scott Burkell, Jody Gelb, Kimberly Hester, Robin Irwin, Larry Keith, Joseph Kolinski, Michael Mulheren, Charles McAteer, Sean McCourt, Matthew R. Jones, William Youmans

On Shore:
    Scott Burkell .... *Frank Carlson*

Songs: "In Every Age" (Thomas Andrews), "How Did They Build *Titanic*?" (Barrett), "There She Is" (Barrett, Bride, and Fleet), "Loading Inventory" (Smith, Stevedores, and company), "The Largest Moving Object" (Ismay, Smith, and Andrews), "The 1st Class Roster" (Pitman, Mrs. Beane), "Godspeed *Titanic*" (Company), "Barrett's Song" (Barrett), "What a Remarkable Age This Is!" (Etches Staff and First-class Diners), "To Be a Captain" (Murdoch), "Lady's Maid" (The Kates and Steerage Passengers), "The Proposal" (Barrett), "The Night Was Alive" (Bride), "Hymn" (Company), "Doing the Latest Rag" (Hartley et al.), "I Have Danced" (Alice and Edgar Beane), "No Moon" (Fleet and Company), "Autumn" (Harley), "Wake Up, Wake Up!" (Stewards and Company), "Dressed in Your Pyjamas in the Grand Salon" (Company), "The Staircase" (The Kates and Farrell), "The Blame" (Ismay, Andrews, and Smith), "Getting in the Lifeboat" (Mr. and Mrs. Thayer), "I Must Get on that Ship" (Reprise, Murdoch et al.), "Lady's Maid" (Reprise, Jim Farrell), "Canons" (Company), "The Proposal" (Reprise, Barrett), "The Night Was Alive" (Reprise, Bride), "We'll Meet Tomorrow" (Barrett et al.), "Still" (Isidor and Ida Straus), "To Be a Captain" (Reprise, Etches), "Mr. Andrews' Vision" (Thomas Andrews), "In Every Age" (Reprise, Company), "Finale" (Company).

    When plans were announced to produce a new musical based on the most spectacular maritime disaster in history, it seemed like *Titanic* madness had reached a new high in tasteless absurdity. This must have been the same Broadway mindset that gave birth to the Lizzie Borden musical. But somehow the Stone and Yeston managed to produce a lively and even comical show with enough weight and substance so as not to be crass. The score is stirring (with "There She Is" a highlight), and the original production's sets and effects helped to set the appropriate somber mood without lapsing into maudlin sentimentality, except to the extent that all musicals rely on overblown emotion. Critics and audiences embraced the *Titanic* for a two-year run, and the musical captured five Tony awards in 1997 (for best musical, book, score, sets, and orchestrations). Especially noteworthy in the original production was the use of elaborate moving decks, which allowed action to be played out simultaneously on different levels of the ship.

    Stone and Yeston achieve the balance mostly by dividing the musical into two acts, with the light-hearted moments and songs about the grandeur of the ship concentrated in Act I, and the more tragic songs filling out Act II. Comic bits are provided primarily by fictional second-class and steerage passengers, including a quibbling married couple (the Beanes, who have different first names from the Beanes who actually traveled in second class), the "three Kates" from steerage, and a hapless Cockney passenger (Carlson) who misses the boat entirely. Martin Moran also does a great comic turn as a Roddy McDowall-ish Harold Bride, with such lines as "Romance and telegraphy do not mix." Fleet marks the end of Act I with his famous declaration "Iceberg, dead ahead!" as he rings the bell three times from a crow's nest high above the audience; the curtain closes on Act I as a scale-model *Titanic* moves across the glassy stage and starry backdrop.

Act II provides an appropriate measure of pathos, mostly from the first-class passengers and officers; Smith, Ismay, and Andrews agonize over who is to blame for the accident in "The Blame" and the Strauses declare their undying love in the a tearjerking romantic dance number "Still."

The $10 million musical, which faced a series of production problems before opening, eventually spawned a book and a CD; since closing on Broadway, it has traveled to other cities.

411 *Titanic: Tragedy and Trial* (1998). By Pat Cook. Published: Florida: Eldridge, 1998.

Act One of this community-theater play has passengers and crew address the audience as they describe the ship and the events of her fateful voyage. Near the end of the first act, the passengers recite names of those who perished and survived. Act Two presents a dramatization of the 1912 Senate hearings. According to the playwright, the play can be performed as a full-length play or either act may be presented on its own (as separate plays, the acts are titled *Voices from the Titanic* and *Echoes from the Titanic*).

412 *The Unsinkable Molly Brown.* Originally produced November 3, 1960, at the Winter Garden Theatre.

Music and Lyrics: Meredith Wilson
Book: Richard Morris
Director: Dore Schary
Choreography: Peter Gennaro
Original run: Winter Garden Theatre, Nov. 3, 1960, to Feb. 10, 1962 (532 performances)
Original cast: Tammy Grimes, Harve Presnell, Cameron Prud'homme, Mony Dalmes, Edith Meiser, and Christopher Hewett
Songs: "I Ain't Down Yet," "Belly Up to the Bar, Boys," "Beautiful People of Denver," "I May Never Fall in Love with You"

A boisterous and brash Irish girl marries a lucky prospector and becomes a Denver socialite. After Molly's efforts to fit into society fail, her marriage falters and she travels to Europe in the company of royalty. After a prince unsuccessfully courts her, she returns to America aboard the *Titanic*, where her determination and lifelong lucky streak help her to survive once again.

Typical of spunky, rowdy musicals of the period, *Unsinkable Molly Brown* was composed by the man who wrote *The Music Man* and a later unsuccessful musical about Christopher Columbus. It produced a soundtrack album and a 1964 film version in which Presnell reprises his role.

413 ***Voyage to the Other Land; Drama in a Prologue and Seven Scenes*** (1939). By Albert Steffen. Published: Dornach, Switzerland: Verlag, 1939. 122 pp., translated by Arvia MacKaye.

Obscure philosophical drama in which unnamed characters representing familiar *Titanic* types—the Line Owner, the Millionaire, First Stoker, Engine-Room Hand—ruminate on their fate and its meaning for humanity.

Albert Steffen (1884–1963), known for presenting complex themes through rather incoherent plots, was one of the early leaders of the anthroposophical movement, a spiritual philosophy that focused on the value of love and individual man as a path to understanding and enlightenment. The movement also decried man's increasingly blind reliance on technology. Although he is considered a major influence in Swiss culture, his work has been largely ignored in the United States.

8 Selected Essays and Articles

In addition to the noteworthy articles and essays below, *Titanic* has of course been the subject of countless news and magazine articles over the years. Many newspapers printed special editions in the days following the disaster, and numerous magazines printed cover stories after the release of James Cameron's 1997 film. Scholarly articles dealing with the cultural meanings and technical aspects of the disaster can also be found in academic databases.

414 Baldwin, Hanson. "R.M.S. *Titanic*" *Harper's Magazine* January 1934.

Naturalistic "true-life danger" account of the disaster that was later anthologized in thriller collections by Alfred Hitchcock (*Suspense Stories Collected by Alfred Hitchcock,* 1945) and others.

415 Ballard, Robert. "How We Found *Titanic*." *National Geographic* December 1985.

One of the most celebrated issues of *National Geographic* features a 20-page spread of the first bluish, blurry photographs of *Titanic* wreck on the bottom of the Atlantic, along with historical photographs and diagrams. At the end of the article, Ballard makes his first plea for preserving the wreck site. A follow-up *National Geographic* feature, with improved photographs and more lyrical text, came in December 1986.

416 Ballard, Robert. "It's a Carnival." *Naval History* September/October 1996.

In interview format, undersea explorer Ballard lambastes those attempting to salvage artifacts from the *Titanic*. The issue also includes an article by William H. Garzke and others called "How Did the *Titanic* Really Sink?"

417 Bride, Harold. "Thrilling Tale by *Titanic*'s Surviving Wireless Man." *New York Times* 28 April 1912.

In this famous first-hand newspaper account, Bride details, among other aspects of the disaster, the initial joking mood of the wireless operators at having to send the distress signal, the violent incident that occurred when a man attempted to steal Phillip's lifebelt, and the band playing "Autumn" as the ship went down.

418 Browne, F. M. "At Sea on the *Titanic*." *The Belvederian* 1912.

Browne's account is reprinted in E. E. O'Donnell's *The Last Days of the Titanic* (1997).

419 Buckley, William F. "Down to the Great Ship." *New York Times* 18 October 1987.

In this article published just before the release of James Cameron's film, conservative commentator Buckley related his experiences visiting the shipwreck as a guest on the French submergible *Nautile*.

420 Candee, Helen Churchill. "Sealed Orders." *Colliers* 4 May 1912.

First-hand account of first-class passenger.

421 Carrothers, John C. "Lord of the Californian." *United States Naval Institute Proceedings* March 1968.

422 Chapin, Howard M. *The Titanic Disaster.* Providence, 1913. 12 pp. Illustrations: Photograph of iceberg as taken by Mrs. Chapin.

Originally published in the July 1912 issue of the *Paignton* magazine in England, *Carpathia* passenger Chapin's eyewitness account also appeared in *Brown Alumni Magazine* before several copies were distributed in pamphlet form. Twenty copies were printed. In his own *Titanic* bibliography, Chapin makes note of another "book," *Graphic Account of Titanic Disaster*, containing excerpts from his own newspaper account of the disaster, as it appeared in the Providence *Evening News*, as well as an excerpt from another article, "The Tragedy of the *Titanic*," that appeared in the August 1912 issue of the *Paignton and Marldon Parish Magazine*.

423 Collyer, Charlotte. "How I Was Saved from the *Titanic*." *Washington Post* 26 May 1912.

First-hand account by second-class passenger.

424 Conrad, Joseph. "Some Aspects of the Admirable Inquiry into the Loss of the *Titanic*." *English Review II* (1912): 581–95.

British novelist Conrad, known primarily for his anti-imperialist novel *Heart of Darkness,* penned two essays for the *English Journal* on the *Titanic.* In this second piece, Conrad in his understated style notes that "heroes funds" will not pay for dead human lives and that he would have rather seen the band members survive than go down as sentimental icons.

425 Conrad, Joseph. "Some Reflexions, Seamanlike and Otherwise, on the Loss of the *Titanic*." *English Review* May 1912: 304–15.

In this first essay of observations for the English Review, Conrad ridicules the American senatorial proceedings as "bumble-like" and ridicules those who could have ever believed the *Titanic* was "unsinkable."

426 Doyle, Arthur Conan. "The Whole Wonderful Epic." London *Daily News* 20 May 1912.

The creator of Sherlock Holmes responded to George Bernard Shaw's essay in this letter, accusing of Shaw of "looseness" and "levity." Among other things, Doyle writes that Shaw distorts facts to support his "perverse thesis" that women were not given priority during lifeboat loading, and that Shaw ignores Captain Smith's last heroic act of swimming with a child to a lifeboat (a story that has never been verified). Shaw responded, in another letter two days later, that it was "really not possible for any sane man to disagree with a single word I have written."

427 Gill, Ernest. *Boston American*, 1912.

Seaman Gill penned what was probably the first article about events aboard the *Californian* the night of the *Titanic*'s sinking.

428 Ian, Jack. "Leonardo's Grave." *Granta 67: Women and Children First.* September 1999.

This essay examines the cultural influences of and impact of James Cameron's *Titanic,* touching on the "J. Dawson" grave in Halifax and the myth of band leader Wallace Hartley. *Granta,* a literary magazine first published in 1889 at Cambridge University, centers each of its issues around a theme. The "Women and Children First" theme focuses on the unraveling of an old code of behavior during such crises as the bombing of Belgrade and the Iraqi conflict.

429 Shaw, George Bernard. "The *Titanic*: Some Unmentioned Morals." London *Daily News* 14 May 1912.

Playwright Shaw, in perhaps the first incisive reaction to *Titanic* mythmaking, decried the false sentimentality and "outrageous romantic lying" in preliminary newspaper accounts, particularly those contributed by such first-class passengers as Lady Duff-Gordon. In this missive, Shaw enumerates the four "romantic demands" of any shipwreck: women and children must be saved first, all men (except foreigners) must be heroes, officers must remain calm, proud, and unmoved, and all victims must face death without tremor, while the band plays "Nearer My God to Thee." The most famous response to Shaw's observations was to come from Arthur Conan Doyle (q.v.).

430 *The Shipbuilder.* Summer 1911.

This British quarterly journal devoted a special issue devoted to the building and outfitting of the *Titanic* and its sister ship *Olympic*, with a focus on reproducing plans and technical specifications. The issue has been reproduced by the *Titanic* Historical Society and also on CD-ROM by *Titanic* Distributors Ltd.

431 *Titanic Commutator.*

The quarterly journal for the *Titanic* Historical Society has been published since 1963, with articles on such tangential matters as the White Star Line flag and the wireless station on Nantucket Island, as well as historical treatises and genealogical profiles of passengers. Many of the journal's articles also deal with the *Titanic*'s sister ships, and the periodical also publishes society news and convention information.

"Commutator" generally refers to a type of electric switch; in the case of the naming of the journal, the word was apparently lifted from a mistake in the testimony Quartermaster Hichens in describing the device used to measure the list of a ship.

9 Selected Poems, Songs and Poetry Collections

432 Ball, Richard. ***The Last Voyage of the Titanic.*** Corsham: Gazebo Books, 1968. 18 pp.

Longish poem by Welsh poet, printed in chapbook form.

433 Banks, William Augustus. "***Titanic, O Titanic.***" In *Beyond the Rockies and Other Poems*. Philadelphia: Dorrance, 1926. 64 pp.

434 Brenner, Henry. ***Titanic's Knell: A Satire on Speed.*** St. Meinrad, IN: The Raven, 1932. Softcover, 58 pp. Cover: Reproduced brown woodcut sketch of the *Titanic* on tan cover.

Pretentious, overwrought poem holds up the *Titanic* disaster as an elaborate metaphor for the wages of sin. In a form imitative of Dante or Spenser, the dreaming storyteller descends deep into "Nature's caverns" and arrives at the resting place of the *Titanic*'s wreck. There he engages in a lengthy, philosophical discourse with a mystic guide on the nature of sin as embodied in pride and the quest for speed and riches aboard the *Titanic*. The satire here is more a matter of form than tone, for although the guide is used as a device to point out man's folly in worshipping technology, the dominant tone of the poem is one of pious finger-wagging.

435 Browne, Francis M. "**In Memoriam.**"

A previously unpublished poem in ballad form by the photographer Rev. Browne, reproduced in E. E. O'Donnell's *The Last Days of the Titanic* (1997).

436 Carson, Douglas, ed. ***Against the Stars: Twelve Poems on the Titanic.*** Belfast: Ulster *Titanic* Society, 1997.

A collection of twelve vernacular and literary poems by different authors, with illustrations by G. O. Fleet.

437 Dixon, J. Qallan. ***Wreck of the Steamship Titanic.*** Buffalo, NY: Sovereign, 1912. 12 pp.

In his early bibliography Chapin describes this collection as "a sympathetic, exciting, and graphic account of the wreck of the *Titanic* and the Horror and Loss of Life, also the Rescue of the Survivors by the Gallant Steamship *Carpathia*." Dixon also wrote a 1904 novel about the Anglo-Boer War.

438 Drew, Edwin. ***The Chief Incidents of the Titanic Wreck Treated in Verse; Together with the Lessons of the Disaster.*** London: W. Nicholson, 1912. Paper, 46 pp. Illustrations include photograph reproductions of the *Titanic* and portraits of Wallace Hartley and John Phillips.

Touted as "the first book of rhyme" devoted entirely to a great wreck (and not just the *Titanic* disaster), this limited-run collection includes such sentimental poems as "Mr. William T. Stead," "The Banquet on the Final Night," "John Phillips: The Wireless Operator," and "Mr. and Mrs. Strauss." The copy housed in the Library of Congress was originally sent by the author as a gift to President Taft. Eager to impress, perhaps, the author also sent a copy to the king of England.

439 Enzensberger, Hans Magnus. ***The Sinking of the Titanic: A Poem.*** Boston: Houghton Mifflin, 1980. Softcover, 98 pp. + viii.

Epic work by an influential German scholar and author, available in English translation by the author. The poem has been performed at literary festivals.

440 Greeley, Horace. ***The Wreck of the Titanic: A Poem.*** Brooklyn, NY: D. Sinclair, 1913. Illustrations by Horace Greeley include one dark sketch. Leatherbound, 52 pp. Dedicated to the *Titanic*'s musicians.

Famed anti-slavery newspaper editor Horace Greeley penned this epic retelling of the *Titanic* in heroic couplets. Greeley relies heavily on antiquated language, dramatic yet fictional dialogue, and other constructions to give his poem an almost Miltonic tone. Yet Greeley focuses on the known facts and celebrates the sublimity of the experience as a whole, rather than playing on the Man vs. Nature angle or falsely sentimentalizing the gentile and heroic behavior of first-class passengers.

441 Hardy, Thomas. "**The Convergence of the Twain.**" Originally published in Hardy's collection *Poems of 1912–1913*.

British novelist Hardy's widely anthologized 1912 poem is the *Titanic* poem most firmly entrenched in the literary canon and most likely to endure. Set in eleven verses numbered with roman numerals (suggesting the hours of a clock), "Convergence of the Twain" speaks of the tragedy as the result of "Immanent Will." The twain — the iceberg and the ship — exist only as two halves of an "august event," destined to come together to create a historical moment in time. Thus in this early, spare poem Hardy elegantly sums up an idea that lesser authors have wrestled with ever since.

442 Howell, J. A. ***The Great Titanic Ship and Its Disaster.*** Diana, WV: 1913, 8 pp.

This limited-circulation poem was written by the so-called "Blind Poet" of Webster County, West Virginia.

443 Jones, Wex. "*The Invincible Armada.*" *New York Evening Journal*, April 16, 1912.

This satiric poem ran on the front page of the *Journal* a few days after the disaster, alongside several scathing articles criticizing the negligence of the White Star Line and a charcoal sketching showing the *Titanic* resting in the hand of God. The poem begins with the rather laughable line, "Hurray for steel! Hurray for steam!" The *Armada* of the title refers to the icebergs of the North Atlantic, which "fly no flag" and "carry no crew."

444 Kilmer, (Alfred) Joyce. "**The White Ships and the Red.**" Collected in *Main Streets and Other Poems*. Classic, 1917.

In this poem by the American modernist known mostly for the 12-line poem "Trees," the *Titanic* meets up with the sinking *Lusitania*.

445 Pratt, Edwin John. ***The Titanic.*** Toronto: Macmillan Co. of Canada, 1935. 42 pp., 1 leaf of plates, 24 cm, Cloth. Cover: Gold lettering embossed on plain blue cover.

Canadian poet E. J. Pratt tells the story of the *Titanic* in this straightforward, narrative form, beginning with her launching in 1911 and progressing evenly through the events of the wreck. Individual passages, set off by telegraph-like datelines in the margins, include the story of the near-collision at Southampton, a lyrical description of the last dinner, and the requisite (but refreshingly concise) drama of the Strauses' decision to go down together. Pratt's descriptive, plain language and his use of free verse and irregular rhyme patterns liberate his vision from the sentimentality and false formality typical of the time. His verse remains palatable to the modern reader and contains not a few memorable, well-crafted lines.

446 Sandburg, Carl. **"Always the Mob."** Cornhuskers. New York: Henry Holt, 1918.

Sandburg's poem on the collective, mob-like experiences of modern man includes the line "The Woolworth on Land and the *Titanic* at Sea?"

447 Shay, Timothy. ***This Cabin as the S.S. Titanic: Poems.*** Winlaw, BC: Solstice Books, 1983. Softcover, 72 pp.

448 Slavitt, David R. **"Titanic."** 1983. Included in Kennedy, X. J. and Dana Gioia, eds. *Literature: An Introduction to Fiction, Poetry, and Drama.* Eighth Edition. New York: Longman, 2002.

Slavitt's cheeky poem begins with the question, "If they sold passage tomorrow for that same crossing, who would not buy?" While the idea of "going first class" in death might hold appeal for some, the poem seems rather to poke fun at the popular literary fascination with a tragedy all too real for those aboard.

449 Songs.

Author Steven Biel provides a survey of the number of folk songs inspired by the *Titanic* in the 1910s, 1920s, and 1930s in his two nonfiction studies (q.v.). (Biel also reproduces many public-domain songs and poems in his later book.) Another fine history can be found in Joe Showler's CD *Titanic Songs* (Canada: Unsinkable Music, 1998), a collection of original phonograph recordings that includes a 20-page booklet with lyrics and record-label illustrations. Among the most significant and enduring folk tunes are the religious "Down with the Old Canoe" (recorded in 1938), blues singer Leadbelly's "The *Titanic*" (1912), and "The Great *Titanic*" (recorded in 1915). One of the versions of the latter song, alternately known as "When the Great Ship Went Down" or "Husbands and Wives," survives as a camp sing-a-long. An interesting version of another early folk song also called "The Great *Titanic*" appears on the 1980 soundtrack to the film *Coal Miner's Daughter*, sung by the actress Sissy Spacek. The song suggests Captain Smith's supposed drinking habits may have played a part in the collision.

African-American oral ballads featuring the mythical heroic black stoker Shine are discussed by scholar Roger Abrahams in his 1964 book *Deep Down in the Jungle*. The character, whose warnings to the captain are ignored, may reflect the ironic satisfaction some African-Americans took in the fact that no blacks took passage or worked on the ship. (A Negro stoker is also mentioned in Logan Marshall's 1912 book.)

Countless forgettable hymns (as well as short memorial verses) were published soon after the disaster, including sheet music hymns such as F. V. St. Clair's "The Ship That Will Never Return," published to benefit a relief fund in 1912.

Also worth noting in the arena of *Titanic* music are the many CDs released in recent years focused on the theme of music "as heard on" the *Titanic*. These have been mostly symphonic or chamber recordings of period music that may or may not have been played on the ship. Titles include Andy Street's *Titanic Serenade: Music from an Age of Elegance* (BCI Music, 1997), the Southampton Pier Player's *Music from the Titanic: 21 Authentic Songs from the Epic Journey* (PPI Entertainment, 1998), the Muzak-like *Music from Titanic: The American Film Orchestra* (Intersound, 1998), a keyboard-heavy rerecording of music from the movie, and Ian Whitcomb's *Titanic: Music as Heard on the Fateful Voyage* (Rhino, 1997), which recreates the sound of the White Star Orchestra and also includes a recording of the poem "The Convergence of the Twain." Also released in 1997 were the official soundtrack to James Cameron's *Titanic* (Sony, 1997) and the original cast recording of *Titanic: A New Musical* (RCA Victor, 1997). The Celine Dion hit song from the 1997 movie was in turn covered in recordings by such soft-pop artists as Kenny G and Neil Diamond. Gavin Bryar's atmospheric *The Sinking of the Titanic* (Point Music, 1994), first released in 1974 by Obscure Records, is a 12-minute experimental composition featuring sounds and music of the disaster. In a similar vein, Ronan Magill released a five-part "atmospheric poem," really an elaborate piano composition, in 1997 (Minerva, 1997).

450 Stahl, C. Victor. ***The Sinking of the Titanic and Other Poems.*** Boston: Sherman, French, 1915. 63 pp.

451 Woodman, Hannah Rea. ***In Memoriam, The Titanic Disaster.*** Poughkeepsie, NY: A. V. Haight, 1913. 60 pp., 22 cm Cover: Small Gothic type lettering on plain cover.

This privately published book of 35 poems (divided into four parts) forms an epic retelling of the *Titanic* disaster, beginning with a meditation on the somber and brooding Atlantic iceberg and moving quickly into familiar and sentimental stereotypes. Women, children, and "sleeping babies" are loaded into the lifeboats with care, without attention to class distinction. Woodman even has Captain Smith bidding farewell and God speed to the lifeboats before romantically plunging himself into the sea. One of the last poems follows the funeral procession of band leader Wallace Hartley. Many of the poems include epigraphs pulled from relevant newspaper stories of the day.

10 Comic Books and Parodies

452 Baloney, Senan. ***A Garbled Titantic: 888½ Disaster Facts, and All of Them Wrong!*** Glarbed Press, 2001. Softcover, 100 pp.

Satirical treatment that targets the *Titanic* media industry, urban legends, the "rivet counting" obsession with an ever-changing set of facts, and the official investigations into the disaster. Much of the humor is straightforward, *Mad*-like silliness—the *Titanic* sails with the White Starched Linen—but the author (a *Titantic* scholar by the name of Senan Moloney) aspires to expose some of the self-serving and posturing aspects of the disaster's legacy.

The book was published in a limited run of 100 autographed copies and was touted as having "35 percent more text" than *A Night to Remember*.

453 Barry, Dave. ***"A Titanic Splash (Again)."*** May 31, 1998.

In this column, the popular humor columnist presented excerpts from his script *Titanic II: The Sequel*.

454 Chick, Jack T. ***Titanic.*** Chino, CA: Chick Publications, 1983.

Religious tract disguised as a comic and designed to aid proselytizing Christians in "witnessing" to doubters. The storyline centers on an unrepentant first-class passenger, Chester, who cares about nothing but money. Predictably, he soon discovers that his money can't save him. The unenlightened Chester panics as other passengers calmly sing "Nearer My God to Thee."

Available online at http://www.chick.com.

455 *Cracked* (May 1998)

Six-page parody of Cameron's movie, with the ship dubbed *Tipanic*. The issue marked the 40th anniversary of *Cracked*, considered by loyalists to be an edgier alternative to *Mad*, and was subtitled, "Celebrating 40 Titanically Disastrous Years!"

456 ***Godzilla: King of the Monsters*** (1996). Dark Horse Comics. May 1996, Issue #11 Cover text: "Terror on the Titanic." Comments: Comic book, 24 pages.

Godzilla is transported to an iceberg in the Atlantic in 1912 and becomes a cause for concern for *Titanic* passengers.

457 ***MAD*** (May 1998). Issue #369.

The wits at *Mad* magazine took aim at James Cameron's film in this *Titanic* cover issue. The cover illustration features Alfred E. Neuman floating head down in a *Titanic* life preserver as the ship goes down in the back ground. In the magazine's main spoof feature, "Trypanic," the ship is captained by the Skipper from television's "Gilligan's Island." Memorable lines include Thomas Andrews (Toomuch Android) declaring, "I've built everything on a giant scale except the rudder.... But I'm not dumb! I put it underwater where no one can see it!" Among others, those who can be spotted being loaded into lifeboats include Bart Simpson and Charlie Brown. *Mad* also ran a series of *Titanic*-related cartoons by its famed artist Sergio Aragones in April 1998.

458 ***The Onion*** (1999).

The popular tabloid and online satirical newspaper ran a story headlined, "World's Largest Metaphor Hits Iceberg" in an "issue" dated April 16, 1912. The cover story did not actually run in an issue of *The Onion* but was included in the book's "retrospective" collection *Our Dumb Century: The Onion Presents 100 Years of Headlines from America's Finest News Source* (Three Rivers Press, 1999).

459 ***Raise the Titanic!*** (1977). United Press Syndicate (Best Seller Showcase).

Clive Cussler's best-selling novel (q.v.) was adapted for a syndicated newspaper comic strip that ran from August 15, 1977, to October 9, 1977. The strip ran in roughly 130 newspapers and the total run included eight Sunday color strips and 48 black-and-white daily strips.

460 Snider, Eric B. ***"Clash of the Titanic"*** (1998). Originally published: *The Daily Universe*, Feb. 9, 1998.

Also known as "*Titanic*: Abridged Version" and "*Titanic*: 5-minute Version," this parody of Cameron's movie was widely circulated on email during 1998 (usually with the author's name deleted).

461 ***Titanic Joke Book*** (2002). Houston: Towers Press, 2002. Softcover, 44 pp.

This tasteless collection includes groaners such as "What kind of lettuce did the *Titanic* serve?" (A: Iceberg) as well as an odd collection of *Titanic* editorial cartoons from the period.

462 Rivière, Francois. ***Titanic: The Search for Sir Malcolm.*** Catalan Communications, 1988. Paperback, 48 pp.

Graphic novel originally published in French as *À la recherche de Sir Macolm* (Dargaud; Albany); 48 pp.

463 ***Titanic: The Unsinkable Dream*** (1998). Florida: Adam Post, 1998. 48 pp. Penciled by C. Foulds; inked by Michael Halblieb; story by Lloyd Chasseur; lettered by Buddy Ackerman.

"Limited edition" nonfiction comic book sold on Internet auction sites in 1999.

464 ***Weekly World News*** (2000).

The August 22, 2000, issue of this weekly tabloid featured a cover story with the headline, "Corpse Found in *Titanic* Life Ring!" The ghastly cover illustration depicts a skeleton with a large ruby ring floating in a life ring. The article claims experts determined the skeleton to be that of passenger Josephine Benton (not the actual name of a passenger). Other tabloid headlines have appeared over the years, of course; collectively, they inspired two short stories by Robert Olen Butler (q.v.).

465 ***Weird Mystery Tales*** (1972). DC Comics. Oct. 1972, Issue #2. Subtitled "A Strange Tale of Destiny Aboard the *Titanic*."

The *Titanic* falls victim to the curse of a deadly ghost. The cover illustration (drawn in the traditional overstated macabre style) shows the sinking ship in the grips of a menacing phantom.

11 Multimedia Software

This listing covers multimedia CDs and other programs, including *Titanic*-related games, educational tools, and informational packages, designed for use on personal computers. Many of the programs have special system requirements.

466 *James Cameron's Titanic Explorer: A Historical Journey on the Ship of Dreams.* CD-ROM, Fox Interactive (1997). Windows/PowerMac, 3 Disks. System Requirements: 166 mHz Pentium, 16MB RAM, 30 MB free hard drive space.

Executive Producer: James Cameron

Multimedia tie-in to the blockbuster movie uses survivor accounts, film footage, computer simulations, blueprints, illustrations, and photographs to expand on the story of the *Titanic* as told in the 1997 movie. James Cameron provides the voiceover for the introduction, and much of the footage is taken directly from the blockbuster film. Other dramatic voiceovers are provided by actors.

Features include interactive passengers and crew lists (with information on whether the person survived and what lifeboat they boarded), a "walk-through" ship tour, a computer simulation of the collision and sinking, ship plans, a detailed scale ship model, a glossary, searchable transcripts of the government hearings, and a list of recommended books, images, and films.

Lead Writer: Alan K. Lipton
Graphic Designers/Illustrators: George Rodgers, Joerg Stierle, Fiel Valdez
Lead Programmer and Architect: Brian Kromrey
Voices: James Cameron, Jim Ward (Narrator), Tony Jay (Captain Smith), Neil Dickson (Bruce Ismay), Benjamin Livingston (Charles Lightoller), Robert Easton (Archibald Gracie), Alexander Siddig (Harold Bride, Laurence Beesley), Michael Gough (Jack Thayer, Francis Dyke), Robert Easton (Sir Cosmo Duff-Gordon, Charles Joughin), Tessa Shaw (Eva Hart, Violet

Jessop), Olivia D'Abo (Marie Jerwan, Edith Brown, Edwina Troutt, Dorothy Cross).

Disc One (Ship of Dreams) presents a smattering of background information (mostly in the form of short narrations and slideshow images) arranged along an interactive timeline beginning long before the actual construction of the *Titanic*. Topics covered include the historical danger of the North Atlantic passage, the growth of the White Star Line in the late 1800s, the excesses of the Gilded Age, Morgan Robertson's novel *Futility*, J. P. Morgan's acquisition of the White Star Line, Ismay's appointment as president, the rivalry between Cunard and White Star, the design and building of the *Titanic*, the launching of the *Titanic*, a "who's who" review of those on board, and the ice warnings. Besides these short informational interjections, Disc One encompasses a "clickable" 3D model and deck plans of the ship.

Disc Two (Tragedy Strikes) continues the narration of the disaster (up to the point of *Carpathia*'s arrival) using footage from the film.

Disc Three (The Legend Comes to Light) covers the rescue and aftermath, official hearings, and voyages to the wreck.

467 *Robert D. Ballard: Titanic: Challenge of Discovery.* CD-ROM, Maris Multimedia, Panasonic Interactive Media Co. Windows95. System Requirements: Pentium 120, 16 MB RAM, 120 MB hard drive space.

Concept: Phil Smith and Nick Maris
Game Design: Phil Smith, Vadim Karpov, and Artem Dobrovolsky
Original Music: Jean-Pierre Garattoni
Consultation: Robert D. Ballard

In this interactive simulation game, the player moves through several levels of training in undersea exploration (using both a ship equipped with sonar and remote vehicles) and as a researcher and pilot on the deep-sea submersible *Discovery*. Training exercises include finding and exploring the Roman merchant vessel *Isis* and the German battleship *Bismarck*. By proving his piloting and research skills, the player is promoted through several levels of play. The player must also interact with several grim-looking crew members, including engineers, archaeologists, and navigators.

468 *Starship Titanic.* Simon & Schuster (1998). Windows95.

Computer game based on the science fiction novel, only nominally related to the famous shipwreck.

469 *Titanic: Adventure Out of Time.* CD-ROM, Cyberflix (1996). Windows95/Macintosh.

This popular time-travel "virtual reality" game invites players to try to divert the course of history (not just the sinking of the *Titanic*, but also World War I and the Russian Revolution) by gathering clues and items from around the ship. More than 25 characters interact with players and "remember" previous encounters. The impressive, navigable 360-degree graphical representations of the ship employ the same type of "walk-through" visuals originally developed for industrial modeling. A tour of the ship in non-game mode is also available.

After its initial retail run, *Adventure Out of Time* was bundled for sale in wholesale stores with *Titanic: An Interactive Journey* (q.v.) and a bonus CD with additional automated tours of the game.

Notes: A hint book was also published by author William H. H. Keith (q.v.).

470 *Titanic: An Analysis.* Diskette, Night Heron Publishing, Houston.

A brief multimedia presentation designed as a demonstration of the capabilities of Microsoft's PowerPoint program. Includes graphs, charts, and photographs.

471 *Titanic: Dare to Discover.* CD-ROM, Expert Software (1998). Windows Only. Program by J. Krapf, E. Haas, and R. Eirich.

Interactive game that challenges the user to discover the "real" cause of the sinking of the *Titanic* by exploring an ancient, underwater city of winding tunnels and monolithic religious structures. The object of the game is mysterious, the way that object is achieved even more so. The player must unlock a number of puzzles and hieroglyphic passages, using a coded amulet, to solve the riddle of the *Titanic*. The dark, watercolor like graphics of the game are intriguing but not dynamic. Includes stereo background music and sound effects.

472 *Titanic: An Interactive Exploration.* Total Vision Inc./Phillips Interactive Media Inc. Phillips CD-Interactive. Approx. 5 hours viewing time. Written and Directed by Jay Woelfel.

Producer: Jennifer Johnston
Narrator: Patrick Stewart

Multimedia presentation made for the now-defunct Philips CD-Interactive system, which was introduced around 1990. The format is similar to the more modern interactive CD-ROM and DVD packages, which allow users to choose topics and areas of interest from a menu, rather than having to view the entire documentary in a linear format. According to one source, the Phillips disk represents the largest source of *Titanic* images, and it certainly contains plenty of footage from the 1985 expeditions to the wreck as well as lengthy discursive monologues by Walter Lord. Menus include "A Ship Takes Shape," "A Tour of the Ship," "Sister Ships," and "Deck Plans." The interactive tour, which allows you to click on different areas of the ship for more information, is invaluable, allowing users to tour the gym, promenade decks, first-class lounge, and hospital. The CD makes good use of graphics, especially in this early stage of multimedia disks, with the inclusion of many Ken Marschall paintings as well as older artwork and posters. The Biographies section includes information on Molly Brown, Charles Lightoller, E. J. Smith, Thomas Andrews, J. J. Astor, Bruce Ismay, and Jack Thayer, who, it is noted, committed suicide years after the disaster. A full clickable list of survivors and a bibliography are also included. Overall, the CD is thorough and accurate, with a good mix of historical, personal, and scientific information, with many little-known facts thrown in for good measure.

473 *Titanic: An Interactive Journey.* CD-ROM, Europress (1996). Windows95/Mac.

This "ultimate reference guide" features an interactive timeline and a virtual dive featuring QuickTime image from *Nautile*. Produced in cooperation with the salvage company R.M.S. *Titanic*, the guide also includes photographs and descriptions of hundreds of objects pulled from the ocean floor, as well as period photographs and survivor interviews.

Note: Bundled with *Titanic: Adventure Out of the Time* in a separate boxed set.

474 *Titanic: The Lost Mission.* CD-ROM, CyberFlix Inc. (1998). Windows Only.

Reduced-price interactive "mini-adventure" based on *Titanic: Adventure Out of Time*. The episode contained on this disk is not included in the full game. Also includes more than 100 screen-saver images.

475 *Titanic: A Voyage of Discovery.* CD-ROM, Titanic Distributors Ltd. (1999). PC/MAC.

Touted as the "largest single collection of *Titanic* material," this multimedia presentation includes 600 photographs, music, deck plans, video clips, fact sheets, and commentary by Ralph White and maritime historian Charles Sachs.

476 ***Total Titanic: A Night to Remember.*** Byron Preiss Multimedia Company (1998). Published under license from Criterion and The Rank Organisation. Windows/Macintosh CD-ROM (two-disk set).

Interactive CD-ROM features the complete film *A Night to Remember* with optional scene-by-scene commentary by Don Lynch and Ken Marschall. The movie itself is in QuickTime format, which does not offer the crispest visual quality. Although the effect is similar to listening to parade color commentary, the authors' analysis on such minutiae as the accuracy of the costumes and Edwardian problems with child labor is fascinating. Other interactive features include a ship blueprint with hot links to scenes from the film, a passenger gallery of biographies with links to character scenes, a timeline, and a search mechanism.

A second "bonus" disc features the 1993 documentary *The Making of "A Night to Remember"* (q.v.).

12 Selected Web Sites

477 The Christian Boys' and Men's *Titanic* Society Home Page
http://www.titanicsociety.com/

This interesting and comprehensive website features much discussion of the ethical issues surrounding the *Titanic*, including the history of the "women and children first" edict.

478 Encyclopedia Titanica
http://www.encyclopedia-titanica.org/index.php

Searchable and comprehensive *Titanic* reference site includes deck plans, crew and passenger lists, animations, message boards, lists, biographies, and articles. The designer and editor, Philip Hind, attempts to verify all information through primary and secondary sources.

479 George Behe's *Titanic* Tidbits
http://ourworld.compuserve.com/homepages/Carpathia/

Of the all the *Titanic* experts, historian and author George Behe is probably the most prominent within the ranks of cyber-culture. Besides participating in e-mail discussion groups, Behe maintains his own site with *Titanic* trivia. The page is a good place to start for those looking for information on well-worn *Titanic* legends such as the man who dressed as a woman to get a seat in a lifeboat. Also includes links to THS member pages.

480 Ocean Planet: How Deep Can They Go?— RMS *Titanic*
http://seawifs.gsfc.nasa.gov/OCEAN_PLANET/HTML/titanic.html

Well-organized page is part of a Smithsonian Institution site on deep-water exploration. Includes such multimedia nuggets as a movie clip from Robert Ballard's wreck dives, a sound file of Doc Hopkins singing the folk ballad "Wreck of the *Titanic*," and a page of text from Edward Park's journal describing the last messages from the *Titanic*.

481 RMS *Titanic*, Inc.

http://www.titanic-online.com/

Official web site for the company that has been awarded the right to recover artifacts from the *Titanic*'s wreck.

482 The Smoking Gun — The *Titanic* Files

http://www.thesmokinggun.com/

Advertised as a "Pierre Salinger–free zone" (in reference to the former JFK advisor who fell for a phony Internet report about TWA Flight 800 being shot down by a Navy missile), The Smoking Gun web site features facsimile reproductions of official court records, police reports, and government documents. (Featured documents at the site include actress Neve Campbell's divorce decree and FBI files on Elvis Presley and Mickey Mantle.) An eclectic collection of *Titanic*-related documents, including a letter from the White Star Line complaining about the early film *Atlantic* and a lawsuit involving 40 cases of lost Roquefort cheese, is included in the site's archive at http://www.thesmokinggun.com/titanic/titanic.shtml.

483 *Titanic* Book Site

http://www.titanicbooksite.com/

Book collector and seller Michael Tennaro maintains this exhaustive and growing site, which attempts to document all fiction and nonfiction books about the *Titanic* and all their editions and reprintings. The site includes hundreds of scans of book covers.

484 *Titanic* Historical Society

http://www.titanic1.org/

The official site for THS includes membership information, *Titanic* trivia, articles, and an extensive list of books, videos, and other merchandise available for purchase. Also includes information on upcoming *Titanic* conferences and organized trips.

485 Urban Legends Reference Pages: *Titanic* Legends

http://www.snopes.com/titanic/titanic.htm

The most well-known site devoted to debunking or confirming urban legends maintains a page on *Titanic* legends, including the stories that the *Titanic* carried a mummy in its cargo and that a man was entombed in the hull during construction. The site's tongue-in-cheek "Lost Legends" page (meant to fool the gullible) also includes the legend of how a silent version of *The Poseidon Adventure* was screened aboard the *Titanic*.

Appendix A: Actors Who Have Appeared in More Than One *Titanic* Film

Michael Ensign played Northacker in *Raise the Titanic!* (1980) and Benjamin Guggenheim in *Titanic* (1997).

Anthony Eustrel played Sanderson in *Titanic* (1953) and Roberts in *The Unsinkable Molly Brown* (1964).

Bernard Fox played Frederick Fleet in *A Night to Remember* (1958) and Archibald Gracie in *Titanic* (1997).

Cloris Leachman played Molly Brown in *S.O.S. Titanic* (1979-TV) and in a 1957 episode of TV's "Telephone Time."

Nancy Nevinson played Ida Straus in *S.O.S. Titanic* (1979-TV) and Sarah in *Raise the Titanic!* (1980).

Norman Rossington played a steerage steward in *A Night to Remember* (1958) and the master-at-arms in *S.O.S. Titanic* (1979-TV).

Vern Urich had a bit part as a man in the water in *Titanic* (1997) and played Thomas Andrews in the dramatized portions of *Titanic: Secrets Revealed* (1998-TV).

David Warner played Laurence Beesley in *S.O.S. Titanic* (1979-TV) and the manservant Spicer Lovejoy in *Titanic* (1997).

Appendix B: Brief Film and Television Appearances of the *Titanic*

- ***Beyond Belief: Fact or Fiction*** (1998), a Ripley-esque Fox television series that asked viewers to decide if stories presented were true or false, featured the story of *Futility*, a novel that paralleled the events of the *Titanic* but was penned 20 years earlier.
- ***Cavalcade*** (1931, 1933). One of the classic scenes from Noël Coward's epic story of two Edwardian families, which was filmed by director Frank Lloyd in 1933, finds honeymooners Edith (Margaret Lindsay) and Edward (John Warburton) aboard the *Titanic*. Note: The life preserver that reveals their fate (in a classic *Titanic* plot device) is mistakenly embossed with the town of "Southampton." In fact the ship's port of registry was Liverpool.
- ***Eeerie, Indiana*** (1991). In episode 4 of the series centered around paranormal happenings, a life buoy marked "*HMS Titanic*" can be spotted in "The Bureau of the Lost."
- ***Ghostbusters II*** (1989). In this sequel to the popular comedy starring Bill Murray and Dan Ackroyd, a spooky-looking *Titanic* arrives at her intended port 70 years too late as part of a string of psychic phenomena that occurs after an oozing plasma wreaks havoc in New York City. The ship has a gaping, rusted hole in her hull, and her ghostly passengers look dazed as they walk into the city.
- ***Pinky and the Brain.*** In one episode from this mid–1990s television cartoon series, Pinky and the Brain (two lab mice) raise the *Titanic* as part of their ongoing plan to take over the world.
- ***Poseidon Adventure*** (1972). In this movie rife with *Titanic* parallels,

the character played by Ernest Borgnine exclaims, "Tell 'em to break out the hymn books and starting singing 'Nearer My God to Thee.'"

• In a 1990 episode of *The Real Ghostbusters*, an animated series that ran on ABC, a scientist claims in a lecture that the *Titanic* sank after crashing into Elvis. The episode was titled "Russian About."

• *Rocky Horror Picture Show* (1975). In this 1970s cult-camp classic, Doctor Frank-N-Furter (Tim Curry) is shown floating in a *Titanic* life preserver.

• A *Titanic* mural can be seen behind the beauty contest in the horror spoof *Scary Movie* (2000). Later, when two characters go to the movies, they see a *Titanic*-esque preview for *Amistad II*.

• The HBO series *The Show* (1997) features a fictional heavy metal band called Titannica.

• *The Simpsons* (various references in this 1990s prime-time animated series). *Episode "Mayored to the Mob":* Episode includes a reference to a television movie by budget film guru Roger Corman, *The $1000 Titanic Movie*, in which a risen *Titanic* attacks survivors. *Episode "Blood Feud":* Mr. Burns visits a mall store called "Plunderer Pete's." One of the items for sale is the safe from the *HMS Titanic*. *Episode "TV Guide":* television executives ask for a show that is *"Titanic* meets *Frasier."*

• *Superfriends* (1970s). Saturday-morning cartoon series featured one episode entitled "Terror on the *Titanic,"* in which the *Titanic* is raised, develops a mouth and teeth, and goes on a destructive rampage.

• *Time Bandits* (1981). Monty Python alum Terry Gilliam uses the *Titanic* to good effect in his time-traveling fable, in which a band of dwarves find themselves taking part in history's most significant moments. Aboard the *Titanic* (simulated with a flimsy mock-up), the dwarves quickly take to the niceties of first class and end up floating aboard a piece of wood (looking rather comfortable) when the ship sinks. An evil wizard creates a whirlpool in the Atlantic, sending them to their next adventure.

• *Trapper John, M.D.* (1970s). In this television medical drama (ostensibly a spin-off of *M*A*S*H*), the young surgeon and Vietnam veteran Gonzo Gates (Gregory Harrison) lives in an RV in the hospital parking lot. The RV, a rusty eyesore that is a constant source of irritation to hospital administrators, is christened *Titanic*.

• *Upstairs, Downstairs* (1973). On this long-running British television drama, the character Lady Bellamy perishes aboard the *Titanic*.

Appendix C: *Titanic* Films Unrealized or Unreleased

Gigantic (1999–2000)
Director: Greg Method

News reports revealed that this script for this film spoof, by writers Mike Bender (*Not Another Teen Movie*) and Chris Bender (*American Pie*) sold to New Line Cinema for $550,000 in 1999. The plot apparently centered around the story of a ship 2½ inches shorter than its famous competitor ship.

Perhaps unknown to the filmmakers, *Titanic*'s sister ship *Brittanic*, launched in 1914 and fated to end its service in similar fashion, was originally to be called *Gigantic*.

Titanic (Alfred Hitchcock project)

Conceived as a sweeping, grand epic by *Gone with the Wind* producer David O. Selznik, the *Titanic* project was to be Hitchcock's entrée in Hollywood. What would have resulted from such a combination of talents (the notoriously controlling Selznik and the meticulous and enigmatic Hitchcock) is interesting to imagine.

Titanic Too: It Missed the Iceberg (1999–2000)
Director: Pat Proft
Screenplay: Pat Proft

This *Titanic* spoof originally was slated for an August 1999 release and was said to have signed on actors David Hasselhoff, Leslie Nielsen, and Priscilla Presley. Presley and Nielsen previously starred together in the popular *Naked Gun* parody films.

Appendix D: Books Carried Aboard the *Titanic*

Although a few books survived the wreck, it is not always possible to tell whether these books were shelved in the ship's libraries, carried aboard by passengers, or stowed among the 86 boxes of books listed in the *Titanic*'s cargo manifest. Charles Pellegrino (q.v.) imagines that perhaps Morgan Robertson's *Futility* would be found in the shipboard library. No official catalog of library books appears to have survived the wreck. What follows is a brief listing of books that were known to have been aboard the ship, in whatever capacity.

Old Dominion, by Mary Johnston, a novel that Archibald Gracie recalls checking out and returning to the ship's library.

A rare, bejeweled copy of **The Rubaiyat of Omar Khayyam**, carried as registered cargo, was among the valuable items lost aboard the *Titanic*.

According to newspaper interviews, a French survivor named Pierre Marechal saved a **Sherlock Holmes** book from the ship.

The Virginian, by Owen Wister, a novel of the American West which served as the basis for the television series. First-class passenger S. V. Silverthorne is said by Walter Lord to have been reading this at the moment of the collision.

Note: In the made-for-television movie *S.O.S. Titanic*, the character played by Susan Saint James complains to Laurence Beesley that the ship's library has only "light shipboard reading," including *Stover at Yale* and *Hopalong Cassidy*. He, in turn, is catching up on some science reading ("Fisher's work on proteins").

Appendix E: Books Written by *Titanic* Passengers (Unrelated to the Ship)

Astor, John Jacob. *A Journey in Other Worlds: A Romance of the Future.* New York: D. Appleton, 1894. Illustrated by Dan Beard. Science fiction novel.

Butt, Archibald Willingham.
Both Sides of the Shield. Philadelphia and London: J. B. Lippincott, 1912. Memoirs published shortly after his death include details of his working relationship with President William H. Taft.
Where Silver Rules. Mexico, 1896.

Candee, Helen Churchill. Candee wrote most of her books after the disaster. She specialized in nonfiction books on antiques and decorating, directed mostly at women. She also kept a diary that has been used by several *Titanic* historians.
Angkor the Magnificient. New York: Frederick A. Stokes, 1924.
Decorative Styles and Periods in the Home. Willy, 1938.
How Women May Earn a Living. Publisher and year unknown.
Jacobean Furniture. Frederick A. Stokes, 1916. Historical background and identification of 17th century antique furniture
The Tapestry Book. New York: Frederick A. Stokes, 1912. History of tapestry and tapestry methods. Churchill was apparently traveling to New York to review the galleys of this book when the ship went down. It was republished in 1935.
Weaves and Draperies, Classic and Modern. Frederick A. Stokes, 1930.

Duff-Gordon, Lady Lucile. *Letters from Egypt.* London: Routledge & Kegan Paul, 1969.

Futrelle, Jacques. The most famous of the authors aboard the *Titanic*, French mystery writer and American transplant Jacques Futrelle was known for his detective tales such as "The Professor on the Case" and "The Thinking Machine" series.
The Diamond Master. Indianapolis: Bobbs-Merrill, 1909.
The High Land. New York: Grosset and Dunlap, 1911.
The Problem of Cell 13. New York: Dodd Mead, 1917.
Collected stories:
Best Thinking Machine Detective Stories. New York: Dover, 1973.
Great Cases of the Thinking Machine. New York: Dover, 1976.

Futrelle, May. Jacques' wife was also a minor, though successful, novelist.
A Secretary of Frivolous Affairs. Great Britain: Gay and Hancock, 1912.

Gracie, Col. Archibald.
The Truth About Chickamauga. New York: Houghton Mifflin, 1911. Military history book on the Civil War battle in which Gracie's father served. The book has not been republished and is a collector's item today. Gracie had been in England researching a book on the War of 1812, the notes for which were lost during the sinking. In addition, he also published an in-depth narrative of the *Titanic* disaster in 1913.*

Millet, Francis D. Primarily an artist, Millet had also served as a correspondent during the Spanish-American War.
A Capillary Crime and Other Stories. Republished by Books for Libraries Press, 1971.
Letters of Francis Davis Millet (1912).

Stead, William T. Primarily an editor and journalist, William T. Stead became known as a progressive, crusading pamphleteer documenting human rights abuses in Britain and elsewhere. Stead was also interested in the paranormal; it is reputed that he is responsible for the story of the cursed mummy being carried aboard the *Titanic.*
Americanization of the World, or, the Trend of the Twentieth Century (1901). Republished by Garland, 1972.
Chicago Today: The Labour War in America. Republished by Arno Press, 1969.
If Christ Came to Chicago! London: Review of Reviews, 1894.
Communication with the Next World. London, 1921.
Maiden Tribute of Modern Babylon (1885), an exposé of child prostitution in Britain.
Real Ghost Stories. Casebook of supernatural stories. Republished by University Books in 1970.

Lawrence Beesley, Comm. Lightoller, and Harold Bride also published accounts of the Titanic *disaster (q.v.).*

Appendix E 178

Satan's Invisible World Displayed, or Despairing Democracy: A Study of Greater New York (1897). Republished by Arno Press in 1974.

The United States of Europe on the Eve of the Parliament of Peace (1899). Republished by Garland in 1971.

Stead also served as the editor of *Review of Reviews* and the *Pall Mall Gazette*, and wrote an oft-cited fictional story in 1892 entitled "From the Old World to the New" about a White Star ship captained by E. J. Smith that collides with an iceberg.

Index

References are to entry numbers.

Abbott, Rosa 64
Abernathy, Lewis 361
Abrahams, M. 69
Adams, Douglas 216
AIDS 153
Aks, Frank 367
Alamo 98
Aluminant 370
Alvin 90, 253, 319, 375
Amerika 113
Andrea Doria 112, 252
Andrews, Thomas 32, 89, 109, 119, 136, 188, 189, 190, 275, 296, 327, 341, 345, 410, 457, 472
Argo 136, 254
The Ark 2
Arthur, King 298
Astor, John Jacob 63, 89, 97, 241, 295, 327, 341, 345, 406, 472, Appendix E
Atlantic (1929 film) 331, 371, 380, 385, 402, 482
Atlantic (White Star liner) 51

Baffin Bay 29
Ballard, Bob 7, 8, 9, 46, 47, 52, 100, 105, 135, 136, 156, 180, 234, 247, 250, 251, 252, 253, 257, 268, 269, 278, 283, 307, 316, 318, 370, 371, 375, 376, 389, 391, 400, 401, 415, 416, 467, 480
ballroom 296, 338, 343
Baltimore 328
Barrett, Frederick 45
Bates, Kathy 254
Beatles, the 192

Becker, Ruth *see* Blanchard, Ruth
Beesley, Lawrence 14, 41, 108, 184, 341
Behe, George 15, 16, 367, 376, 479
Belfast 22, 323, 364, 407
Bell, John 174
Benbow, John
Bermuda Triangle 195
Biel, Stephen 359, 449
Blanchard, Ruth Becker 79, 253, 367, 375, 376, 396, 401
Boothe, John 67
Borden, Lizzie 410
Boxhall, Joseph 105, 337
Bride, Harold 6, 87, 108, 156, 170, 184, 322, 410, 417
Britannic 4, 20, 51, 252
"brittle steel" theory 27, 300
Brown, Edith 72, 137, 376, 380, 394
Brown, Margaret Tobin ("Molly") 11, 12, 63, 64, 87, 97, 104, 118, 124, 134, 208, 254, 258, 287, 309, 327, 341, 344, 345, 346, 349, 354, 382, 394, 412, 472
Browne, Francis 130, 317, 371, 418, 435
Buckley, Daniel 45
Bucknell, Mrs. William R. 125
Butler, Daniel Allen 33, 359
Butt, Archibald 125, 207, Appendix E

Californian 26, 33, 42, 55, 60, 73, 74, 97, 105, 123, 133, 135, 140, 168, 203, 308, 427
Cameron, James 4, 50, 54, 93, 107, 116, 134, 156, 291, 346, 361, 365, 366, 388, 395, 428, 446

179

Index

Cameron, Mike 361
Capone, Al 369
Carpathia 19, 36, 48, 66, 67, 87, 97, 108, 111, 143, 146, 155, 341, 364, 376, 422, 437
Challenger (space shuttle) 76, 136
Chapin, Howard 39, 59, 422, 437
Clarke, Arthur C. 200, 241
Coast Guard, U.S. 154
Cohen, Gus 168
Columbus, Christopher 185, 412
Conan Doyle, Arthur 58, 185, 240, 295, 426; *see also* Holmes, Sherlock
Conrad, Joseph 156, 424, 425
Costner, Kevin 346
Coutt, Willie 252
Coward, Nofil 403
cummings, e.e. 205
Cunard Line 19, 337, 466
Cussler, Clive 202, 339, 459

Danes, Claire 134
Dante 211, 434
Dawson, Jack 257, 346, 393, 428; see also *Titanic* (1997 film)
"Dawson's Creek" 2
Dean, Millvina 67, 367, 376
DiCaprio, Leonardo 346, 366
Dodge, Washington 48, 156
dog survivors 41, 54
Douton, Mrs. W. J. 56
Drury, James 370
Dublin 89
Duff-Gordon, Cosmo 67, 125, 429
Duff-Gordon, Lady Lucile 49, 64, Appendix E

Eastland 78
Eaton, John P. and Charles A. Haas 215, 225, 371, 375, 386, 390
Empress of Ireland 52, 252
Exxon Valdez 35

Fay 370
Fleet, Frederick 16, 372, 410
Flying Dutchman 69, 353
Forbes Magazine 381
Ford Pinto 76
Fortune, Alice 83
Futility see Robertson, Morgan
Futrelle, Jacques 120, 201, 213, Appendix E

Galveston Storm 56
German-language films 331, 334, 343
Gibson, Dorothy 164, 340
Gilnagh, Katie 255
Godzilla 456
Goldsmith, Frank 68, 168, 370
Goodwin Sands 69
Gorman, Louis 362
Gracie, Archibald 14, 70, 184, Appendix D, Appendix E
Great Eastern 174
Great Lakes 34, 78
Grimm, Jack 41, 79, 362, 370, 371, 378, 382
Guiness, Alec 339
Gyre 370

Haas, Charles *see* Eaton, John P.
Haisman, Edith *see* Brown, Edith
Hakkarainen, Elin 128
Halifax 144, 323, 428
Halley's Comet 136
Hamilton, Linda 134
Harland & Wolff 114, 260, 263, 392, 394
Harper, John 1, 289
Hart, Eva 67, 75, 79, 168, 360, 367, 368, 377, 380, 388, 392, 394, 396, 401
Hartley, Wallace 428
Hartman, Phil 351
Henner, Marilu 345
Hesiod 211
Hichens, Robert 431
Hitchcock, Alfred 414, Appendix C
Holmes, Sherlock 213, 233, 236, 295, 426, Appendix D; *see also* Conan Doyle, Arthur
Hopkins, Doc 480
Hume, Jack 89
Hurd, Carlos F. 66

iceberg 28, 29, 33, 41, 56, 67, 125, 238, 280, 326, 345, 357, 408, 441, 443, 451
Indiana Jones 295
Irwin, Howard 135
Isaacs, Sir Rufus 175
Ismay, Bruce 27, 45, 63, 87, 114, 131, 189, 209, 224, 341, 343, 345, 356, 376, 392, 410, 466, 472

J. Peterman catalog 346
Jason 136, 391

Jessop, Violet 89, 120
John, Bert 69
Johnson, the Rev. Andrew 56
Johnson, Samuel 345
Jougin, Charles 135
Joyce, James 185

Kenyon, Mrs. Frederick 168
Kipling, Rudyard 185
Knorr 251
Koppel, Ted 375

Leachman, Cloris 341, 354, 382, Appendix A
Leonardo da Vinci 357
Lightoller, Charles 67, 87, 95, 159, 184, 270, 360, 374, 472
Lillie, Beatrice 103
Littlejohn, Alexander James 96
Llewelyn, Doug 382
Lloyd's Weekly News 65
Lord, Capt. Stanley 73, 74, 97, 133, 140, 168, 169, 174
Lord, Walter 5, 7, 97, 98, 105, 113, 136, 215, 295, 336, 337, 365, 376, 380, 472, Appendix D
Lusitania 4, 8, 52, 113, 176, 252, 290, 353, 444
Lynch, Don 257, 346, 361, 366, 388, 394, 401, 476

Mackay-Bennett 125
MacQuitty, William 103, 365, 380, 394
Malachard, Noel 341
Mann, Sally 346
Marconi, Guglielmo 63, 114
Marschall, Ken 4, 100, 251, 252, 253, 257, 294, 322, 346, 361, 366, 388, 401, 472, 476
Marshall, Logan 26, 59, 108, 449
Marvin, Daniel 341
Mauretania 4, 8, 113, 176, 207
Mauro, Philip 111
Mayflower 327
McGough, James 108
McKenzie, Edwina *see* Troutt, Edwina
McKinley, William 56
Melville 136
Melville, Herman 58
Mersey, Lord 63
Millet, Frank 63, Appendix E
Moloney, Senan 122, 123, 452

Morgan, J.P. 40, 466
Mowbray, J. Henry 125, 352
Muller, Bill 13
mummy legend 218, 234, 485
Murdoch, First Officer William M. 28, 97, 108, 162, 345, 346
musicians 52, 211

NASA 136, 160, 204
Nautile 394, 419, 473
Navratil children 120, 135, 171, 297, 367
"Nearer My God to Thee" 22, 52, 56, 65, 331, 337, 338, 343, 378, 389, 429, 454
"negro stoker" 108, 208, 449
Neil, Henry 56
New York 394, 445
A Night to Remember (film) 103, 121, 152, 336, 337, 341, 346, 350, 365, 375, 378, 380, 382, 397, 476
Nimoy, Leonard 362, 399
Norfolk county 10
Normandie 113

Oceanic 95, 110
Olympic 4, 8, 20, 51, 60, 89, 106, 118, 130, 170, 174, 182, 184, 263, 364, 376, 394, 401
Omont, Alfred 169
Orwell, George 402

Padfield, Peter 133, 168, 362
Park, Edward 480
Paxton, Bill 361, 366
Pearl Harbor 98, 180, 232, 404
Pellegrino, Charles 135, 136, 361, Appendix D
Peuchen, Major Arthur G. 95
Phillips. John G. (Jack) 6, 259, 417, 438
Pirrie, Lord William James 24, 54
Plunkett, Sir Horace 32
Poseidon Adventure 485, Appendix B
Prentice, Frank 135
Presnell, Harve 347, 412
Puget Sound 127

Queen Mary 113

Republic (White Star liner) 51
Reynolds, Debbie 254, 349
Rivera, Geraldo 369
RMS *Titanic* (salvage company and

Index   182

exhibit) 7, 8, 53, 179, 180, 253, 358, 391, 398, 400, 416, 473, 481
Robertson, Morgan 61, 88, 109, 168, 172, 232, 259, 336, 352, 372, 394, 466, Appendix D
Roosevelt, Theodore 56
Rostron, Capt. Arthur H. 36, 66, 67, 97, 143
Russell, Edith 67, 360
Ryerson, Emily 45

Sachs, Charles 475
Salinger, Pierre 482
San Francisco Earthquake 56
Sanderson, Harold 392
Sandstrom, Beatrice 367
Savalas, Telly 38
Saved from the Titanic (1912 film) 121, 164
Schefer, Eilen 367
Scientific American 76, 174
Scott, George C. 345
Scott, Robert Falcon 187
Serling, Rod 353
Shackleton, Sir Ernest 54
Shakespeare, William 211
Shaw, George Bernard 58, 426, 429
Shipbuilder 176, 182, 184, 430
Shuman, Elanor Johnson 367
The Simpsons 457, Appendix B
Smith, Capt. Edward J. 14, 22, 24, 27, 33, 41, 44, 67, 87, 94, 95, 104, 125, 135, 156, 170, 189, 194, 224, 259, 264, 275, 296, 312, 319, 320, 343, 345, 371, 380, 389, 394, 400, 410, 426, 449, 472
S.O.S. Titanic (TV movie) 151, 341
Southampton 86, 135, 445
Spacek, Sissy 449
Spedden, Douglas 118, 317, 359
speed record 13, 16, 125, 193, 344
Stanley, Amy 64
Star, Kenny 370
Stead, W. T. 61, 63, 150, 158, 183, 438, Appendix E
Stekel, Wilhelm 103
Straus, Ida 89, 95, 327, 410, 438, 445
Straus, Isidor 89, 95, 327, 410, 438, 445

Taft, William Howard 438
Thaxter, Celia 61
Thayer, Jack 108, 163, 322, 472
Tillett, Ben 169
time travel 91, 203, 205, 207, 227, 235, 272, 298, 302, 311, 312, 356, 357
Titan see Robertson, Morgan
Titanic (1953 film) 129, 356, 385
Titanic (1997 film) 50, 54, 107, 116, 134, 147, 152, 168, 206, 215, 241, 249, 257, 316, 320, 333, 346, 350, 351, 366, 371, 373, 383, 388, 393, 395, 401, 428
Titanic: Adventure Out of Time (computer simulation) 386, 390, 469, 474
Titanic: A New Musical 156, 161, 401
Titanica (IMAX film) 397, 399
Tower, Lucky 52
Troutt, Edwina 41, 168

Upstairs, Downstairs (TV series) 228, Appendix B
U.S.S. *Missouri* 127

Wagner, Robert 344
Walker, Betty 380
Walker, E. D. 52, 54
Wall, William 308
Ward, Anna 69
Weaver, Sigourney 408
Webb, Clifton 344
Welles, Orson 370, 378
White, Jay 56
White Star Line 3, 14, 16, 20, 40, 45, 51, 89, 99, 114, 118, 131, 193, 221, 331, 337, 339, 343, 376, 389, 392, 393, 399, 431, 443, 466, 482
Widener, Harry 63
Winslet, Kate 50, 346, 366
Woods Hole Oceanographic Institute 90, 282

Yasbeck, Celiney 64
Yeager, Chuck 47
Yoerger, Dana 375
Young, Filson 58, 185

www.ingramcontent.com/pod-product-compliance
Ingram Content Group UK Ltd.
Pitfield, Milton Keynes, MK11 3LW, UK
UKHW042014140426
5217IPUK00015B/1170